THE MACMILLAN COMPANY
NEW YORK · BOSTON · CHICAGO · DALLAS
ATLANTA · SAN FRANCISCO

MACMILLAN AND CO., Limited
LONDON · BOMBAY · CALCUTTA · MADRAS
MELBOURNE

THE MACMILLAN COMPANY
OF CANADA, Limited
TORONTO

THE AMERICAN COLLEGES

AND THE SOCIAL ORDER

by Robert Lincoln Kelly EXECUTIVE

DIRECTOR, ASSOCIATION OF AMERICAN COLLEGES, 1917-1937

New York · The Macmillan Company · *1940*

wGE

This publication was authorized by the Association of
American Colleges in 1937 and is issued under its
auspices. The work has been made possible through
a grant from the Carnegie Corporation of New York
to which grateful acknowledgment is now made.

"When the waters of the world are troubled, the gift of progress may be to shed oil upon them, or produce gyrostatic devices for equilibrium or craft which can make new records of smooth sailing, or a knowledge of weather lore and safe channels and a higher order of navigation.

"When the waters of the world are still and stagnant, green and dead, the gift of progress may be any stick which stirs them, any gas which aerates them, any breeze or tempest which chases over them, any swift motive power which traverses them."

—SIR JOSIAH STAMP

PREFACE

THE primary theme of the following pages is that it is the function of the colleges to promote the general welfare. A secondary theme is that for three hundred years this has been a conscious purpose of the colleges and that they have made a very appreciable contribution to this purpose. A third proposition is that the colleges are now rallying to their primary task as never before.

Certainly if the general welfare is to be promoted there must be an informed and responsible public opinion. There must be men and women of tested capacity and of good will. These men and women cannot be isolationists: they must work cooperatively. They must maintain contacts with the hopes and aspirations of the people. The colleges and the community must develop together. Each must react upon the other.

The term "general welfare" is borrowed from the Preamble to the Constitution. The judges of all the courts have attempted to point out its abundant and pregnant content. A complicated structure of government has been built upon it. It is the basis and justification of the vast and perplexing variety of American colleges.

In no country on earth is public opinion sufficiently informed to exert the power which rightly belongs to it. Our vanity as a people prevented us from accepting this pronouncement when Lord Bryce first enunciated it. Today the titanic convulsion from which civilization is suffering has persuaded us of its truth, for public opinion has been cast to the winds.

In the light of such realistic and far-reaching facts the efforts of American education to contribute to human progress may appear insignificant. Certainly schools and colleges cannot at all times and in all circumstances be guided by the ebbs and flows of current and of localized opinion and custom. The social order like the law lags behind knowledge. It is recognized by the colleges that the contemporary scene has its significance, which it would be suicidal to ignore. It is also recognized by some that "the larger and fuller life must have an abiding sense of the past and the future in every passing moment of the present." It is the task of the liberal colleges to show that all history and experience are potentially, and may become actually, contemporary.

There is validity in the age-old distinction between the town and the gown. The expectation, frequently expressed, that this distinction may be entirely wiped out can rarely be realized. Since the ends which the community seeks are usually very volatile, the colleges are called upon to assist in maintaining a balance of individual and social forces. They have the function of serving as balance wheels, thermostats, governors in the total machinery of a free society. The colleges help to steady the ship of state.

But they are more than balance wheels. They are also dynamos for the generation of power. They are effectual as well as effective. If they do not immediately and institutionally attain social ends, they arouse some of their members to the realization of social needs. The colleges generate good will, inspire students to understand and to develop the courage if need be to resist destructive regimes. They are very jealous of their areas of reserved freedom. They have developed a remarkable capacity for self-examination. They are able to serve more fully as agencies of conservation because on occasion they stimulate the freedom to warn and the power to oppose. They cannot be expected, chameleonlike, to change the color of their skins in response to every external stimulus or pressure. While they are in the current of events they are fortunately not entirely of it. They strive to preserve the objective view.

The groups with which they identify themselves are not all here and now. Their horizon extends beyond. The social con-

cepts of the epoch may not coincide with the national genius
of the people which has a far deeper grounding. Still more
ultimate than either is the nature of man and of the universe
of which he is a part.

Individual colleges are free to take the short-range view as
the time and the community are likely to demand, or the
median view, attempting to interpret the national or racial
genius, or the long-range view which envisages the "starry
heavens above and the moral law within." The liberal colleges
are interested most of all in the gradual development of man's
creative powers and the part these powers may play in helping
men and society to understand themselves and the universe by
which they are encompassed.

Most colleges try to understand all these concepts. The liberal colleges are obligated to seek and find what they believe
to be enduring values and base their programs upon them.

ACKNOWLEDGMENTS

My experience has been enriched through contacts with
college men and women during a period of more than half a
century. I am indebted to all of these men and women but
cannot here make specific acknowledgments to all. The Association of American Colleges provides that a manuscript to be
published under its auspices be read by its Committee on
Publications. By virtue of this provision I have been fortunate
in having as readers and critics Presidents Meta Glass and
Edward V. Stanford and the Executive Director, Guy E.
Snavely. Every chapter has also been read at my request by
Eric T. Clarke, the Director of the Association's Art Program.
One or more chapters have been submitted to Presidents
Trevor Arnett, Walter A. Jessup, Donald J. Cowling, Henry
M. Wriston, John L. Seaton, Frederick C. Ferry, Directors
Stephen P. Duggan and Walter W. Van Kirk, and several other
Association colleagues of long standing. Secretary Frank W.
Padelford of the Board of Education of the Northern Baptist
Convention and Secretary Gould Wickey of the United

Lutheran Board of Education and the Executive Secretary of the Council of Church Boards of Education have read selected chapters.

Of great assistance in the preparation of the manuscript have been my former staff associates, Ruth E. Anderson, Research Secretary, and Martha T. Boardman, Editorial Secretary.

All of these colleagues and consultants have made most helpful suggestions. The book therefore is a cooperative product, although the author must be held responsible for its deficiencies.

References arranged by chapter groups are presented, for the convenience of the reader, alphabetically in terms of the authors mentioned in the text. Both to these authors and to their publishers grateful acknowledgment is made.

In the preparation of the manuscript I have enjoyed the hospitality of the Associated Colleges of Claremont. I wish to make especial mention of the presidents and the library staffs of the three colleges. The libraries have placed their rich treasures at my hand and on rare occasions have drawn from other libraries located in this and other parts of the country.

ROBERT L. KELLY

CLAREMONT, CALIFORNIA
July, 1940

TABLE OF CONTENTS

xi

THE AMERICAN COLLEGES
AND THE SOCIAL ORDER

CHAPTER I

THE EARLY AMERICAN TRADITIONS

THIS discussion proceeds upon the hypothesis that in the history of our country a period of continental expansion continuing for some 250 years was followed by a shorter one of concentration of power in many social groups, and this in turn by an era in which centrifugal and centripetal forces have been in conflict. It is in the midst of these slow but decisive transitions in the social order that American colleges have developed. What part have they played in these transformations in American life?

There is a popular misconception that the great transition began with the appearance of the telephone, automobile, moving pictures, and the radio. Such manifestations of a new day do not indicate beginnings but more recent extensions of the new age.

During the first historical period, the foundations of the Republic were laid; during the second, some indications appeared of a major transition; during the last half century, progress has been made in establishing "a more perfect union." In spite of clouds and fogs which have frequently enveloped us, the sun of democracy has guided us on our way and still shines over a highly favored, if not a contented, people.

It would be possible to oversimplify the statement as to why the colonists crossed the Atlantic. It is frequently said they came because they sought religious liberty. Many of them did so, but the motives of most of them were not unmixed. The passengers on the *Mayflower* were seeking more than religious liberty. They had had that in Holland for ten years. They wished also to preserve their language and customs, which they could not so easily do, even among the hospitable and tolerant Dutch. They sought also political liberty, and in time this motive gripped the people in all the colonies. It was over an economic question—the question of taxation—that they first broke with the mother country. "Taxation without representation" was an initial shibboleth of the Revolution.

Remarkable interpretations of the frontier period from the standpoint of political theory and institutions, and of individual and social life, have been made by James Bryce,* and more recently by a multitude of penetrating students. The brilliant analyses of Henry and James Truslow Adams, Van Wyck Brooks, George Santayana, Odell Shepard, T. J. Wertenbaker are illustrations which readily come to mind. They are in general agreement in their various pictures of the spirit, character, and achievements of the long line of pioneers. The "First Americans," the "American Dream," the "American Way," are apt and striking and well-known symbols of those adventurous men and women who dared to stake their lives and fortunes in an apparently unequal contest with the disciplined troops of the mother country, with the unorthodox methods of warfare of the American Indian, and with the untamed forces of nature. The present writer has no disposition and is not equipped to make a further contribution to this picture. He may be permitted, however, presently to point out that as the pioneers pressed forward in their task, many of them were impelled by ideals and inspirations which had arisen in the mother countries and which formed one of the most significant movements of thought in the history of man.

There must be deep-seated reasons why the United States now has the oldest government among the great Powers, and also has a very influential group of institutions of higher learning which were well established in the seventeenth and early part of the eighteenth centuries. Harvard's history

* See References, p. 348.

before the Constitution was adopted in 1789 covers as many years as her history since that pivotal date. One institution at least, as was remarked at Harvard's tercentennial, has come of age.

All this must mean that America has great and rich traditions. While these are American traditions, not all of them were made in America. The life of America is, after all, but a continuation and development of phases of the life of the mother countries from which our forebears sprang. This life has been greatly modified during the years by new and strange environmental conditions to which the early colonists, as well as the newcomers, have been subjected. These inherited and acquired characteristics, however, modified by our rich soil and stimulating atmosphere, have contributed to keeping American character and institutions true to our great adventure in representative democracy. By striking down into our own soil we have discovered a surpassing richness and potentiality. Our happiness has been measured in large degree by the consistency with which we have striven to preserve, and have been constrained to cherish, our inheritances.

James Truslow Adams has traced the majestic march of these ideas and impulses during the era of expansion across the Alleghenies, Old Man River, the Plains, the Desert, and the Rocky Mountains until the frontier met the incoming tides of the Pacific Ocean. Other analysts have dealt with more restricted sections of the country.

In spite of the remarkable interpretations of our early national life, very little has been done in setting forth a detailed history of the relationships of their educational progress to the life of the people as expressed in their religion, politics, economics, art and social development. Detailed histories of New York and Illinois are exceptions to this statement, and the Ohio State Archaeological and Historical Society is now committed to the production of a six volume history intended to set forth authoritatively and accurately an account of Ohio's complicated development as a state, as well as in its relationship to developments in the country as a whole.

The present volume manifestly deals with trends recently pointed out and generally accepted in the total life of the people, and attempts to interpret the progress of the colleges in terms of those trends.

In the nature of the case, the pioneers who laid the foundations of civilization in the Western hemisphere were concerned with immediate problems. They were confronted with the necessity of learning the art of living in a primeval wilderness: in the forests, on the plains, in the valleys, among the mountains. They could not learn this art from books. There were no books, except such as the face of nature provided.

Their greatest teachers at first were the wild Indians and they learned their lessons in the school of experience. Their physical existence depended upon their ability "to hunt, to trap, to build fires, to follow trails, to blaze new paths, to hew logs, to cure skins, to identify medicinal herbs, barks and roots, to make maple sugar, to cook without utensils, to till the ground with home-made implements, to make and use moccasins and snow-shoes, to construct and navigate birch-bark canoes, to use smoke as a signal, to detect the approach of enemies, and to be wary of ambushes." All of this eventually led on to communication and trade. A frontiersman after some years in this school of life declared that he had learned to think Indian thoughts so readily and unfailingly that he could anticipate the thought of the Indians themselves. We reluctantly recall the vivid recitals of facts which demonstrate that the pioneers were apt students in deception and cruelty, and we must not forget that their activities in these respects were not altogether due to the power of example. An array of incidents like the diversion of many thousands of beaver pelts belonging to the Indians into the hands of the hated peddlers could be listed.

All this was an American adventure in the "new education." It was a form of adult education and the students enrolled were men of virility and women of endurance. They were not seeking "security"; they were seeking the opportunity to carve out their own destiny. They sought the great boon of liberty through the means of thrift and industry. They feared neither exposure nor starvation. They took conflict for granted. Many of them combined the audacity of the explorer, the shrewdness of the big business man, and the temerity of the warrior.

With the territorial expansion of the country from the forests into the plains and the mountains, the informal curriculum of the new education was greatly enriched. We have no more honest interpreter than Mark Twain of trans-Mississippi life during the period following the War between the States. In his *Gilded Age,* while recognizing that the settlers whom he described were "uncouth, not cultivated, not always particularly industrous," he insisted they "were nevertheless honest and straightforward, and their virtuous ways commanded respect." Yet his delineation of character in the same book gives us Colonel Sellers, who was utterly unable to distinguish between the figments of his imagination and the facts—certainly a characteristic of this age of discovery and exploitation. Mark Twain was impressed, too, that their patriotism was strong, that their love of country amounted to idolatry. They hated Benedict Arnold "because he had broken faith." Twain's story seems to buttress the claim often made by economists that some of the settlers were "refugees" from a life with which they could not successfully cope. They certainly were not without defects.

These settlers and pioneers were endowed with very definite qualities of intelligence and imagination. They were always pursuing ideals, hopes, dreams. They faced the future in the midst of their present struggles. They revelled in the vapory realms of speculation as to the rewards which awaited them at the end of the rainbow. They were always on the heels of success; only the faint-hearted turned back. It is not strange that men confronted with such challenges as

these were disposed to break loose from traditions, to lose
sight of the past with all its lessons, to become detached from
what had been and expectant of what was to be. This
accounts for what has been called the legal vacuum in the
trans-Mississippi area. The Ordinance of 1787 neutralized
this tendency to a certain degree in the old Northwest Territory. It is not surprising that the artificialities of race and
rank should be forgotten or despised. The conditions of
their lives developed a type of character which justified G. K.
Chesterton in saying, "Americans are of many races; but wish
to be of one rank." They wished to be judged, and they were
disposed to judge others, not by their past but by their
future. They wished to have no limitation on their liberty.
The sight of smoke from a neighbor's chimney was looked
upon as an unwarranted encroachment. They were pre-
eminent in the power of physical resistance, of strength of
will, of certain types of courage; by saving their own lives
and the lives of those dependent upon them, they were
advancing the cause of liberty.

With such a program, it was inevitable that they often
became impatient of any form of restraint. The frontiers
of our early history constituted an ever active school of democracy for those who were able to pay the tuition. The
helplessness of the disciplined troops from Europe which led
to Braddock's defeat, in warfare under forest conditions, is
a striking demonstration of a type of education among the
colonial troops which the older education could not furnish.
Through the school of experience, even at great cost, these
English and other pioneers were transformed into Americans. A careful American historian has pointed out that the
galaxy of great Virginians who came upon the scene at the
opening years of our constitutional history, were the product
of the life of the tobacco plantations. Tobacco had brought
in something entirely new, certainly in no sense European.

All this is said, however inadequately, lest we forget at the
beginning of our study of American higher education that a
race of giants went before us and prepared the way. They

leveled down many inequalities, they made many paths straight. We do well to search out and find those paths, and to acknowledge our indebtedness to those who went before us, as they would acknowledge indebtedness to the fatherlands whence they came, and more immediately to the Indians and the wild beasts of the forests and plains. The essential elements of the pioneer spirit were the same on the Atlantic Coast, in the South, the Mississippi Valley, the West, and on the coast of the Pacific Ocean. The men and women who were impelled by it were, in varying degrees, restless, discontented, ambitious, vaguely optimistic, youthfully buoyant. They were developing a receding frontier of free government lands, of expanding railroad construction, of staked claims, of golden dreams.

CHAPTER II

THE GENIUS OF CITIZENSHIP

ALL MEN and all races have their underlying philosophy of life. Some of them are consciously guided by this philosophy; most of them follow it unconsciously. The pioneers of America were no exception to the rule. Particularly among the English-speaking people of Europe during the seventeenth and eighteenth centuries, conceptions of the worth of human personality were expanding men's minds and dominating their spirits. They were revolting against all forms of tyranny. They were claiming their rights as free men. They were setting over against the divine right of kings the natural rights of all men.

*John Locke.** Among the many creative minds of these centuries there was no one who had a more profound influence upon the destinies of America than John Locke. Milton had written his *Areopagitica,* and many others had prepared the way for a new movement of thought. However, the greatest of the European philosophers measured in terms of his influence upon the early makers of America was John Locke. The early state papers bear the impress of his thought. A mere catalogue of these Declarations and Contitutions would take too much space for their insertion here.

Notable illustrations of familiarity with Locke's doctrines are the Constitution of Carolina, the Articles of Confederation, and the Constitution of the Confederate States. Locke had set forth the cause of political freedom and religious toleration. He aroused the people of England to an appreciation of their "just and natural rights," and he interpreted

* See References, p. 349.

the meaning of "the consent of the people." He proclaimed "the natural liberty and equality of mankind," and reiterated the thought that this state of perfect freedom impelled them "to order their actions and dispose of their possessions and persons as they saw fit within the bounds of the laws of nature." "Men are by nature free and equal and independent," and the purpose of government is "to preserve their lives, liberties and fortunes." Over and over again, great teacher that he was, for many states and for at least two centuries, Locke repeated these and similar sentiments.

Locke and the Schoolmen. To say all this is not to say that Locke coined all the shibboleths of the Natural Rights metaphysics. Locke's main support against his adversaries was the "judicious Hooker," of whom he wrote, "But I thought Hooker alone might be enough to satisfy these men." Another renowned scholastic, Francis Suarès, in his work *De Defensione Fidei,* had refuted the theory of the divine right of kings (which defense King James ordered to be burned), and had propounded the democratic theory of civil power. The democratic concepts of the scholastic, Robert Bellarmine, were selected by Robert Filmer, the author of *Patriarcha, or The Natural Power of Kings,* as "the strongest argument for the Natural Liberty of the Subject." Locke displayed familiarity with these and other subtle schoolmen or jurists imbued with the scholastic philosophy—such as Grotius, Puffendorf, Fortescue—in his attack upon the *Patriarcha* delivered in the *Two Treatises on Government.* Thus the citizen arose out of the crucible of debate. As the citizen increased, the subject decreased.

Hobbes and Locke. It is frequently asserted that Locke was indebted to Hobbes in developing his theory of the state. Locke and Hobbes both held to the social contract theory; they were both profoundly interested in political philosophy. Hobbes furthermore furnished Locke much to combat, just as, as has been pointed out, Bellarmine set up targets for Filmer. Their essential differences placed them in entirely separate schools of thought. The American leaders at these

points of difference followed Locke rather than Hobbes.
Hobbes made war the state of nature, and fear the impulse
to government. This conception was obnoxious to Locke,
and as to the American idea, read the Preamble to the Constitution of the United States. Hobbes justified a "Common
Power,"—including absolute monarchy:

> as if every man should say to every man I Authorize and give
> up my Right of Governing myselfe, to this Man or to this
> Assembly of men on this condition that thou give up thy
> Right to him and Authorize his Actions in like manner.
> This done the Multitude so united on one Person is called
> a *commonwealth,* in latina *Civitas.* . . . And he that carryeth
> this Person is called *Soveraigne* and is said to have Sover-
> aigne Power: and everyone besides, his *subject.**

Locke took the crown off Hobbes' *Leviathan.* The Americans did the same, though it was not without a struggle, for
we had our Hamilton and there was a considerable sentiment
in favor of making Washington king. If Thomas Jefferson
drew inspiration from Locke's *Treatises,* Adolf Hitler might
find justification for his theory of the state in Hobbes'
Leviathan.

Among the natural rights of men Locke lays especial emphasis on liberty. It is true the Declaration of Independence
says all men are created equal, but our acceptance of Locke's
ideas of property led us at first to the same result in respect
to liberty and equality that it did Locke. Locke grounds
the state in the consent of the governed, which in turn is
grounded on the acceptance of property. The crystal clear
statement of the natural rights free from limitations and
conditions was made by Montesquieu. Locke stood midway
in time among this interesting group of political thinkers
and gave the theory the philosophical formulation generally
accepted by democratic groups.

Such sentiments as these impelled the adventurers in the
cabin of the *Mayflower* to formulate the first practical application of the doctrine of the Social Compact. A. Lawrence

* See References, p. 349.

Lowell has pointed out that many American statesmen and judges looked upon the Constitution as a compact, and it was upon the strength of this assumption that several of the colonies acceded to it. The Constitution would not have been adopted but for the promised inclusion within it of the first ten amendments carrying into it the Bill of Rights.

Locke and Samuel Adams. Adams dedicated himself early to the task which eventually won for him the title, "Father of the American Revolution." His first acquaintance with Locke's writings was made while a student at Harvard. The extent of Locke's influence upon him is indicated by the fact that his thesis for the Master's degree in 1743 was *An Supremo Magistratui Resistere Liceat, si aliter Servari Republica Nequit.* He became the great popularizer of Locke's sentiments on this side of the Atlantic, as Rousseau did in France, and Montesquieu did in Europe at large. A characteristic declaration of Samuel Adams was this: "There should be one rule of justice for rich and poor, for the favorite at the court and the countryman at the plough."

The usual human method in dealing with a problem is to act first and to rationalize the action afterward. Locke had rationalized the English Revolution after the event. Samuel Adams reversed the order and rationalized the American Revolution before the event. It was a striking forecast of a function of the higher education on this side of the Atlantic. Samuel Adams became a propagandist for what Americans still think was a good cause.

Locke had said:

> Great mistakes in the ruling part, many wrong and inconvenient laws, and all the slips of human frailty will be borne by the people without mutiny or murmurs. But if a long train of abuses, prevarications and artifices all tending the same way make the design visible to the people and they cannot but feel what they lie under and see whither they are going, it is not to be wondered at that they should then rouse themselves and endeavor to put the rule into such hands which may secure to them the ends for which the government was at first erected.

Locke and Jefferson. When on the basis of this and other indications of Thomas Jefferson's intimate acquaintance with Locke's theory of government, he was accused of plagiarism in writing the Declaration of Independence, and the accusation was fortified by the deadly parallel, he defended himself on the ground that his assignment was not to produce a new document, but only to interpret the genius of the Revolutionary movement. Jefferson asserted that in composing the Declaration he turned to no book or document. An indication of his appraisal of the place of John Locke among this group of Natural Rights thinkers is found inferentially in a letter he wrote to a friend delineating the character of General Washington. Jefferson wrote: "His mind was great and powerful without being of the very first order; his penetration strong, though not so acute as that of Newton, Bacon, or Locke." Jefferson looked upon Locke as a key man in the unfolding of the human race.

There is no doubt but that Jefferson was greatly influenced as well by French thought, as was assuredly Benjamin Franklin. Rousseau was fascinated with the idea of equality and was withal the champion phrase-maker of the Natural Rights philosophy on the other side of the Atlantic, as Jefferson was on this side. Patrick Henry, John Adams, and James Otis, as well as Jefferson, undoubtedly were familiar also with the writings of Locke, Rousseau, Montesquieu, and other European philosophers. They were the common possession of the pioneers who pressed their victorious way across the continent. If they may be designated as an army of occupation, they were also in revolt against the triple combination of king, lords, and commons, against edicts, against any extreme concentration of power, against unjust laws and, at times and places, against all man-made laws.

Tom Paine. The minds of the people were stirred by all these devotees of the Natural Rights, but the eloquence and earnestness of the leaders had come short of releasing the energies of the people. At this moment the wisdom of Benjamin Franklin came into play. He discovered Tom Paine in London. The meeting was a turning point in Paine's life and contributed to great events. Paine and Franklin found much in common. In 1774 Paine sailed for America. Less than two years after his arrival—early in 1776—his pamphlet *Common Sense* appeared. Franklin had known his man. Franklin was a personal embodiment of common sense. Jefferson sympathized with Paine's opposition to the Deism of the eighteenth century and his defense of natural religion. The open movement for independence broke loose. Washington testified that *Common Sense* worked a powerful change in the minds of many men. From Paine's *The Crisis* was taken up the battle cry: "These are the times that try men's souls."

Pitt is quoted as having said, "Tom Paine is in the right, but what am I to do? . . . As things are, if I were to encourage Paine's opinions we should have a bloody revolution." Paine's fiery pamphlets were ammunition for Revolutionary guns, for they were in revolt against the authoritative state and the authoritative life.

Thus a birthright Quaker, with a background of mysticism, whose personal life was not always an ornament to the Society, developed into "a rough and ready passionate controversialist." He advocated conceptions which were part and parcel of the Natural Rights metaphysics, with such moving words that he was branded as unorthodox and an infidel, which he certainly was as measured by the prevailing claims of most of the Christian churches, and even as an atheist, which he probably was not, as was neither Franklin nor Jefferson. In any event, the potential power of the Natural Rights became dynamic, and as Lincoln said in the Gettysburg Address, "Our fathers brought forth . . . a new nation."

Locke was far more, however, than a medieval metaphysician. He was not content to rest his case on the validity of the Natural Rights. Metaphysics was his servant, not his master. He recognized the necessity of placing the Natural Rights formula in legal statutes. He was a worthy forerunner of the modern scientific, constructive statesman whose perfect representative perhaps has not yet appeared on the earth. If it be said that Rousseau maddened the populace of France by his brilliant and extreme exposition of Locke's theories, it may be countered that Blackstone also quoted Locke approvingly and was under the spell of the Natural Rights. As many copies of Blackstone were sold in America as in England. The American student of law thus became acquainted with Locke's political theories, and with their practical application.

Having set forth his faith in progress, his optimistic outlook upon the possibilities of men, Locke addressed himself to the practical application of his principles to the English government. In this he had the confidence of William the Third and of the Parliament, and in the long run his general method of procedure may have been more powerful in the development of our country than his metaphysics.

Somers, the chief advocate of the Comprehension Bill and the Toleration Bill, and the leader of the committee appointed to consider the redress of grievances out of which grew the Declaration of Rights and the Bill of Rights, wrote to Locke: "Your former favors make me bold to presume upon you, and your judgment is such that I can depend upon your instructions as to the rules of my behavior."

Again, when a censorship bill came up for reenactment, a conference of the two houses was held "18th April 1694-95," to which Edward Clark read Locke's strictures on the Act, and the Lords gave way at once. The Commons had approved his recommendations before the conference.

One other illustration of Locke's method of doing things must suffice. In May 1695 commissioners were appointed "for promoting the trade of the Kingdom and for inspecting and improving the plantations in America and elsewhere." Locke was the chief director and controller of the commission. He set on foot a careful investigation of his problem in its numerous and diverse phases. Statistics and data were collected in reference to the pauper class, the interests of the quarrel between the white and brown paper makers, the condition of the woolen trade—domestic and foreign, the condition of commerce with Sweden and the Baltic, and with Holland, the American settlements, Jamaica, etc., etc. That is to say, in a word, Locke began the use of the methods of the practical economist, politician, and business man of our own day: the methods of compromise, of attaining equilibrium by setting over against each other a multitude of conflicting claims and interests, the hearing of evidence, the investigation of allegations, the admission of qualifying propositions, the setting of bounds and fixing of innumerable limitations.

In Locke's active campaigns he produced a multitude of pamphlets and did much by example to perfect the method of pamphleteering which was used with such remarkable success in America during the colonial period and leading up to the final adoption of the Constitution. No more brilliant state papers have ever been produced here than during this formative period in our history. Statesmen rather than politicians stood on the bridge of the ship of state. They displayed sincerity, earnestness and conscience.

Here was a man so richly endowed that he could both think and act. He was a philosopher who made distinguished contributions to metaphysics, to psychology, to ethics, and to the science of government. He was a statesman who dealt successfully with the details of administration, and withal gained and held the confidence of those to whom great responsibilities had been entrusted. He was a profound scholar, a wise counselor, and a valued friend.

His metaphysics inflamed the minds of a Rousseau, a Patrick Henry, a Samuel Adams, a Tom Paine. He was a father of revolutions. He furnished ammunition of thought and feeling which led up to 1776. His science of politics animated those who would frame what became the most remarkable document ever struck off at one time by the brain and purpose of man. Today the Constitution of the United States is the oldest functioning, written constitution in the world.

Locke's methods of administration led up to 1787. So completely did the framers of the Constitution address themselves to the practical adjustment of strains and tensions in the framework of that document, to the practical rather than the theoretical side of Locke's teaching, that they momentarily lost sight of the metaphysical implications of their task. But the people did not forget. They proceeded to attach the Bill of Rights to the document. They wanted fundamental law, which might serve also as metaphysics on a rainy day. Political oratory had used both in America, and still does. All this led up to 1789, when Washington was inaugurated as the first president of the new nation.

As the years have gone on, the theoretical and the practical have characterized American thought and aspiration. We have learned that the "Natural Rights of man" had their uses: they have not gone with the wind. Thomas Babington Macaulay was a false prophet when he wrote in a letter recently discovered, "Your Constitution is all sail and no anchor." Daniel Webster clearly perceived the relationship between liberty and wholesome restraint. He recognized the safeguard of liberty and union in the Constitution. God grants liberty, he said, only to those who love it and are ready to defend it. Goethe's phrase was: "What our fathers bequeathed to us, we must earn to possess."

The American people know now that they do not *possess* their rights as a free gift of heaven. Many of them believe that they are granted the *opportunity* to defend their rights by a higher law than the law of the existing state. They have learned by experience that their rights must be continually fought for, safeguarded, and defended, if they are to be possessed. Never more so than today.

It is worthy of note that Americans have made another important distinction. The acceptance of the theory of Natural Rights generally did not involve the acceptance of the theory of "natural religion," to which many of the early English and American political philosophers adhered.

Those who spied out this land of Canaan were an intrepid

outpost breed.   They were the scouts and the skirmishers of the great American migration.   A new kind of courage was required to *remain* in sight of the smoke from neighbors' chimneys and create an indissoluble union.   The colleges began to function in the frontiers of the mind and spirit. They helped to prepare the way for a new social order.

CHAPTER III

WHY COLONIAL COLLEGES?

THE prevailing attitude of critics has been and is, down to the present moment, that the colonial colleges missed the boat. To paraphrase George Fox's observation applied to the ministers of religion of his time, "They did not speak to the condition of the people." There was a wide chasm between the colleges and the people and, according to the critics, no effort was made to bridge it.

It must not be forgotten that most of the twenty-six colleges that were founded before the British army withdrew from Yorktown, were British colleges—if you prefer, British provincial colleges. There were King's College at New York, Queen's College at New Brunswick, and William and Mary at Williamsburg. With rare exceptions, such as William and Mary and the University of Pennsylvania, where Scotch and European influence was more marked, they were modeled after Cambridge and Oxford, which had been the well-nigh unchanged centers of the higher learning of England for some five hundred years. How thoroughly unchanged Cambridge and Oxford were has been generally forgotten, if ever known, on this side of the Atlantic. Morison, the Harvard historian, has recently commented upon it. An abridgment follows:

> Galileo and Kepler and Copernicus had come and gone, but Oxford and Cambridge continued essentially unchanged. The celestial system of Ptolemy was good enough for them. Magellan and Vasco da Gama had rounded the Cape more than a century before, but the cosmology of

Plato's *Timaeus* and the geography of the pagan scholars of the first century suited their every need. The generally accepted political tenet was obedience to the king. Religious and moral indoctrination was the vogue of the church. When Harvard was founded, Descartes' *Essais Philosophiques* furnished stimulating material for discussion in the Dutch universities, but it is improbable that any of the university trained founders of New England were acquainted with Descartes.

Indeed, to quote directly, Morison says:

It is doubtful if anyone who had to do with the founding of Harvard except John Winthrop, Jr., had accepted Bacon's inductive and experimental method which was destined to revolutionize science, and indeed all learning. . . . The great mass of Cambridge alumni probably assumed that the ancients had said the last word on statecraft, the schoolmen on philosophy, and the reformers on divinity. . . . The University of Cambridge had introduced her children destined for New England to the best minds of antiquity and had made them through all wilderness toils and pains companions of the deathless muses.*

Admit with Van Wyck Brooks that "the college was a little realm as fixed and final as a checker board";—Greek, Latin, Hebrew, grammar, theology, natural religion and logic—the "Golden Calf of Cambridge." "Logic moved forward in terms of perfect definitions." "Unless we knew logic we could not read Locke; and who that had not read Locke could ever be certain that his Christian faith had a solid bottom?" And yet the colonial colleges laid the foundation for what is now the world's greatest aggregation of colleges and universities.

While the early settlers in America brought with them the same stock of ideas, principles, and habits as those which had prevailed in their own groups in the home countries, the vicissitudes of life here tended to produce a condition of instability, and even incoherence. This condition may ac-

* See References, p. 349.

count in some measure for the "marvel" expressed by Bryce, that a country so new and supposedly full of energy should have disclosed so meager an appreciation of the things of the spirit. It was recognized by some that the stability of the old culture must be preserved, and that, whether the majority believed it or not, colleges might be especially equipped to supply this need. The strange and rugged life on this side of the Atlantic must be grafted into the old culture if an American culture was to emerge. The settlers at their peril would ignore the past. The college founders seemed to recognize what Erskine in the light of more recent events has aptly generalized: "A nation which has dropped its past has thereby dropped the instruments of expression."

Some of the elements of this culture have been referred to in the preceding chapter. The colonists and later settlers were insistent upon realizing their political and religious aspirations. They had learned well the lessons taught by John Locke and the other apostles of Natural Rights. They had determined to perpetuate those rights and they had incorporated into their life some of the European institutions for their implementation—town meetings, churches, legislatures, courts, executive departments. With the founding of Harvard, William and Mary, and Yale, they carried over another institution—the English and the Scotch college, and dedicated it to the perpetuation of their church and their civic life. Thus their political, church, and civic life was transplanted. The budding processes of the intellectual life followed later. At first the roots must strike down into virgin soil.

When Harvard was established in 1636, its founder had endowed it with 320 books. By 1671 the Cambridge Press had published 157 books, of which 63 were upon religious subjects. Throughout New England the intellectual life expressed itself very largely in theological disputations. By the end of the seventeenth century, seventy-six of the eighty-six clergymen of Massachusetts, and thirty-one of the thirty-five clergymen of Connecticut were Harvard graduates.

But the circumstances of growth, as well as the educational ideals, were markedly different in Virginia and Massachusetts, at William and Mary and at Harvard. The Anglican Church was the ruling church in Virginia, a typical old world institution. While a majority of the settlers were church members, the membership of many was evidently inactive. The plantation, not the church, was the unit of life. The population was scattered. There was not sufficient cohesiveness to build many strong congregations or to offer sufficient support to clergymen to justify prolonged preparation. Relatively few candidates were sent to England for confirmation. The standards of scholarship and of morals for clergymen were not too high.

Current literature was neglected in the colleges and by the people in general except in the realm of politics. This was not due to the lack of the production of literature in the home countries. The Puritans exercised a strict censorship on books. The age which brought the settlers to Massachusetts and Virginia was the age of Shakespeare, Spenser, Milton, Bacon, Harvey, Newton, Cromwell, Hampden, Jeremy Taylor, and John Bunyan.

Naturally the typical pioneer and prospector centered his interest on the task in hand. While he projected his life in large, round terms into the future, it was remote from Shakespeare and Milton, not to speak of Plato and Aristotle. He held to his textbooks—the forests and the plains.

One innovation followed another in rapid succession. That they were apt students of their new environment and gifted in initiative and ingenuity is evidenced by the well-authenticated fact that by the end of the seventeenth century the standard of living in America was higher than in England. The countryman at the plough did his work well.

The founders of the early colleges have often been criticized for not adjusting their programs to the manifest needs of the people. It now appears that this is exactly what the colonial colleges did do. They adjusted their programs to the needs which were manifest to them. Most of all, in their judgment, the people needed spiritual and intellectual leadership. They made these adjustments with such devotion and consistency that their programs are now inaptly called "professional." No greater tribute could be paid to their ability to hew to the line. In most of the colleges they sought to develop a "learned" ministry, in the church and civil state. They got what they wanted. The critics forget that they were working in lines familiar to them and thoroughly approved by them. For mass education they dared to wait. The charters of the New England colleges are eloquent in the expression of the singleness of aim of the founders. The conservatism of the college pattern grew out of their immediate sense of need in the realm of the mind and of the spirit. Still emblazoned on the Harvard gate is the quaintly phrased demand for a continuous supply of educated ministers. Emanuel College, Cambridge, Harvard's model, had been operating a half-century on a "Puritan foundation" established for the special purpose of providing the church with a preaching ministry. Most of the American colleges felt this to be their dominant need. Strikingly enough, their conception of the ministry began very soon to expand. This is a way education has.

They held to one other conviction, that the classics were the only subject matter for the mental discipline of the future intellectual and religious leaders of their several communities. They felt profoundly that those who were to become ministers, whatever their fields of activity, should be inoculated with the thought and experience of the race; more accurately, with selected portions of such thought and experience. The colonial colleges did not pass a Declaration of Independence. They were content to follow the pattern of Cambridge and Oxford, of Edinburgh and Aberdeen. If there seemed to be a professional purpose—the training of ministers, there was a liberal, even classical subject matter. They sought an objective which we now call professional, through an unprofessional program. They considered education more important than training. The minister and scholar were different names for the same person. A minister was a man of learning. In those days and for many generations to come, a college likewise was a college.

The colleges, then, did not forget the contribution of the past to human welfare. They were unwilling to break with classic traditions. They felt the need of conserving racial memories. If the people lived in large open spaces, the colleges lived in an eternal world. That they contributed this larger phase of life to a period in peril of losing the accumulated values of history and experience, was their greatest glory. That the principle of conservation was the dominant one in their total influence is evident, since its momentum determined the pattern of college life very largely for 250 years after the founding of Harvard. That most of these colleges were oversteeped in tradition is but another illustration of the power of habit.

The colleges did not attempt seriously to achieve unity between the life of the people and the traditions of academic patterns. "Life" was largely left on the outside. The colleges that were founded even up to the period before the Civil War were more concerned in preserving knowledge and virtue as inseparable objectives of formal education than in transforming them into direct agencies in meeting the fluctuating exigencies of contemporary life.

If the colleges of the present period seem to have lost something of the keen appreciation of these fundamental necessities, it is well to recognize the contrary forces now operating in society. In the transition from individual knowledge and individual virtue to socialized knowledge and socialized virtue which has been going on during the last half century or more, countless ramifications and interdependencies have been introduced.

But the early pioneers were manipulating their balance, not ours. To attempt to measure their problem in terms of the problem of such a pioneer on the social front as the late Graham Taylor, Chicago's noted practical sociologist, has described would be to make the same mistake in kind which the early pioneers are almost uniformly condemned for making. Graham Taylor in describing his experience said his life for fifty years had "swung like a pendulum between the privileged few and the struggling many, between the town and the gown, between landowning farmers and tenant farm hands, between crowded tenements of day laborers and the homes and offices of captains of commerce, between industrial wage earners and the employers, between trade unions and manufacturing associations, between academic circles and the masses of the people, between native born and foreign born population, and in politics and religion between conservatives and progressives, reactionaries and radicals."

The colonial colleges had no such background. Present day colleges will ignore these modern problems at their peril. To the credit of the colonial colleges it may be said that they were reaching down that America might build up. The present day superstructure is now being built in conformity with a confusing array of codes. We may boast of our variety. We have yet to agree upon our principles of unity.

To bring what we have called "adult education" in the pioneer school of experience into close juxtaposition with the classical education then prevailing in the colleges, is to emphasize the contrast, even what some would call the conflict, between them. One was essentially expanding, the other essentially conserving. On the one hand was a free, energetic, resourceful people bent upon occupying new land; on the other was a self-contained, traditional, stabilized institution, well content with its definitive program.

It has been hastily concluded there was no unity between the colleges and the life of the people. As a matter of fact, there was inherent relationship between them. Both ends are necessary to a balance. Just as one end goes up, the other goes down. The people were forever pulling up stakes and venturing forth into unexplored territory. They were seeking more elbow-room—less contaminated air. They were ill at ease under restraint, even the restraint of law. The colleges would enrich this life. It would be quite too much to say that the colleges fully met the intellectual and spiritual needs of the people. They certainly did not do so. Their program was not broad and inclusive. The absorption of the settlers in the problems of physical existence, and of the colleges in their Neo-Platonic studies, had excluded development in medicine, the arts, and literature. Indeed, in such fields as these, there had actually been recession. The colleges did tend to counteract the ultra-obsession with immediacies. Their influence tended toward a definite form of enlargement and enrichment. Their influence was supplementary, complementary; it was not comprehensive. They applied checks and balances before the framers of the Constitution did. However consciously or unconsciously, they furnished the conservative element so necessary in a rapidly developing and progressive society. Neither of these tendencies of itself, nor indeed both of them together, could guarantee a broad and comprehensive unity of body and mind and spirit, from which would develop a collective national consciousness on this side of the Atlantic. That was the problem of a later generation.

In course of time the Supreme Court made a powerful contribution to this preservation of balance. Justice Marshall gave to that tribunal weight and dignity, injected stability into the American government, and strengthened the wavering assurance that democracy could and would accept great learning and be guided by sound judgment. The Supreme Court then as now exercised strong centripetal power. It has been a nation founder and builder. It has been and remains our final crucible of reasonable determination. The fact that American higher education is relatively so effective as a force for human conservation is largely due to John Marshall's refusal to permit the New Hampshire Legislature to divert the funds of Dartmouth College. This decision carried far-reaching implications. The end is not yet.

The churches, too, with which the colleges for the most part were closely identified, were bulwarks of conservatism, but their conservatism assumed such rigidity and impenetrability as to make them divisive in their influence. They drove many thinking men out by their very threats of doom. Their influence became more and more centrifugal as the multitude of sects developed. The churches helped to make of the American scene "a plate of sand," as Sun Yat-sen said of China in the earlier days of the Chinese democracy. It is not strange that the churches furnished less receptive soil than the colleges to innovations of thinking and toleration. Neither the colleges nor the churches, however, thought of the people as a whole. Both encouraged sectional and racial differences. There were occasional exceptions, but, speaking in the large, they were not crusaders for the American "race" now forming, much less for the human race. The colleges were pursuing an abbreviated form of Greek thought, sans music, sans art, sans gymnastics, in a word, sans Plato's lively sense of the completely balanced life. They did contribute to a partial balance, largely, it may be, through the law of inertia. With the gradual separation of the educational and ecclesiastical influences, these types of conservatism continued in each group.

The most remarkable fact, then, that confronts us as we view the situation in the large is the contrast between the expanding physical life of the people and the relatively contracted intellectual and cultural life and methodology of the colleges. Each made a necessary contribution to the foundations of the nation. Fortunately, we still refuse as a people to be wholly individualized or wholly socialized.

CHAPTER IV

PROPAGATING THE SPECIES

AMONG the epics of mankind, include the epic of the American colleges. They sprang up across the continent in scores and hundreds, as if by magic. But there were discoverable causes: religious zeal, private benevolence, and to a much less extent, state action. Donald G. Tewksbury in his study of the founding of colleges before the Civil War, in which he used the Session Laws of the several states as a primary source, has recently given statistical confirmation to a conviction largely held.* Discarding the claims of the colleges themselves and of their zealous friends, he has listed them on the basis of their charters, legally authorized, and has demonstrated what had not been accurately authenticated before, that the vast majority of them were of church origin, and that the prime motive of the founders was the development of a supply of educated ministers. By this painstaking process Tewksbury discovered that, before the Civil War, 182 college enterprises were launched, which still in the year of our Lord 1927-28 sailed the academic seas. Until the decade of 1830-40 they were primarily of Congregational and Presbyterian origin.

In a few instances referred to in Chapter XXII, there were concerted efforts on the part of nationally organized churches to found colleges. The work was done largely through what might be called personal evangelism. It was the home missionaries who did it, more particularly Yale and Princeton men.

While the chief influences emanated from colonial insti-

* See References, p. 349.

tutions, not all such institutions exhibited this missionary spirit. Harvard did not, Brown did not. Dartmouth had a plan for educating the Indians, but it did not eventuate in the form projected, nor in any form in the extensive multiplication of colleges. The college movement was inaugurated, propelled, and largely financed by church and college men with strong Puritanical convictions.

There were settlers in most of the communities who looked upon colleges as veritable citadels of religion and democracy, and in certain groups, of culture. They foresaw that the spiritual conquest of the continent must come in large measure through the implementation of the colleges.

There were others who thought of the college as an instrument of the devil—sure to undermine the religious faith of young people. A third group, not holding so extreme a view, placed a higher value upon religious fervor than on intellectual balance, an attitude that still persists in some quarters. Colleges of the type of Oberlin were condemned for being too progressive and tolerant, standing as Oberlin did for "perfectionism," for coeducation, against slavery, and later, including in their enrollment Negroes and other minority races. Oberlin also adopted the manual labor device which soon fell through there and elsewhere of its own weight. The proposed charter of Illinois College was held up by the legislature for several years, the ground stated being that legal recognition would be a deterrent to the principle and growing practice of the separation of church and state. It is said by a prominent Catholic authority that that Church later was stimulated to found colleges through the encroachments of the state system of schools. An official of a leading Protestant society wrote, "The Jesuits are willing, nay longing, nay plotting . . . to become the educators of America." From the annual report for 1853 of the same society, Paul M. Limbert quotes: "In our associate capacity, in conjunction with kindred organizations, we meet the Society of Jesus to decide the question whether Protestant evangelical institutions or the institutions and influences of Rome shall cover that field, and mould the forming population." Here then we find democracy working with a very considerable admixture of fear, suspicion, vengeance.

Even in the old Northwest Territory, as a trustworthy historian has testified, "There was a lively mistrust of Yankees, pianos and colleges," a century after the Ordinance of 1787 had declared in its Preamble, "Religion, morality and knowledge being necessary to good government and the happiness of mankind, schools and the means of education shall forever be encouraged." This distrust is all the more significant because this Ordinance had preceded and helped to mark the way for the Constitutional Convention, and, because of its advanced provisions on the subject of free government, it had attracted to the Territory the "thrifty Yankee from New England, the enterprising Dutchman from Pennsylvania, the conscientious Quaker from Carolina and Virginia, and some of the sturdiest pioneer stock from the frontier of Kentucky."

There were interesting techniques of college founding. For illustration—several Yale graduates before going into the trans-Mississippi region made a "compact" in true early American fashion. Each was to found a church and when these first steps were taken all were to combine in getting behind a college enterprise. From such labors a present day worthy college came forth.

With the Congregationalists in general another procedure was adhered to. A New England community was first transplanted into soil farther west, and soon a college was placed in this setting as its bright particular gem. It was so at Marietta, Oberlin, Beloit, Knox, Olivet, Carleton, Grinnell, Colorado, Whitman and Pomona.

The early procession of colleges was preceded by all sorts of bands—the Yale Band, the Andover Band, the Western Collegiate Society, the Iowa Band, and other bands and societies indigenous to the soil. The colleges were founded by the people. They sprang up through the exigencies of the times. The impulse to found colleges ran riot. No wise educational philosophy was injected as an element of control.

The way to do it was to form a committee and go out and do it. The founders were "God sakers."

As a result, many more colleges were founded than could possibly survive. If the plan had been in vogue of placing a wooden cross where each college had expired, the landscape would show a widely extended burying ground. The ravages of academic diseases—chiefly due to malnutrition—were ter-rific. Colleges died literally by the hundreds. Tewksbury found that the average mortality rate for the sixteen Western States studied was 81 per cent. In these same states and dur-ing the same period he lists 412 deceased and 104 living colleges.

Through the influence of the various organizations, the foundations were laid for such substantial institutions, in addition to those mentioned above, as Wabash College, Lane Theological Seminary, Illinois College, Western Reserve University—to mention typical examples.

The detailed history of these bands and societies has been set forth by competent authorities. In the very early years the Methodists and Baptists declined to participate in the movement. A group of Methodists feared the influence of the educated ministers as likely to dry up the springs of emotional life and therefore of right conduct. The Baptists, then a minority and persecuted group, attributed their status to the influence of the educated ministers of other denomina-tions. The changed attitude of these two groups was wrought through the acceptance by the church leaders of more toler-ant views, and through the increased success of the groups which had founded colleges as a necessary step in building a civilization permeated with religious faith.

The Triennial Convention of the Baptists in 1820 under the influence of their creative leader, Luther Rice, altered their constitution so as to bring education under the opera-tions of the church. The shibboleth of the Baptists in due time became, "Every state its own Baptist college." The resolution was not put into effect by the Convention, which, according to Frank W. Padelford, Secretary of the Baptist

Board of Education, soon showed a disposition to control their schools but evaded the obligation to support them.

In 1824 the General Conference of the Methodist Episcopal Church transferred from one form of zeal to another and voted to establish a college within the confines of each Annual Conference. Thus arose a multitude of "Wesleyan Universities," of which those of Ohio, Illinois, Dakota, Nebraska, Iowa are examples. The General Conference declared at that time, "The church college is the bulwark of the Christian church." Randolph-Macon in Virginia (1830), and Wesleyan, Connecticut (1831), are considered the "parent institutions of the Church." Within the decades of the forties and fifties the founding of Methodist colleges reached large proportions. The peak of the movement was reached in the fifties. The Methodist *Almanacs* and General Conference *Journals* list 200 schools and colleges founded between 1835 and 1860. The list of Methodist schools and colleges in 1860 contains 100 names, of which twenty-five were those of colleges. Up to and including 1870 there were nearly 300 institutions, of which not more than 100 still survive as Methodist. A Methodist historian observes, "Throughout this period the Methodist Episcopal Church as a denomination was powerless to prevent the wasteful multiplication of these schools, or to control this lack of educational standards which was injuring the reputation of the church and bringing disrepute upon the denomination." Because of this situation the General Conference soon took the steps outlined in a later chapter for bringing order out of chaos.

Three vivid forebodings of the extinction of "our Protestant civilization" were observed by some of the earlier workers in the field: increased immigration from certain parts of Europe, infidelity, and Roman Catholicism! In each case they were wrong. Divisions among the Protestants themselves have had a much more weakening effect than any influence from without.

Nothing can demonstrate more conclusively the lack of

foundation for the fear that the Catholics were likely to monopolize the college field than the actual statistics. The first Catholic college which appears on Tewksbury's list is Georgetown University, which, founded in 1789, was chartered in 1815. St. Joseph's College, Emmitsburg, Maryland, a college for women, followed one year later. St. Mary's College, Baltimore, not in the Tewksbury list since it was closed later, was the first successful attempt at higher education in Maryland. Three Catholic colleges were chartered in the '30's and five in the '40's. The Catholics concentrated largely on elementary and secondary education in the earlier period. At the beginning of the World War, 115 institutions were listed as colleges by the Catholic educational authorities. Since that time some seventy Catholic colleges have appeared, although the dates of the chartering for the baccalaureate degree are not at hand. More detailed reference to the influence of the various churches will be found in the chapter dealing with the changing relationship of the colleges and the churches.

Eventually the most prominent and influential of the societies devoting their energies to the building of colleges was the Society for the Promotion of Collegiate and Theological Education at the West. It represented a non-denominational adventure: to prevent duplication and waste in founding colleges; to protect Eastern donors from beggars who were seeking by hand-to-mouth feeding to keep their academic children alive; to guide gifts into worthy channels. Up to 1858 about three out of four of the dollars contributed through this Society came from Congregational sources. This Society eventually became the Congregational Education Society. Under whatever name, it has consistently opposed denominational control of educational institutions.

The leading spirit and for twenty-five years the president of the Society for the Promotion of Collegiate and Theological Education at the West was Theron Baldwin, a graduate of Yale and a member of the Yale Band, whose services to American education were later officially recognized by his

Alma Mater. A typical quotation expresses the spirit which impelled him. In 1856 he wrote:

> It is one of the glories of our American colleges that their doors are alike open to all classes of society, and that the only nobility known within their walls has its basis in intellectual power, high attainment, and moral worth.

The panic of 1837 accentuated the difficulties of the under-nourished colleges. In many cases where the home committees failed to secure the needed means of sustenance for their infants, they left them crying on the doorsteps of the churches and ran away. When the Iowa College Association, led by a group of ministers, was organized in 1844, an agent was immediately sent to Boston to secure funds. The Society already referred to, whose title was alphabetically embellished, condemned the plan and advised that "aid may be obtained when the plan and the system of instruction shall be so matured that they can secure the confidence of the Eastern mind." The report of this rebuff spurred the wives of the home ministers to raise one hundred dollars "out of their own resources," and eventually with many small supplementary gifts from the Society for Western Colleges and others, "Grinnell University, the soul, the animating spirit of the colony," entered upon its brilliant career.

It will be recalled that in 1819 Thomas Jefferson had established the University of Virginia as a definite protest against the dominant sectarian influence in American higher education. He suggested, however, that the churches might well establish agencies about the University but not organically connected with it. According to Tewksbury, permanent colleges were founded before the Civil War with denominational affiliations as follows: Presbyterian, 49; Methodist, 34; Baptist, 25; Congregational, 21; Catholic, 14; Episcopal, 11; Lutheran, 6. Two or more denominations cooperated in founding a number of the colleges included in the above figures, so that some institutions are counted two or three times.

During the same period there were twenty-one permanent institutions founded or eventually taken over by the state, and three others which became city colleges. Particularly were colleges founded through Presbyterian influence destined to become state institutions. Their development into universities was to come later.

Meantime the life of the people was an expanding life. The leaders of the movement to found colleges were *en rapport* with the genius of the times. They were not so much educators as promoters. It should be pointed out, however, that neither the religious nor the educational motive was entirely uncontaminated. Conditions were not so simple as that. The representatives of real estate, all the business men in the several local communities, and particularly the railroads which had the power to dispose of vast areas of government land, had a stake in the matter.

The location of colleges, therefore, followed upon the heels of the expanding empire; the colleges generally followed the railroads. A railroad map during the latter part of this period is also a map of college sites. One may be superimposed to a large extent upon the other, and this despite the fact that the active and influential Congregational group sought to set each new college within an isolated community.

In 1850 Virginia, the oldest settlement, had eight colleges, nearly all of which were on railroad lines; William and Mary was on a waterway. The main lines in railroad building were from East to West, and the belts established by the railroads were also the college student belts. In each decade, as railway mileage increased across the continent, the number of colleges and college students increased. The decade from 1850 to 1860 was the greatest of all the railroad building eras and in that decade more colleges were founded than in any other decade in our history. Later, the tendency had become established to found institutions not merely on railroads but at railroad centers.

The bare recital of this story, however, brings to light the diversity of ideals and purposes of the people. Many of the

people had a passion for religious orthodoxy, a passion which
had led Horace Mann, a Unitarian, to deplore the fact that
the representatives of Calvinism got control of the largest
number of colleges.

There were some indications of an impulse toward cooperation, signalized by the abortive effort of the Congregationalists and Presbyterians to adopt "A Plan of Union," and
by the formation of the Society for the Promotion of Collegiate and Theological Education at the West. The Congregationalists furnished the leadership for this Society and
about three-fourths of the money. The Presbyterians eventually took control of most of the colleges. According to
Limbert, "The Secretary of the Presbyterian Board of Education in 1847 deplored the fact that the number of colleges
strictly under Presbyterian control was very small, and expressed the hope that every new institution of this kind
would commit itself to the management of the Church,
instead of to a 'comparatively irresponsible body of self-
perpetuating or state-elected trustees.'" On the other hand,
the Congregationalists individually and through their various
societies consistently opposed denominational control of institutions of learning. This was one of the reasons why the
"Plan of Union" of the two churches referred to in more
detail in a later chapter was not achieved.

There was a recognition of intersectional dependence.
There were some unsuccessful attempts at mergers, and some
transfers of college control from one denomination to another. There was almost a consistent demonstration of the
reproductive power of the college pattern. There was the
struggle between independence and initiative, between tradition and liberty, between external control and self-determination both on the part of the college and the individual
student.

The modern problems of college administration and teaching were slowly arising. Manifestly with such differences of
viewpoint among the people on practically all subjects,
whether religious, political, economic, or racial, the college

could not continue to reproduce unaltered the colonial patterns of instruction. Perforce the colleges must be forums for the discussion of vital issues of life. Changes in the college program were inevitable in spite of the persistent power of inertia. The seeds of expanding life within the colleges as well as among the people were being sown. The leaven was beginning to work.

A leading historian has declared, "It is safe to say that by these and other similar institutions the cast of character for intelligent morality and religion and civil probity has been largely affected in these great interior commonwealths and also in those of the regions beyond."

This exposition has held thus far to the title of the chapter—"Propagating the Species." Emphasis has properly been placed on the administrative side. It is not inappropriate to ask: What was the nature of the species?

Albea Godbold has drawn a vivid picture of the colleges of the ante-bellum seaboard South. He has been guided not only by official documents but by many intimate diaries of teachers and students.

Churches are exhibited in Godbold's thesis which were pawns of politicians, were aristocratic in membership, were prejudiced against education, were prompted by jealousies and rivalries, were fearful of the proselyting power of other churches and their colleges which "decoyed and entrapped" their children. It is not strange that both churches and colleges died by the hundreds. Other groups were particularly vehement in their denunciation of Presbyterian activity in founding colleges and in assuming leadership in state universities. They opposed the "Presbyterian monopoly." These are not all generalizations, to be sure. It is pointed out, however, that dissenters were often more numerous than church members.

There was a disposition among the churches to deplore what they called their own "educational inferiority"; they bore ill will toward the North because of the slavery question; they held that students lost their religion at college;

they criticized the University of Virginia and all state universities for inculcating "infidelity and skepticism." The faculty of one of these universities was once denounced as "a parcel of inveterate demons from among the damned."

While the reason usually given for founding colleges was the need of an educated ministry at home and abroad, yet at no time or place were a majority of the students candidates for the ministry. The graduates became lawyers, teachers, physicians, farmers, and merchants as well as ministers. Colleges were needed, it was recognized, for "the rising culture of society." Many churches regarded themselves as a part of the nation and therefore obligated to render public service. They recognized educational institutions as of strategic importance in the life of the country. Many church people agreed with Washington—also a founder of colleges—that "reason and experience both forbid us to expect that national morality can prevail to the exclusion of religious principle." They expected colleges to promote evangelism and looked upon revivals as times of recruiting membership.

The typical colleges had daily prayers, Sunday services, Sunday Bible classes, Sabbath observance, grace at table. While the emphasis was upon conversion, the number of converted students who became church members was relatively small. Randolph-Macon College had a church composed of students and the community from its founding. There were curriculum courses meeting once a week in Evidences of Christianity, Moral Philosophy, Natural Theology. In 1856 one college dropped Wayland's *Moral Science* from the curriculum because of its chapter opposing slavery. A textbook in algebra "exhibiting strong sectional feeling" was written by a professor in one of the colleges. In 1861 President Wingate of Wake Forest exclaimed, "Lift your eyes above the prejudices of the hour!"

Work began at sunrise but educational standards were not high. There were many restrictive rules. Students were ranked in discipline, morality, and scholarship. The colleges of Virginia followed the educational standards of their state university. Libraries and scientific equipment were meager throughout the entire system. The libraries were open one or two hours each week. It was not unusual for the college literary society to have more books than the college library. One college so advertised in its catalogue. In the matter of developing libraries the University of South Carolina was especially progressive. The curriculum of the ancient languages, mathematics, and English composition and declamation changed little.

The college students took themselves seriously. Often they were the sons of the most fortunate classes. They were ambitious to become leaders and to render service in education and religion. There were always a few good students.

For the most part, slavery was defended by the colleges. One college president wrote a book on "The Philosophy of Slavery." Presidents and heads of Departments of Theology were slave owners. No evidence is submitted that the colleges favored secession. At the University of Georgia students debated the slavery question and often decided against it. The colleges reflected the martial spirit in the South. A military company was organized at Davidson College in 1853. Commencements were great occasions. They lasted for almost a week and drew large companies of people. There were speeches and music. The Commencement "party" in the church colleges became a great occasion as a substitute for the "ball" of the state universities. The state universities also gave attention to religion. In this matter there was no separation of church and state.

In general and contrary to conditions which usually prevailed in the North even long after the War between the States, educational standards of the state universities were higher than those of the denominational colleges. In this respect the Universities of Virginia and North Carolina were notable and their influence was widely extended.

All this is submitted as an impressionistic picture of colleges of the period in the Southeastern area of the United States. Much of the spirit that was characteristic of churches

and colleges in the Southeast was also found in other sections
of the country. Of course, the manifestations of this spirit
varied with the local aspirations and prejudices and gave
peculiar local color. In all areas there were notable exceptions.

Unfortunately there is no fully documented story of ante-
bellum colleges as a whole within the other sections. Many
intimate histories of individual colleges have been written.
In other sections the ground has not yet been so thoroughly
covered.

A number of institutions have submitted lists of colleges
founded or presided over by their former students, which
will be found on pages 337-339 of the Appendix. The statistics are not comparable as the data have been prepared on
different bases and often for purposes of publicity. The information is much more complete in some instances than in
others. Such factors as the age and academic standing of the
institution, and the number of graduate and professional
schools must also be taken into consideration in evaluating
the contributions to leadership in the field of higher education.

Other universities undoubtedly made significant contributions to the multiplication of colleges, as they have to their
later development. By some of these the data have not been
assembled; for others they are not at the author's hand. Several of the smaller institutions have remarkable records in
this respect. It is to be observed that in some of the instances
cited, the college of liberal arts of the university has played
an insignificant part. The university must share credit for
the achievements of graduate students with the smaller undergraduate institutions.

CHAPTER V

THE RISE AND FALL OF THE "INTELLECTUALS"

The University in a Changing World, edited by Kotschnig and Prys and published on the authority of the International Student Service, deplores the "grand betrayal of the Intellectuals."* It declares that the oneness of learning which once united all universities is now broken down. The unity of truth and learning has been lost. Likewise the singleness of aim as to the kind of individual the university would produce. The oneness of the *unitus intellectus,* it is asserted, grew out of the acknowledged oneness of God, which was propounded so trenchantly by Abelard. Since then there has been consistent deterioration following a series of decadent philosophic conceptions. An adapted and condensed statement from the book just named would be:

> Humanism brought heaven and earth together; the Enlightenment enthroned the Goddess of Reason; Utility confined the conception to Reasons of State; Romanticism momentarily discovered anew the unity of the world; Positivism ceded the supreme place of honor to Natural Science and her methods—"Science without presuppositions carried the claim of the Absolute"—and (to make the descent to Avernus complete as well as easy) at last the "immorality of Einstein" made all values relative!

Of course, science does have presuppositions, does not parade in the livery of metaphysics, does not admit the "immorality of Einstein." If the summary reflects the present

* See References, p. 351.

philosophy of the European university, it certainly does not that of the university of the United States. In bringing the university to the people, the present writer denies that education is tobogganing toward doom. But the main point now under consideration is the break with tradition. The answer of the universities to that indictment is "Guilty," and in the light of considerable experience they are inclined to add the word, "fortunately." There is justification for the view that the present variety of American colleges, perplexing though it is, is better than an enforced uniformity. To approve variety, is not to condemn a wholesome unity.

There has been a corresponding descent, according to the book cited, in the excellence of the individual product of the university.

> The Middle Ages knew the scholar-saint; Humanism with its great traditions, the sage; Romanticism had its concept of the scholar and ethical Personality; Positivism produced the idea of leadership in the words, 'Knowledge is power.' "Today there is no common idea of the elite any more than there is a common idea of truth and learning."

The Platonic revival at Cambridge, England, in the seventeenth century had furnished the immediate intellectual background for Harvard. It was derived from Plato, but it did not fully represent Plato. The proportion, the balance, of his teaching had been lost. It placed emphasis on the intellectual at the expense of the mystical, the esthetic, the ethical, and the sensory. It was Neo-Platonic, and as such it sought "retired and cloistered virtue." Harvard knew she had a good thing and she brooked no interference.

The present condition of many universities abroad is deplorable enough—certainly from the American point of view. The boast—"Our youth will never be free but they are happy," was made by Hitler in 1938, not by any proponent of American representative democracy at any time, least of all during the last fifty years.

It is also true that, without boasting of it, our early educators and ecclesiastics denied freedom to youth. They would mould them to a predetermined pattern. The college curriculum was fixed. Orthodoxy was thunderously defined, but there was plenty of lightning to give visibility. The church and the college were under the dispensation of law. No one ever suggested that the students were or ought to be happy.

The 1840's are frequently referred to as the era of the "march of intellect" in and around Boston. For the most part the intellect was kept well within prescribed bounds. The squirrel marches in her cage, too. The Harvard ideology was generally well accepted and firmly established.

The New England character is portrayed by James Truslow Adams: "The gristle of conscience, work, thrift, shrewdness and duty became bone. It was good bone, all too lacking today, but the flesh was missing from it." Harvard's first great teacher, Andrews Norton, who caused his students to think by antagonizing them, was a representative of the old school. He wrote a celebrated book on Christian Evidences, and as a master of definitions expounded it to his students. The students are reported as saying that the only evidences of Christianity at Harvard were Norton's daughters. Many students favored changes in the curriculum, but the administration ignored their suggestions.

Ticknor and Channing were great intellectuals representing a more tolerant point of view. Ticknor had some of the qualities of a reformer: "He had the sense of an enthralling purpose which dominated all of his other thoughts, that is of 'reforming Harvard College.'" He failed to accomplish his purpose. He would have found a more congenial atmosphere at the University of Virginia if he had accepted Jefferson's invitation to become a member of the faculty there.

Charles W. Eliot once characterized Channing as the outstanding Unitarian of Harvard and of all time. Channing gave Unitarianism its unequaled exposition. He stood for intellectual and spiritual liberty. He had a flexible mind and was suspicious of dogma. He could not follow the hideous theology of the Cottons, the Mathers, and the Edwardses. He, too, like Ticknor, was a reformer. He taught Emerson, Thoreau, and the rest of the Transcendentalists.

Ticknor and Channing were two Harvard teachers who looked upon scholasticism in any form as a closed system, who sought an Open Sesame to truth, who felt the stagnation of the ideology and orthodoxy of the time and sought the enrichment of diversity, who were convinced that life is too spontaneous to be uniform; in a word, who had the biological view of nature and man without Darwin's method or his facts. These bold leaders were genuine democrats in the realm of the spirit. The *unitus intellectus* of Harvard was in danger because of their presence. They were not interested in the missionary bands from Yale and Princeton enlisted in founding colleges west of the Hudson any more than were the rest of the Harvard men. They were interested in Harvard. They were among the first *causae belli* which made of Harvard the battleground *par excellence* of the intellectuals.

Outside of the sacred Harvard pale, a much larger group of freer thinkers was forming. These thinkers are ordinarily referred to as the Transcendentalists. They may have been forming a dogma of another kind, but in any event, they were dissenters. They were quite willing to be dubbed heretics. They were concerned more with the inward look and the forward look than with the backward look. Bronson Alcott chronologically was their leader. Emerson became their greatest prophet.

It is no part of the present task to attempt an evaluation of the complex of thought and feeling known as Transcendentalism. Among the many evaluations which have already been made is that of William James: "The source of Emerson's optimism is the philosophic direction of his states of mystical ecstasy." Yet James discovered in it "the doctrine which has marked all the periods of revival—the early Christian age, Luther's age, Rousseau's, Kant's, and Goethe's, namely, that the innermost nature of things is congenial to the powers which men possess." These strange ideas began to have a disturbing effect upon the intellectual *status quo.*

Bancroft identified the new philosophy with Quakerism's doctrine of the Inner Light. Other sources for it have been traced. While it found fructifying soil in the pioneer spirit of New England and eventually across the continent, many of the seeds of it, like the seeds of our political philosophy, had been transplanted from across the sea. They are to be found in Plato's *Timaeus.* Oriental philosophy flavors much of Emerson's writing, and the *Compensation* has been likened to the *Karma.* Adrienne Moore recently listed many magazine articles printed in America during this period in which expositions were made and discussions were carried on concerning phases of Oriental philosophy. Such material frequently became "first page news." There were evidently many readers. From Germany had been captured the insight of Fichte, Schleiermacher, Kant, Schiller, Herder, and Jacobi. Much of this German influence reached New England through Carlyle, who leavened Emerson's thinking as Locke did that of Thomas Jefferson.

Emerson and Carlyle comprehended each other's language. Carlyle said Emerson was the only man who ever understood him. Through Emerson, *Sartor Resartus* was published first in America, and here it found its first large circle of readers. Carlyle reciprocated by publishing some of Emerson's works in England before they appeared in America. They dug down into the same wells even if they often tapped different streams of water, for, while Emerson was a philosopher of hope, Carlyle was a philosopher of despair.

It is not necessary to become a devotee of the intuitive philosophy of Emerson which conceived the purpose of life to acquaint man with himself and considered the highest revelation as that "God is in every man," in order to discover that it became a divisive influence at Harvard and served as a transforming purpose of the first order in determining the future of American college history. It was an interpretation of the spirit of the pioneer. By its tendency to free the college mind from English and European patterns and standards, it, too, marked the change which was to come over the colleges.

Let Emerson speak for himself:

> Our age is retrospective. It builds the sepulchres of the fathers. It writes biographies, histories, and criticism. The foregoing generations beheld God and nature face to face; we, through their eyes. Why should not we also enjoy an original relation to the universe? Why should we grope among the dry bones of the past, or put the living generation into masquerade out of its faded wardrobe? The sun shines today also. There is more wool and flax in the fields. There are new lands, new men, new thoughts. Let us demand our own work and laws and worship.

Emerson's proposed substitution of a new philosophy of intellectual development for the intellectualism of his Harvard predecessors was a very important contribution to the progress of the American college. This statement does not carry with it the assumption that the colleges began immediately, or even later, to teach in any thoroughgoing way the text of the Emersonian philosophy. Emerson's contribution was more in terms of method than of substance. He demonstrated at least that scholarly minds in America could devote themselves to philosophic thought which was without the bounds of accepted tradition. Emerson drove in an entering wedge.

The influence of this movement of which Emerson was the outstanding product brought Boston and the rural centers into closer touch with one another. Numerous societies were organized, and Brooks states that "almost every eminent man in New England joined in the general effort to propagate knowledge."

The striking movement of which the Transcendentalist teaching was the final outcome, in spite of its excesses and vagaries, stood for a collective impulse. Men found that by living together and working together, there came added zest and energy in their endeavors. It was chiefly to Alcott that we are indebted for this impulse toward "association as the only sure means toward individual freedom and happiness." Out of such impulse as this grew eventually the present day method of cooperative study, research, and administration, which has contributed so profoundly to our educational advance.

Emerson was fond of quoting the phrase of Simonides, "Give me twice the time, for the more I think, the more it enlarges." The word "maturation" has recently been invented as expressing an important element of the educational process. Emerson liked the word and was devoted to the process. This process was not only familiar to Simonides and Emerson, but it was advocated by Gideon Hawley who became superintendent of common schools in New York State one hundred and twenty-five years ago. He outlined a process of development adjusted to the maturing powers of students, and clearly recognized not only the principles which within recent years have been known as maturation, but also the principle we now call motivation, likewise inherent in Emerson's philosophy. Basic English would now say growth.

Emerson was not merely a New Englander; he was an American. He was passionately interested in the enlargement of horizons. He learned the resources of the country, going to school to the prairies. He did not distrust "the rough, wild, incalculable road America would have to travel to find itself. The Hoosiers and the Badgers of the West, the hard heads of Oregon and Utah, the rough riders and legislators in shirt sleeves, let them drive on as they might. Better than to quote English standards and miss the sovereignty of power, he believed that no strong nation could ever develop without its own strong, wild will."

Before Emerson died, he realized that the Transcendental philosophy had spent its force in New England, but his imagination kindled as he fared forth into the West and Northwest, and his faith was strengthened in the ultimate achievement of a philosophy more in keeping with American ideals.

Emerson was not the only New Englander who became an American. Bronson Alcott was also a scout, venturesome enough to travel into the regions west of the Hudson and spy out the Promised Land. Everywhere in the West he was heralded as the Sage of Concord, the master of Emerson, and the founder of the Concord school of philosophy. Emerson was a spectator and an oracle. He set forth the truth from his secluded eminence. Alcott, on the other hand, was an investigator and a sharer. He delighted in the conversational method. He knew how to take as well as to give. He made some great discoveries and brought back certain wild men of the West as exhibits of a culture not so fully comprehended in Boston, as he at first did not fully comprehend it himself. Over and over, from 1855-82, he made these conversational tours, ten of them in all, and received an increasingly cordial welcome at the centers of learning in Ohio, Illinois, Missouri, and Iowa. He peddled his Yankee notions and picked up new ideas so that his bag was always full. He was an unofficial ambassador at large. He glorified vagabondage.

He found at St. Louis a philosophic society composed of what he called "loaded brains." The member of it best known to succeeding generations was William T. Harris. Harris and the rest of them were studying Hegel's philosophy. St. Louis began to be known as the Athens of the West. There is evidence that Alcott fertilized Harris' thinking, who, in turn, was to give the set of Hegelian thought to much of the educational process of America. Hegel and his American disciples taught that the spirit of man realizes itself through what is about it, that the secret of man's nature is embedded in the energies of his moral and intellectual life, and that conflict and competition among the elements of society serve eventually to direct and enrich that society. The impact of these disturbing influences tended to weaken Harvard's carefully built fortifications.

That President Eliot belonged to the same school of

thought is evidenced by a declaration he made as early as 1853:

> The other day I came to the conclusion that this eternal cultivation of the intellect is not the source of all the happiness in the world, nor even a large part of it; that the continued effort to improve one's mind is too selfish and unfruitful to be very satisfactory, and that this everlasting digging can at best produce but a fruit with a stone at its heart.

If the traditional conception of the "Intellectuals" fell, that of a sound and more inclusive scholarship began to take its place. Emerson, while he could not foresee the contribution science was to make to the conception of scholarship, became ere long the symbol of "the American scholar."

William James and John Dewey later carried on the Hegelian tradition. It is well to observe that the Hegelian philosophy developed first at St. Louis, not at Boston. Alcott and Emerson, the two wise men from the East, had unobtrusively shuttled between the East and the West, between the past and the present, and helped "to weave this country into one seamless robe."

The Transcendentalist movement, whatever its inherent values may have been, has indirectly been a potent influence on American higher education. It produced in an increasing number of minds a distrust of the imitation of the English college pattern, which was not only characteristic of New England, but had become practically universal. Emerson transferred the immediacy which had characterized the life of the colonists and pioneers into the life of the mind. He performed the miracle of giving philosophic justification by the method of the scholar to the life of the common man. The youthful mind welcomed these appeals toward heroism and mysticism. Later Eliot testified, "When I had got at what proved to be my life work for education, I discovered in Emerson's poems and essays all the fundamental motives and principles of my own hourly struggle against educative routine and tradition, and against the prevailing notions of discipline for the young."

CHAPTER VI

THE SCRAMBLED DECADES

IF THIS chapter appears to lack unity, it has to that extent been true to the era with which it is concerned.

In *The Gilded Age* Mark Twain said, "The eight years in America from 1860 to 1868 uprooted institutions that were centuries old, changed the politics of a people, transformed the social life of half the country, and wrought so profoundly upon the entire native character that the influence cannot be measured short of two or three generations."*

This gem of wisdom is somewhat dimmed by Twain's habit of exaggeration. It is true that the measuring of the influence of those tragic years has not yet been accurately made, but violence is not the most effective method of changing the spirit and outlook of a people. While the habits and aspirations of generations could not immediately be abandoned, there was, after the shock of war had ceased, a gradual slowing down of centrifugal forces. The world could not shrink over night, but the processes of contraction under manifold legal and social pressures began.

Lord Bryce relates an incident that came to his notice at which he was amazed. His story is that but twenty years after the end of the War General Sherman attended a banquet in Atlanta and was introduced with great nobility of spirit in a speech which ended with the words, "The General has the reputation of being rather heedless in the use of lucifer matches." Was it then that Sherman declared that "war is hell"?

* See References, p. 348.

Dr. William S. Beard set forth a more reliable principle
for the interpretation of events when he said, "Everything
with which the student of American education deals seems
to impinge upon a multitude of other things—the general
content and unfolding of all things relevant, pertinent, tang-
ent, and contingent." The growing recognition of this indissoluble connection of all things tends to confuse the vision
of those who would attempt to interpret or even record the
trend of events. Some old things were passing away: not all
things were becoming new. There was an impact of conflicting forces which produced the most chaotic period of our
history. New forces broke loose during the decades of the
'70's and '80's, forces which had been gathering for some
decades before.

The effort is not made here to clarify these seething years
of the nineteenth century, but only to indicate some of the
currents and counter-currents, the tides and "tide-rips" which
followed in the wake of the preceding storm.

While cultures do not develop on a calendar schedule, the
life of a people does follow general trends at rather definite
periods. The year 1870 and the years immediately before
and after were remarkable as years of endings and beginnings. Details could be multiplied here indefinitely. Be-
neath the confusion confounded of the next two decades, two
general trends emerged. Centrifugal and centripetal forces
began to operate on a grand scale.

Population Shifts. On the one hand the pioneer spirit
which had already manifested itself in conquering the
strategic points of the continent still impelled adventurous
souls. Twenty years had elapsed since Horace Greeley's injunction, "Go West!" had been uttered, but the war had
interfered with the processes of migration. The Homestead
Act had been on the statute books for almost a decade, and
the Congress had passed a law making it impossible for people who "had taken up arms against the government" to take
advantage of the purchase of new government lands. A new
sectionalism began to develop. Vast numbers of people con-

tinued to look outward and beyond. The president of a college located in eastern Indiana on the old National Road later remarked to the writer that, standing on his campus during the '70's, he had in one day often counted as many as forty to sixty covered wagons wending their way westward.

The rush for the free government land developed into a remarkable technique, in comparison with which the modern intercollegiate football game would appear as child's play. These land rushes became America's chief outdoor sport. The newspapers of the nation furnished the people with thrilling stories of the successive occupations. The rushes in the Cherokee country toward the end of the period were the last in the series. In 1890 the Census Bureau announced that the frontiers "had all been taken up."

In marked contrast to this population movement was one in the opposite direction—not toward the land but toward the city. Harold Ward in *Travel* has given an excellent account of this development. It was in 1872 that the term "city planning" was first used in America in connection with projected improvements for Boston. This presaged a remarkable transition in American society. Soon after the opening of the first transcontinental railroad in 1869, San Francisco began to assert itself as the principal seaport on the Pacific coast. It was not until 1880 that New York became our first metropolis to pass the million mark.

Gradually our people learned to pool their interests within strategic areas, social, industrial, financial, and cultural. During the pioneer period, except among the missionaries, the social impulse was confused and irresolute. Such concentrations as developed outside of missionary circles were usually made for purposes of protection against hostile forces. This motive was one of prime consideration also in the early growth of our cities. In the beginning, all of them were located on deep water—on the Atlantic coast, the Great Lakes, and the rivers of the Mississippi basin; Roanoke, Jamestown, New Orleans and New York were on islands.

The military advantages of city location gave place in time

to the demands of commercial and social life. The development of science, the promise of greater profit, more leisure, more freedom of movement both of body and of mind, were contributing factors to city development.

Signs began to appear during these scrambled decades that agrarian democracy was beginning to disintegrate. Human impacts began to beat down the "inalienable rights." The first steps were being taken in a movement which in time promised to substitute a unified industrial society. In these first steps a series of hierarchies began to form, not only in industry but, in ways characteristic of their fields of operation, in politics, economics, social life, and even in religion: railroad building, the manufacturing of farm machinery, pork packing, oil refining, banking, political machines, stock exchanges, intense denominational consciousness. In these and other areas of our national life power was being concentrated in the hands of small groups of men. Before the trek of the covered wagon which marked the peaceful conquest of the continent was over, Jay Cooke's Juggernaut was fully under way, and many sought to profit by his example. Certainly the days of new kinds of pioneering were just beginning on a grand scale. These concentrations of power became so characteristic of so many phases of our life that the period has been called that of the American feudalism.

Corporations. Vast sums of money were needed for colossal enterprises. Temptations to exploit their fellows could not be resisted by greedy men. Ruthless waste of natural resources was certain to ensue. Excesses on the part of the "buccaneers" and "robber barons" in business and politics characterized the break from the vague optimism of youth to the beginnings of national growth. Transportation seems to have been the mother of the corporation. The year 1869 marked the completion, near Ogden, Utah, of the first great transcontinental railroad. Other great railroad enterprises were to be contemplated, and they could not be achieved without the use of the combined capital of many individuals.

After the completion of the Union Pacific, the nation was shocked at the disclosures of the Crédit Mobilier, an organization "into whose chest the gains from contracts for the whole Union Pacific building had flowed." Leading men in political life at Washington and elsewhere were stockholders in the Crédit Mobilier, congressmen having received the stock without cost. "A crowd of millionaires emerged from the Union Pacific adventure." The opportunities and the temptations involved in this process of building transcontinental railroads are strikingly illustrated by a quotation from one of Jay Cooke's publicity men concerning the region of the Northwest:

> There is nothing on the American continent equal to it. Such timber, such soil, such orchards, such fish, such climate, such coal, such harbors, such rivers! And the whole of it is but the western terminus of our railroad. The empire of the Pacific Coast is to be enthroned on Puget Sound. Nothing can prevent this—nothing. There is no end to the possibilities of wealth here. . . . Jay, we have got the biggest thing on earth. Our enterprise is an inexhaustible gold mine.

Even today new depths of the degradation which accompanied these phases of "winning the West" are being discovered.

The Civil Service. But just as there was a reversal in population shifts, so there were beginnings of reform in business and politics. The reformers for the most part were college men. They entered the picture as early as 1870 in behalf of an improved Civil Service. That year Carl Schurz introduced the first Civil Service Reform bill. The next year George W. Curtis was appointed chairman of the advisory board which during the administration of Hayes became the Civil Service Commission under the chairmanship of Dorman B. Eaton. During these same years Grant, ironically enough, proposed the annexation of Santo Domingo, believed by many as a mask for internal troubles, and the political orators began to speak eloquently on manifest destiny. Sumner, chairman of the Senate's Committee on

Foreign Relations, opposed the proposed annexation and staged an oratorical but not actual demolition of the political bosses.

In 1884 the Mugwump Party was launched. A new revolt of the people was beginning. This revolt, under the initial leadership of that great American, Carl Schurz, who in his native country had imbibed a decent respect for the authority of law and morality, attracted such public-spirited men— young and older—as Trumbull, Nast, Charles Francis and Henry Adams, White of the Chicago *Tribune,* Greeley and Reid of the New York *Tribune,* Watterson of the *Courier Journal,* Halstead of the Cincinnati *Commercial,* Ottendorfer of the *Staatszeitung,* John Hay, W. C. Bryant, Charles W. Eliot. These men had faith in disinterested intelligence, however unwarrantedly optimistic they may have been. The intellectuals, who knew little of practical politics, crossed swords with the bosses who were armed with the powerful spoils system. The first victory went to Goliath. Only such a prolonged and bitter struggle could disclose the Gargantuan growth of the "practical necessity" of the spoils system. Not even Dana's exposure in the *Sun* of the Tweed Ring scandal during the early part of this conflict could shake the confidence of the great mass of the voters in the political bosses. During the struggle Horatio Seymour wrote to Tilden, "Our people want men in office who will not steal, but who will not interfere with those who do."

As is characteristic of all political struggles, not all the bosses were as black as they were painted by the tarred stick. But municipal, state, and federal rings were disclosed as piratical monopolies. At least it was demonstrated that the phenomenon of the reform movement is as natural to our politics as the tendency toward corruption.

President Hayes attempted to stem the tide by appointing Schurz to the Department of the Interior and designating Eaton as an official student of the British Civil Service. He at once placed the post offices and customs on a competitive basis. Eaton had, in 1866, drafted the famous Metropolitan

Health Law which gave New York City its present Health Department, and before the century closed established the Eaton Professorship of Municipal Sciences at Columbia University. The Pendleton Act of 1883, framed by Eaton, has remained the basis of the Civil Service system. By the end of Arthur's administration, 16,000 positions were filled on a competitive basis. The opposition of the Mugwumps to the candidacy of Blaine placed Grover Cleveland in the presidency. The progress in Civil Service reform thus begun during the "scrambled decades" has been augmented by every president from Cleveland to Hoover. At the end of Hoover's administration about three-fourths of all federal employees were so classified. The laudable purpose of President Hayes to apply to our Civil Service the effective methods of the British Government has unfortunately not yet been achieved.

Another constructive trend of a very different nature was signalized by the Philadelphia Centennial Exposition of 1876. During this period the Metropolitan, Boston, Chicago, Corcoran, and other Museums of the Fine Arts were established, as were schools of industrial art in Philadelphia and Providence, schools of architecture at Columbia, Cornell, and Illinois. These followed the lead of the Massachusetts Institute of Technology founded in 1865. Art faculties were brought together at Pratt Institute, the Chicago Art Institute, Newcomb College of Tulane University, Washington University at St. Louis. In New York the Metropolitan Opera House was built. Music, opera, the theatre were making what strides they could, depending largely on foreign talent. The power press appeared, Thomas Nast became the Shakespeare of caricature. Drawing had been made a common school subject in 1870. In the minds of the masses, however, all these manifestations of the better life remained superfluous.

Among the Churches. The prevailing spirit of combination was caught by some of the churches and put to good purposes. A striking illustration may be taken from a group of churches which never has displayed strong cohesive tendencies. In 1870 the Fifth Jubilee of the landing of the Pilgrims on Plymouth Rock was being celebrated. Descendants of the Puritans, whose influence in community and college building during the 250 years had extended across the continent westward and southward, conceived and dramatized this celebration. The American Congregational Association and the American Congregational Union joined hands in certain concrete plans and persisted in them until, years later, the formulated ends were achieved. These plans looking toward the new era of consolidation were formulated in the same year which marked the death of Theron Baldwin, the great apostle of collegiate expansion. Striking trends were taking shape which were destined to transform the American church as well as the American college. Almost immediately the great Chicago fire intervened, the Boston fire, and the panic of 1873. Through all these adverse conditions the Congregational leaders held steadily to their purposes.

Here was an early illustration of the projection of a plan with stated objectives. These involved a half-dozen definite aspirations. It was proposed to raise a memorial offering of $1,000,000 for general Congregational purposes; to erect in Boston a great memorial structure which should perpetuate the memory of the founders of Puritanism on this side of the Atlantic and serve as a conservatory of "historic and sacred mementoes, as well as a social center"; to establish a rallying point for the church membership, not only on this continent but "from the four quarters of the globe"; to devote funds not so much for the extension of denominational influence into new territory as for the building of church edifices for churches already organized; to lead in "a re-discussion of the great principles upon which our institutions are founded, not for purposes of propaganda but for purposes of a better understanding," declaring that they had "much more to gain than to lose by thorough ventilation"; and finally, the most comprehensive objective of all, to stimulate the denomination itself "to begin to realize its unity." Other religious groups developed much greater cohesiveness.

These are typical trends selected from a confused era. Out of it all has grown the conviction that combinations, even corporations, are not essentially evil. The evil, if it exists, is found in the motives and methods by which they are organized and controlled. Theodore Roosevelt was right: there are good and bad trusts. But these were mere beginnings. The end is not yet.

Now suppose the colleges had acted upon the demand that they adjust themselves immediately to all the contradictory elements of this expanding life. Only the pieces would have been left to tell the story. How were they to be both teachers and reformers? For the most part, they wisely exercised the suspended judgment. They made combinations a subject of study. For this they have been sufficiently condemned. They began to study their own objectives, and later to enter upon concerted policies.

CHAPTER VII

COLLEGIATE VARIANTS

THE Declarations of Independence by the colleges came a century later than those of the English colonists. For 1775, made famous in Mecklenburg County, North Carolina, and 1776 in Philadelphia, the colleges substituted 1862, when Lincoln signed the Morrill Act, and the various declarations of the '70's. It would not be too much to say that Senator Morrill was the Samuel Adams of the American college revolution. Through successive discouragements and defeats he carried on until the seal of government was placed upon a new form of American higher education. His conception is now embodied in the "land-grant colleges," adjusted to the needs of farmers, mechanics—the people. Interrupted by the war, these colleges began to take form during the scrambled decades.

Another educational revolutionist had appeared a third of a century before. Horace Mann, the Samuel Adams of the American public schools, had read his Declaration of Independence to the Massachusetts State Board of Education in 1832. After years of persistent labor in a not too friendly atmosphere, Horace Mann, upon the acceptance of his plan for the free education of all the people, is reported to have said: "Now let the stars look out for my head." These revolutionists and their colleagues were laying the foundations of a democratic system of education. They would educate the people's children and confidently leave the impending issues with the children, grown to manhood and womanhood.

While the rulers of American society, therefore, were organizing a series of concentrations into a form of feudalism, the general trend of education was in the opposite direction. Education was becoming democratic. Population shifts, industry, politics, even art and religion moved toward diverse forms of centralized power and devised special machinery for its direction. Great industrial and financial leaders emerged, political bosses rose to eminence, corruption and reform fought for supremacy. Education, like art and religion, began to devise new methods of implementation also, but it did not make machinery paramount. The greatest leaders of education held fast to the conviction that its product must be self-made, or at least hand-made. One tendency to which the German influence contributed was to become more "efficient" through mechanization, but the colleges did not go so far in this direction as did industry and politics. Many of the bosses were out for the main chance; the colleges had a more altruistic purpose.

The year 1870 stands out on the frontier of the mind. Dramatic and momentous changes in the thinking of all English-speaking peoples were in the making. It was in 1870 that Emerson delivered his lectures on "The Natural History of the Intellect" at Harvard.* It was a fitting culmination to his own powerful influence in the realm of philosophy and poetry and education. It was his last great effort in the movement to liberate American thought from slavish imitation of English and European patterns.

In 1859 Darwin's *Origin of Species* appeared, and in 1871 *The Descent of Man.* Emerson and Darwin were moving by different routes toward the same end. Philosophy and science in their upper strata, without entirely understanding each other, began to become allies. If Emerson dealt with ideas, Darwin dealt with facts.

In 1872 Herbert Spencer's *First Principles* was thrown into the caldron of thought. He launched the synthetic philosophy, "All the world currents were making for questioning." Above all else, the scientific method began its revolutionary career.

* See References, p. 350.

Among the currents of doctrine to which these years gave impetus were several which had a profound influence upon higher education in the United States. First, there was this new birth of science. Second, there was the democratic trend which expressed itself in (1) the great extension of the common school system; (2) the opening up of unexplored educational areas by the land-grant colleges and the state universities; and (3) the establishment of both separate and coeducational schools and colleges for women. Third, there was greatly extended recognition of a new conception of the place of youth in the processes of education. Fourth, there were multiplying signs of new methods of administrative organization and of curriculum building in the old line colleges.

The Trend for Public Education. The Ordinance of 1787 had provided that from all the regions reaching to the Mississippi every sixteenth section of every township was to be devoted to free schools. In this instance the central government had created permissive legislation which could not at the time be realized in any thoroughgoing fashion, but which was conspicuous in setting forth a remarkable challenge to the five states which were later carved out of the Northwest Territory. Personal leadership was required for the accomplishment of this comprehensive ideal, and Horace Mann had become the acknowledged founder of the public school system.

The high schools had made considerable advance and were enrolling more girls than boys. Measures were being established for the founding of normal schools for the training of the public school teachers, most of whom were to be women. The girls were demanding further educational opportunities, and the "female seminaries" were multiplying in response to this and other demands.

The Education of Women. For several decades these female seminaries had been developing, particularly in the South, and some of them became foundations of colleges. In New England the prevailing tendency was to establish colleges for women on new foundations, Mount Holyoke being a notable exception to the rule. In the West the higher education of women became dominantly of the coeducational type, while in the South seminaries persisted longer than in either of the other sections. Almost fifty years later there was a Southern Association of Colleges for Women made up for the most part of institutions which had not been accepted for membership in the Association of Colleges and Secondary Schools of the Southern States.

In the annual report of the United States Bureau of Education in 1872 about one-half of the 187 schools formerly called seminaries were designated as colleges. The terms college and seminary were often used interchangeably, but the institutions were distinctively of secondary type. The use of the term "college" was not the result of any standardizing process, but was the indication of a growing national sentiment. Georgia Female College at Macon, now Wesleyan College, had been established in 1836 and must be credited as one of the very first institutions offering education on a college basis to women. The establishment of the separate colleges for women added to the momentum of the educational revolution. Mount Holyoke Seminary became a college in 1888, and three years earlier Bryn Mawr was opened, largely following the Johns Hopkins pattern. It was in such institutions as these, as well as in a few coeducational ones like Oberlin and Antioch, that the significant demonstration was being made that women possess the nervous, physical, and mental capacities for higher education. This crusade for the education of women reminds one of the earlier crusade of the churches for the establishment of colleges for the education of the clergy. Eventually, the greater proportion of women seeking higher education were to be enrolled in coeducational institutions and, interestingly enough, west of the Mississippi River. The West and Far West were leading in the realization of greater freedom in the educational process.

Coterminous with the advance of woman in educational

opportunities, was her progress in attaining political rights. Suffrage had been granted to the women of Wyoming in 1869. In 1871 a national convention of women was called by Isabella Beecher Hooker, in which a demand was made for recognition of women as citizens entitled to become voters. This was followed by the first international convention of women under the same leadership in 1888, in which Mrs. Hooker read the first printed arguments dealing with the constitutional rights of American women. Susan B. Anthony, Elizabeth Cady Stanton, and Lucy Stone, all drawing inspiration from Lucretia Mott, became champions of phases of this movement, and their views were merged in 1890 into the program of the National American Woman Suffrage Association.

The first consideration with which these pioneers were concerned was the right to the privileges of formal education. Perforce they were concerned with proving their intellectual parity with men. At Johns Hopkins, M. Carey Thomas, later to become the president of Bryn Mawr and one of America's great college executives, was at first grudgingly allowed to sit behind a screen in the classroom and listen to the lectures and recitations of the men who were duly enrolled.

The question of the *nature* of the college for women was to be faced later. It is generally agreed that in the construction of the curriculum there have never been fundamental differences between liberal arts colleges for women and those for men. In coeducational institutions it was assumed that no important distinctions would be made. We have it upon the authority of the American Association of University Women, to which the author is indebted for carefully prepared data, that, thus far, the women's colleges have not changed their objectives. However, as Mrs. Charles L. Moncure of the American Association of University Women's staff writes, "Due to social conditions during the period while the women's colleges were developing, there have been certain factors that influenced administrative differences, which in turn have had some influence on the whole development of the liberal arts college." According to Mrs. Moncure, the claim was made in an article by the late President Pendleton of Wellesley College that the women's colleges had made significant contributions in the fields of health, housing, the orientation of freshmen, college government, personnel work, and the arts.

It is easy to see that, initially, women in making their demand for the opportunities of higher education were on the defensive. They must demonstrate that they were physically equal to the strain of college life, that they were not abandoning the home-making instinct, that they were instinctively domestic, that they were not ignoring regulatory disciplines, that they were able to participate in college and community government, that they were determined to hold on to cultural values; in a word, that education was far more to them than the "training of the intellect." The first colleges to demonstrate the capacity of women along these lines were Vassar, Wesleyan, Mount Holyoke, Smith, Wellesley, Goucher, Sophie Newcomb. Colleges more recently founded, such as Converse, Sweet Briar, Mills, the Woman's College of the University of North Carolina, Connecticut, Keuka, Hood, have continued the same traditions.

It has been pointed out, especially by Kathryn McHale, Executive Secretary of the American Association of University Women, in books and periodicals, that the women's colleges are leaders in constructive forms of experimentation. There is evidence to show that these colleges have paid more attention to the individual student than have the men's colleges. Chapter and verse by way of confirmation might be cited except for the limitations of time and space.

Land-Grant Colleges. When in 1862 the land-grant colleges were authorized by the Federal Government, it was claimed that a new era had dawned in American education. The basis of this claim grew out of the authorization in the Morrill Act of these colleges "to teach such branches as are related to agriculture and the mechanic arts." While the Civil War and the firm resistance of the church-controlled colleges delayed the development of these institutions, this authorization eventually resulted in the horizontal extension of our program of higher education. Their status was made more secure through the recurrent aid of the government. The Hatch Act of 1887, supplemented by later appropriations, vitalized their work by providing for the organization of an experiment station in connection with each institution. By these means the solution of agricultural problems by scientific research entered on its benign and generally effective course.

As the states generously supplemented the aid of the Federal Government, vast opportunities were opened up to the boys and girls from the farms and the shops for a higher type of educational preparation than had before been accessible to them. In several of the states great schools devoted in part to rewarding research and to the applications of science in many realms have been developed. The land-grant colleges, whether operating as detached institutions or as units in great state universities, have demonstrated their usefulness and effectiveness, and have justified the early dreams of their founders. That in recent years there has been a recession in their enrollments in courses in agriculture, does not detract from their total serviceableness to the nation. As a group they hold fast to the section of their charter which has been quoted above.

In November 1937, there was celebrated the fifty-first annual convention of the Association of Land-Grant Colleges and Universities, the seventy-fifth anniversary of the first Morrill Act, and the fifteenth anniversary of the Hatch Act. It appears from the problems considered at these anniversaries that the land-grant colleges are still holding definitely to the provision originally made for agricultural and engineering education.

It is of both historic and philosophic interest that the provision of the Morrill Act for the teaching of agriculture and the mechanic arts was sandwiched in between two other coordinate provisions. Before this provision, it was stipulated—"without excluding other sciences and other cultural studies," and immediately following, a further re-enforcement of the same educational policy was added—"in order to promote the liberal and practical education of the industrial classes."

In recent years several of the land-grant colleges have made notable advance in emphasizing their charter provisions for liberal education. As a group these colleges are centers of religious life.

Conservation of Values. It is apparent, then, that the new era which was struggling for expression was consciously grafted into the old era which had been in operation for more than two centuries. The pioneers in these new fields were unwilling entirely to sever their shore lines.

This same conservatism and caution was manifested, as has been pointed out, by the colleges for women. After all has been said about the chaotic condition of American colleges, it still remains true that, on the whole, they are striving to emphasize the same values.

The Adolescence of the State Universities. A somewhat different treatment must be given the state universities. They appeared as offshoots from the main stem, as scions of the royal stock, much earlier than the variants just enumerated. Before the Civil War, twenty-one state universities had been founded. Six of these had been established in as many of the original states—Virginia, Maryland, Georgia, North Carolina, South Carolina, Delaware, without the aid of congressional land grants. In fourteen new states fifteen state universities had been founded—Vermont, Kentucky, Tennessee, Ohio University, Miami, Louisiana, Indiana, Mississippi, Alabama, Missouri, Michigan, Iowa, Wisconsin, California, Minnesota, usually with the aid of congressional land grants. As universities, they had functioned feebly. Ten of them, in addition to the major units dealing with liberal arts, had the beginnings of departments of law. Michigan was outstanding with an enrollment of 649 students

in law and medicine. California, Lousiana, Vermont, and
Virginia had small groups of medical students.

A few of these universities were originally organized as
private institutions. Delaware was not brought entirely
under state control until 1913; Maryland, until 1920. The
church influence, particularly that of the Presbyterians, was
definite in almost every one of them. Even at Virginia, after
the death of Jefferson, religious influences almost controlled
the University until the Civil War. In many of these the
presidents were ministers of the gospel, and the boards were
made up largely of church representatives.

The religious interests regarded the teaching of the classical and liberal subjects as their prerogative. This encouraged
Wisconsin, in 1859, to direct its work into the practical
sciences and teacher training. Because of their attitude, the
churches must assume their part of the responsibility for
the alleged "secularization" of the public schools, including
the state institutions of higher learning.

Because of these conflicts between the state and the church,
and for other reasons, it came about that the state universities
as well as the land-grant colleges were of slow growth. In
nearly every state the enrollments of students in the stronger
privately controlled colleges exceeded those of the state
university. In several of the states the leadership in higher
education was distinctly in the hands of one or more of the
private institutions. It has only been within the last few
decades, and especially in the Middle West and Far West,
that some of the state universities have come to dominate the
educational work of their respective states, and only within
a few years that the total enrollment of college students in
tax-supported institutions throughout the country has exceeded that of the privately controlled colleges. Now, the
state universities, in the aggregate, lead not only in the
number of students but in building operations, and, what is
most important of all, in budgetary provision for faculty
salaries.

The statistics in the first report, in 1870, of the United

States Commissioner of Education are not complete or well analyzed, but they include data from 167 institutions for men only, 54 for women only, 77 for both men and women, and 71 which were reported as unknown as to the sexes enrolled. Of the total of 369 institutions, 25 were reported as state, and one as a city institution.

The state universities in 1870 then had far to go to justify their name. Nebraska, opened in 1871, is representative of the Middle Western institutions which are now so powerful. Thirty years after her founding Nebraska had only passed the 200 mark in enrollment. In another thirty years she had approximately 6,000 students enrolled in ten colleges and three schools. This number had increased by 1938-39 to 6,810. The College of Liberal Arts and Sciences remains the largest single administrative and teaching unit.

During 1931-32, of approximately 13,000 students enrolled at Illinois, 3,827 were in the Liberal Arts College, and 11,454 were listed as undergraduates. In the Graduate School there were 1,480. In the professional schools—undergraduate and graduate—there were 8,423. In the 1938-39 enrollment of 13,872 students, the liberal college heads the enrollment list among fourteen units of administration. This distribution of students is found in nearly all the state universities. Indeed, the largest liberal colleges are in tax-supported institutions.

Urban Universities. By 1870, there were a score of urban universities, some of which were municipal in that they received financial support from the cities in which they were located. A number of these were beginning to respond to the immediate needs of the citizens of the community and were setting patterns for many such institutions to follow.

Colleges for Negroes. A dozen or more colleges for Negroes had been opened in 1870. Among these Lincoln University, Howard University, Fisk University, Talladega College, Wilberforce University, Morehouse College, Shaw University, are now accredited by regional accrediting agencies, as are numerous others more recently founded.

Technical Schools. A differentiation between the "general" and the "technical" had also been made which resulted in the establishment of Rensselaer Polytechnic Institute, Lawrence Scientific School, Sheffield Scientific School, and Massachusetts Institute of Technology.

The humanitarian impulse is not now, and never has been, monopolized by the institutions under private control. There are still those who consider that there is a chasm which cannot be bridged between the old ideal and the new. The state university from the first has incorporated both ideals into its organization and function. As Norman E. Foerster puts it, "The natural man of the old regime has become the economic man, the conqueror of physical nature, and the creator of an industrial order." The state universities have made a marked contribution to this transition.

Old Line Colleges. While there were incipient indications such as have just been referred to of a new conception of American education, the forces of conservatism were still operating dominantly in the college field. The old type college still held fast not only to its name but, in the main, to its educational program. In 1870 no political science or sociology was being taught at Yale; practically no history at Columbia. As a class, the privately controlled colleges of liberal arts, whether for men or women or of the coeducational type, did not boldly strike out in new directions. They were not yet ready for radical reforms.

As a concrete illustration of the departure from the old tradition, it may be cited that a number of the colleges began in the '80's to offer, as alternatives to the classical course leading to the A.B. degree, a modified course including science but excluding the ancient languages, leading to the B.S. degree, and a second alternative which omitted the Greek but afforded an opportunity to students to hold on to Latin with one hand and to science with the other. This course led to the Ph.B. degree, conferred for several years by quite a number of colleges. These departures were made with great caution and with general recognition that the B.S. and the Ph.B. represented a lower quality of academic achievement than the A.B. degree.

The keen awareness of the colleges to the changing trend of American life and the sense of social responsibility were destined to characterize a later period of development. This was to come after the old geographical frontier had entirely passed away and new forms of implementation had been developed. At the same time, there was a disposition on the part of the colleges to quell the occasional manifestations of student revolt against the prescriptions in religion. It was in 1870 that Emily Dickinson declined to take part in a pre-Christmas fast approved by the principal of Mount Holyoke and consequently severed her connection with that institution. Her refusal was an indication of the inevitable decrease of that peculiar type of religious fervor which had generally characterized the administrators of the schools and colleges of the earlier era.

At the last meeting of the National Teachers Association before it changed its name to the National Education Association (1877), President Fairchild of Oberlin was discussing the question, "How the College Shall Control the Religious Instruction of Pupils." He was greatly disturbed at the developments of freedom at Cornell and Wisconsin, and declared that not to require religious instruction would be ruinous to the college and the state. At an early meeting of the National Education Association President McCosh of Princeton eloquently urged the importance of an American educational system in which "the high school and the normal school shall educate for and feed the colleges." He was not prepared for coming events. The high school had not definitely won its place in the sun, for Dr. Harris during this period was using his marvelous powers of persuasion in behalf of that unit of American education. The high school was still on the defensive. Dr. Harris, with insight and understanding, faced the new era of expanding life. The time was ripe for a more comprehensive philosophy of education and he met the demand.

CHAPTER VIII

A NEW ERA EMERGES

To SPEAK of the period beginning about 1890 as a "new era" is not to imply that the country at that time turned over a new leaf, clean and white, upon which to begin the history of the last fifty years. On the contrary, the forces of evil which were unleashed during the period of the "American Feudalism" continued their course. Many of the problems then raised have become more aggravated and few of them have been permanently solved. During the "scrambled decades" the administration of President Hayes had adopted a policy of reconciliation and reform, and some of the ugly scars produced by the Civil War had been partially healed. But the wavers of the bloody shirt were in the ascendancy, and they won many victories.

However, instruments of control were introduced about 1890 which, at least, have placed restraints upon greedy men. The Sherman Anti-trust bill became a law; the Supreme Court defined the corporation as a person and therefore not only entitled to certain rights, but bound to assume definite responsibilities. Civil Service reform has made some progress; to a large extent a spirit of national unity has replaced the old sectionalism. In numerous sectors the good has been overcoming the evil.

Some of the currents of life referred to in Chapter VI may now appropriately be followed further. The full significance of city planning, to the beginnings of which reference has been made, was not appreciated until the extraordinary architectural and engineering operations of the Chicago World's Fair in 1893 made many Americans architecturally

conscious. There are today more than three thousand urban
communities which together account for more than one-half
of the population of the country. This shift from rural to
urban population has reached its climax in our "dinosaur"
cities. On the Atlantic seaboard the mercantile motive was
dominant in the great massing of population. Farther west
the dominant motives were agricultural and industrial production. These were the great centers for the manufacture
of farm machinery, for the location of packing houses,
granaries, and mills.

Be it said, the city type of American dinosaur has had the
intelligence not to commit suicide by its sheer bigness. On
the one hand, it is the verdict of the National Resources Committee that Americans are the most inveterate town dwellers
in history, and, on the other hand, this Committee and many
city planning commissions are now leading in the study of
movements of the population away from congested centers.
In New York, for a typical example, business large and small
is carried on largely on Manhattan Island, but the City
Planning Commission of New York has projected no less
than one hundred zone divisions and now includes the suburbs and towns within a radius of fifty miles from the City
Hall, so closely interrelated with the metropolis as to be
a part of a vast super-urban area with a population of twelve
million. This includes nearly five hundred separate municipalities. In the same fashion Pittsburgh dominates 135
neighboring municipalities, Chicago 115, Philadelphia 92,
Detroit 45, and San Francisco 38. Inevitable extinction is
being obviated by definite remedial movements in the opposite direction. Perhaps in time this movement away from
ultimate disaster will aid also in clarifying political as well
as industrial and social organization. Dwight Morrow once
observed that "hope is greater than history."

As to the "robber barons" of business, be it said that until
the muck-rakers appeared, the people were disposed largely
to justify their means by the large ends which were achieved.
The discussion of the rights and duties of vast aggregations

of wealth has rocked the foundations of the nation in the transition from individual to corporate control. At times the conflict over the strict and loose construction of the power of the corporation has taken precedence over that of the strict and loose construction of the Constitution. In spite of all this, a distinguished journalist has recently declared that "the use of the corporation as an instrument of business enterprise is one of the greatest, perhaps the most indispensable, of modern social inventions."

The corporation is but an illustration of the instruments of social control which have become necessary in ordering our society. New organs of government have been created to deal with increasingly complex situations, and, adding to the complexity, to them has been delegated a mixture of legislative, executive, and judicial power. To make the matter still further complicated, these agencies have been placed in the hands of politically minded men who have used their power very often for partisan purposes. To those who have faith in democratic principles, the most promising development in the management of industrial combinations is the elimination of absentee directors, many of whom perpetuate the power of old families, the relocation of central offices, and the appointment of men who have grown up in the business on corporate boards of control. Here college men are beginning to enter the picture.

When one turns to the colleges it appears also that the wheat and tares had grown up together. In this field, about fifty years ago, a process of more intensive gardening began. The same two purposes were in view. First, to destroy the most noxious of the weeds. Secondly, to graft some new buds on to the old stems and let nature do her work. The soil was stirred at times, it now appears, by tools ill-adapted to their purpose. There was much done by way of "enrichment." Most striking of all was the introduction of brand new processes of aeration. Group discussions, conferences, founders' days celebrations, presidential inaugurations, commencements, meetings of multitudes of associations, individual and group surveys, publications without end—all these kept the atmosphere stirred. When it was announced to a man with much potential power to help the colleges that the Association of American Colleges was being organized, he responded,—"Another place for college presidents to go." There were many overcast days and many frosts, but the sun continued to shine, and the colleges grew, some of them in stature, some in wisdom.

In the college world also the general direction of events became somewhat more definite. Out of all this the present-day colleges have developed. Some valuable lessons have been learned. The colleges are on their way toward a science and art of administration and teaching. In recent years leading universities have organized departments dedicated to this objective.

At the opening of this era, about fifty years ago, at least one academic conception had been not without honor for two hundred and fifty years. This conception had been wrought into the policies of many colleges: "Nothing can make a university (or college) without scholarship, learning and high standards." Upon this foundation our best colleges were determined, "having done all, to stand."

But some unorthodox ideas had gained ground and were winning their way. Prophets were announcing the necessity of widening the scope, deepening the work, and liberalizing the spirit of the American college. Specifically, they would introduce the method and spirit of science, they would liberate the power of student interests, whether those interests were in humanistic or scientific studies, and they would carry out the spirit and work of the colleges through the introduction of the free elective system applicable both to teachers and students.

Of course, these were not new ideas. Many persuasive voices inspired by study in Germany or sympathetic with European ideals and methods—Ticknor at Dartmouth and Harvard, Everett and Bancroft at Harvard, Jefferson at Virginia, White at Cornell, Wayland at Brown, Barnard at

Mississippi, Alabama, and Columbia, Folwell at Minnesota, Tappan at Michigan—had been heard, even if crying in the wilderness, in behalf of greater freedom. Then, all these dreams had found their advocate pre-eminent in Charles William Eliot. The death knell of the old order was sounded in his inaugural address. He proceeded to put the free elective system into operation. "Students are to be considered adult men."

Practically coincident with the introduction of the free elective system, and indeed as furnishing an immediate motive for it, was the scientific movement, with Huxley and Agassiz and Gray and David Starr Jordan, as well as Eliot, as prophets, advocates, and exemplars. Shortly appeared John Dewey at Michigan and Chicago, destined on the side of philosophic theory to be the greatest American guarantor of liberty in the educational process, with his interpretation of the significance of interest, his appeal in general to experience, and in particular to the dynamic power of student aspirations and capacities.

All of these impacts were beating on the body and soul of the college in the '90's. Here were three planks, quite unseasoned, shortly to be placed permanently in the American college platform: the scientific spirit and method, the discovery of the student, freedom of election and freedom from what Cotton Mather called "the collegiate way of living," with all the individual and social implications involved.

The rest of the nineteenth century was devoted largely by forward-looking colleges to efforts to interpret and apply these three principles. During this process the skies fairly gleamed and the air resounded with the lightnings and thunders of heavy artillery. Huxley, champion of science in education among English-speaking peoples, made his campaign more difficult through exaggeration. In a bitter tirade against British backwardness, he wrote:

The foreigner who should wish to become acquainted with the scientific or the literary activity of modern England would lose his time and his pains if he visited our universities with that object.

And as for works of profound research on any subject, and, above all, in that classical lore for which the universities profess to sacrifice almost everything else, why, a third-rate, poverty-stricken German university turns out more produce of that kind in one year, than our vast and wealthy foundations elaborate in ten.

Huxley pronounced the German universities "the most intensely cultivated and the most productive intellectual corporations the world has ever seen." He stimulated the fighting instinct among the educational standpatters, by his famous dictum: "There is only one kind of knowledge and one method of pursuing knowledge, scientific knowledge and scientific method." As for the other side of the debate, he was denounced in the pulpit and the press as irreligious, immoral, and unscrupulous.

Eliot put the case of science more moderately. He said, "The student of natural science scrutinizes, touches, weighs, measures, analyzes, dissects and watches things. By these exercises his powers of observation and judgment are trained and he acquires the precious habit of observing the appearances, transformations and processes of nature." * Furthermore, he declared, "This University recognizes no real antagonism between literature and science and consents to no such narrow alternatives as mathematics or classics, science or metaphysics. We would have them all at their best." Even as late as the Harvard Tercentenary Eliot was placed among our chief public enemies on the boldly expressed indictment, "It is a hard saying, but Mr. Eliot, more than any other man, is responsible for the greatest educational crime of the century against American youth, depriving him of his classical inheritance." Within these fifty years science has supplanted the humanities in student interest, and until the outbreak of the World War German influence had superseded that of England. Almost ten thousand American students had

* See References, p. 351.

studied in Germany and become teachers in American colleges. Now the picture is changed in both particulars.

All American leaders of the educational revolt were committed to the democratic spirit in education, which, of course, always has its weaknesses and dangers. The necessity for adaptation and control was soon recognized. A true democracy must preserve the values indigenous to its own life. This idea, during the same period, was being consciously safeguarded. Johns Hopkins, the Baltimore Quaker, understood this need. America's pioneer graduate school was the result. Charles W. Eliot, Andrew D. White, and James B. Angell, by invitation, advised with the trustees of Johns Hopkins University, and the result was the appointment of Daniel Coit Gilman as president. The opening address, significantly enough, was delivered by Thomas E. Huxley. Soon Clark University was founded, under the presidency of G. Stanley Hall, who also represented the German influence. Neither of these institutions would have a college. They were not interested in housing. They represented a new conception of an American university. These enterprises, as the programs developed and as the graduate idea was taken up by other universities, promised for the colleges of the United States a supply of educated teachers. Thereafter American colleges did not have to depend entirely upon England and Germany and other European states for leadership in philosophic insight, in scientific production, and in teaching method.

Here then was a fourth new plank in the college platform. Provision had been made for the conservation and enrichment of the scholarship of American college teachers. A great gain came to the colleges through the gradual enlivening of the mental heaviness to be found in many a faculty.

But there were other suggestions for improvement yet to come. Before the century closed, another major prophet appeared in the person of William Rainey Harper. Through his energy and genius the members of the colleges and schools of the Middle West were given the opportunities for stimu-

lation and study which for many years before had been
enjoyed chiefly in the Eastern states. The University of
Chicago opened in 1892 and fairly bristled with new educational ideas. It had, for example, a bifurcated college—a
junior college and a senior college, with a certificate—Associate in Arts, at the end of the sophomore year for all who
cared to accept it. Next to the magnetism of President
Harper's personality, which drew to Chicago from the ends
of the earth a notable faculty of investigators, scholars, and
teachers, was his power to analyze the elements of the university and the college. He organized the University on the
quarter basis. He placed dormitories on the campus. He
returned to the residential pattern which had been all but
lost under the preponderant German influence. In this
respect the English university example is again in the ascendancy.

Immediately the Summer Quarter at Chicago became the
rendezvous of educational administrators and teachers in
service, largely from the Middle West and South. Harper
organized a mock college faculty of which he was the president, and he selected Fellows representing different departments of the Graduate School of the University, who were
invited to become heads of departments in this faculty. This
group met on stated evenings in the president's home and
canvassed the problems of college administration and teaching. Harper had a schedule of teaching equivalent to that
of any head professor.

But Harper's most far-reaching contribution to the colleges was set forth in his little book, *The Prospects of the
Small College*. This was the most remarkable analysis of the
detached college which, up to that time, had ever been made.
Harper was at once heralded as the prophet of doom for the
undergraduate college, as Eliot had been for the old line
college. President Harper said that most of the small colleges would be unable to stand the pragmatic test, that
within a quarter of a century not more than one-fourth of
them would be in existence. Now, the quarter of a century

has passed and a few years have been thrown in for good measure since this death-knell of the college was announced. Now is being challenged the right to be, not only of the detached undergraduate college but of the liberal college as well, which is still found at the heart of every great American university, including Hopkins and Clark, Chicago and Stanford. The cry, "Away with the small college!" has become the cry, "Away with the liberal college!" Incidentally, in all these years the number of colleges, large and small, has been constantly multiplying. Like kites and airplanes, colleges rise against the wind. The number of students they instruct has increased 800 per cent. And this in spite of all the sifting processes which have been placed in operation, particularly in the privately controlled institutions.

Among the menacing agencies to the small college, President Harper listed the high school, the junior college, the professional school, the university—particularly the state university; and among the menacing influences, the tendency toward specialization, the decline of the sectarian spirit, migration, and finally poverty. Except for the menacing influence of poverty, Harper's pronunciations have failed to come true. Even on the point of poverty, the colleges, and the institutions with which they are connected, have greatly increased in permanent endowments as well as in equipment, since the prediction was made.

Of course, most of this increase—which amounts to 1,000 per cent—has gone to those institutions which already had endowment and equipment, but not much has been taken away and something has been gained by many of those institutions which a third of a century ago were very poor. There are colleges today which are undernourished and small, but smallness as such is no necessary deterrent to usefulness. The college in the state of Pennsylvania whose students have led all other students for a decade in passing rigid examination tests has never had 400 students. Incidentally, its graduates are practically all employed. This particular college is not poor, but its most precious asset is to be found in the endowment of mind and heart of its faculty.

In the meantime, the high school, which it was prophesied would become the people's college and thereby largely displace the established liberal college, has become its greatest ally. Indeed, the increase in high school attendance has amounted to 4,000 per cent. This, then, made necessary the junior colleges, and the junior colleges have quite recently been absorbing a considerable part of the high school product. In performing this service and thus affording opportunities for further study to multitudes of students whom the liberal colleges are not prepared to accept, they also have become cherished allies of these colleges.

The experience of the colleges in the striking loss of freshmen and sophomores before the junior colleges came to their rescue has been repeated in large measure by the tremendous mortality in the latter. In this cooperative task the junior colleges are devoting themselves preponderantly to what President Conant has recently referred to as the "Jacksonian tradition,"—some education for all the people, while the liberal colleges are set free more fully to devote themselves to the maintenance and extension in our American democracy of what Jefferson called "an intellectual aristocracy," and what we prefer to call "high achievement in the realm of the mind and spirit." Among the differences between these two types of institutions, there is the marked difference between the extent of their respective horizons.

In the light of all the developments during the twentieth century, the question will be raised, "How then can President Harper be listed among the prophets?" The answer is that the greatest feature of his *The Prospects of the Small College* was to be found in its methodology. He drove the friends of the college to a detailed and ordered study of their jobs, and indicated the essential method of doing so. Before this, a *laissez faire* policy had been in vogue.

The heightened appreciation of the need for fresh facts, fresh thoughts, and fresh methods in the ordering of college life has led to the unprecedented era of college planning and experimentation—unprecedented in any time or in any country—which has affected during the last few decades almost every college in the land—all but the complacent ones. The colleges have achieved the liberty, guided by their own experience and that of others, to define and promulgate their own programs and the methods by which they are to be carried out, knowing full well that ultimately they will be judged in terms of their fruitage. The colleges of America, speaking broadly, are not dominated by any system, either of federal or state control. Among their assets, they prize most of all their areas of reserved freedom. Each tends to constitute a free association of free academic personalities, and all together have been building up a guild spirit in an atmosphere of camaraderie.

One of the great achievements of the colleges during the present century has been their voluntary association in the study of problems common to all, in the free communication of their tentative conclusions, and in the sharing of knowledge concerning their several aspirations, successes, and failures. Millions unprecedented in the history of education have been available for studies and publications. Books and professional magazines bearing on the work of the colleges have sprung into being like wild flowers on the desert. The colleges, more fully than any other American agency, are postulating the human spirit as the basis of their work. Their problem involves such questions as, "How to formulate the industrial, social, economic, political, and religious problems of this generation that mankind may be the better served; how to discover, and if possible, to guide the irresistible energies of human behavior?" Perhaps it may be safely said that they are contributing more than any other agency to the present movement toward all forms of intelligent synthesis—interdepartmentalization, intercommunity action, and action intercollegiate, interstate, interparliamentary, interracial, international. At this moment, if any group of agencies was ever called to a task monumental and apparently unsolvable, it certainly is the universities and colleges. But universities in the past have undoubtedly played an important part in guiding human destiny. At least one thing seems certain to the friends of the liberal college: men and women cannot contribute to such vast intellectual and moral tasks who have been too impatient to allow time for the growth of their powers and insight. These are not tasks for sophomores.

CHAPTER IX

THE COLLEGES LEARN TO COOPERATE

A LEADING characteristic of the new era has been the development of the spirit of cooperation. Following the law of substantial growth, the cooperative spirit was of slow development. The natural rights tended toward individual effort, at the present moment. Cooperation involves the recognition of duties as well as rights, the disposition to grant concessions, the willingness to share experience.

President Eliot, despite the stiff and continuous fight which he made in the advocacy of his revolutionary principles of education, set some high marks in cooperation. His correspondence with George Brush of Yale, in which he admitted Yale's superiority in philosophy and Harvard's need of visits from selected Yale men in order that the Harvard mind might be fertilized, was a new and strange thing in American college administration. Well did Eliot remark in the midst of this correspondence, "There is frankness for you."

Of course there were others who had the disposition to cooperate. Among the early manifestations of this spirit were the organization in 1882 of the Association of Collegiate Alumnae, which was of national scope, and the New England Association of Colleges and Preparatory Schools in 1884. Each of these was of a special significance, the first because of the leadership of women, and the latter because it emanated from the most provincial section of the country. This New England organization, with slightly modified name, has held true to its initial purpose of serving its constituent institutions. From its beginning until the present time it has been restricted in membership. Its meetings are

84

not open to the public. While not a standardizing or even an accrediting agency in any formal sense, it served in certain ways as a model for the several sectional standardizing agencies which came later. The Association of Collegiate Alumnae became the American Association of University Women, which has functioned and still functions within certain areas as a standardizing agency.

It will be recalled that President Eliot was a leader in establishing in 1900 the College Entrance Examination Board, which he had suggested long before. This was followed two years later by the New England College Entrance Certificate Board.

The Association of Agricultural Colleges and Experiment Stations, now the Association of Land-Grant Colleges, came into being in 1885. This also was of truly national scope, and preceded the National Association of State Universities by ten years.

The representatives of the tax-supported institutions and the college women were blazing out new paths through the educational wilderness. They were fighting for a place in the sun, while New England was strengthening her claim to intellectual supremacy.

The University Senate of the Methodist Episcopal Church was the pioneer in the field of standardization. Through the effort of its Board of Education, the General Conference established in 1892 the University Senate to function as a standardizing agency for colleges of the Church. It drew up definite requirements in 1893, and the next year the Board applied them in the classification of Methodist Episcopal institutions. These agencies introduced a certain coercive element into the process of cooperation.

The Association of Colleges and Preparatory Schools of the Middle States and Maryland, organized in 1888, was the first of the regional agencies. It later developed a program of standardization considered effective in that day. The North Central Association of Colleges and Secondary Schools, and the Association of Colleges and Secondary Schools of the Southern States, although organized in the '90's, did not begin to apply standardizing tests to member institutions until more than a decade later.

These associations, some with modified names, all include secondary schools as well as colleges in their operations. The New England and the Middle States Associations have substituted "Secondary" for "Preparatory" in their official titles.

In 1900 the Association of American Universities, whose membership is determined primarily in terms of graduate schools, was formed. Its immediate purpose was "to secure in foreign universities, where it is not already given, such credit as is already due to the advanced work done in our own universities of high standing, and to protect the dignity of our Doctor's degrees." The approval of colleges on the basis of their ability to prepare students for graduate work was begun in 1913, and is given only after a careful inspection by representatives of the Association. These inspections are looked upon by the colleges as constituting the acid test of accreditment.

In the restricted field of scholarship, especially in recent years, Phi Beta Kappa is stimulating a similar contribution to achievement.

The North Central Association has displayed remarkable capacity for adjustment as the science of educational administration has developed, and today constitutes the vanguard of leadership in accreditment, which term it has substituted for the harsher and more rigid term, standardization. It has recognized institutional differences, has abandoned the questionable effort to apply minimum objective standards alike to all institutions. It is seriously addressing itself to the process of discovering "optimum principles," in terms of which to measure adequacy of performance. It judges institutions individually in terms of their stated objectives. This Association has maintained powerful leadership by precept and example for all types of institutions throughout the nation, whether publicly or privately controlled.

The standardization of institutions with Methodist affiliation also has exerted and still exerts a marked influence throughout the entire country, particularly in all institutions related to the churches.

The Southern Association has not moved so rapidly. It has not recognized so clearly the principle of self-determination, and the result has been the recent organization of the Southern University Conference, which is concerned with the progress of institutions which may be described as in the "upper brackets." This organization now enrolls some thirty-three universities and colleges in the Southern States.

Quite recently, the Northwest Association of Secondary and Higher Schools, modeled largely after the North Central Association, has assumed jurisdiction in the Western Mountain States.

It is to be noted that federal influence has not been exerted on these agencies of cooperation. They are "free and independent." After one adventure on the part of the United States Bureau of Education some decades ago into the field of classification, which was disclosed by a premature publication, it returned to its original policy of fact finding. Its successor, the Office of Education, finds great scope for its activities outside the field of classification, standardization, or accreditment.* It issues much information in increasingly serviceable ways.

In several states the state board of education and the state university have contributed to the accrediting process. Their requirements, however, except in the field of teacher preparation, have not usually produced so high a degree of educational achievement as have those of the regional associations. Several state universities have high school inspectors who render valuable service. The recognition of a secondary school or a college by the New York State Board of Regents, or by the University and State Board of Education of California, is considered as of distinct professional significance.

During the time of the early development of college stand-

* See References, p. 352.

ardization, the National Committee on Standards of Colleges and Secondary Schools functioned as an advisory body. It was composed of representatives of various educational associations, including several of the regional standardizing agencies, members of the Carnegie Foundation staff, and the United States Commissioner of Education. It devised standards which in substance, and frequently in phrasing, were adopted by the regional associations. It was a super-educational agency without official status.

The American Council on Education, by which the Emergency Council on Education was superseded immediately after the armistice, took over the functions of the National Committee on Standards of Colleges and Secondary Schools. This was not done in a formal way but was a natural response to developing needs. The Council's activities now cover a wide range, including not only various types of standardization but practically every other major interest of American education. In a sense it has become the unofficial substitute for a United States Department of Education. An important element of its strength, along with its remarkable leadership since its organization, has been its unofficial character.

The standardizing process has been criticized not only because it concerns itself chiefly with minimum standards and is apt to include certain coercive elements, but on the ground that its use is largely responsible for the "sameness" of American colleges. It was for these reasons, as well as others, that the Association of American Colleges declined to enter this field. Despite their inadequacies, experience has shown that the agencies of standardization have exerted a powerful influence for good. They serve as an incentive and guide to institutions in their formative stage. However, when strong and courageous undergraduate institutions have broken away from accepted procedures, their students have usually been given special consideration by the graduate and professional schools. In view of the usual application of standards to minimum objective tests, such standards cannot be held responsible for objectionable "sameness." Above and beyond these minimum tests, the colleges have had plenty of room to grow. Below these tests, assuming that they were wisely administered, the weaker institutions have had to bow to the concerted judgment of their colleagues or pursue their individual ways.

It must be pointed out, however, that free and independent agencies do not always see eye to eye. Shortly before and for some time after the turn of the century, there were unfortunate manifestations of contention between the tax-supported and the non-tax-supported institutions of higher learning in several of the states, particularly in the Middle West. The tax-supported institutions in these states were rapidly moving forward in enrollment, in buildings and equipment, and in the support of their educational programs. In the judgment of many of the privately controlled institutions their own security was being threatened. The state normal schools and the state universities were rapidly assuming practical although not formal control of the entire area of public education. They drew students from many or all of the counties of the state, and those students who as alumni were distributed throughout the state became effective recruiting officers for their several Alma Maters. With the development of special courses for the training of teachers outlined usually by the state boards of education, and upon their recommendation given legal status by the legislatures, the possibilities of building up state educational monopolies seemed promising, or threatening, depending upon the point of view.

During this period, in several of the states, certain privately controlled institutions had higher standards and larger enrollments than the state institutions. It was claimed that the latter institutions were entering upon a process of duplication of educational effort, and in a number of instances the privately controlled institutions organized state associations within whose membership the tax-supported institutions were not included. Some of these state associations tried their hand at practical politics. As a concrete indication of this state of war, when the Rhodes Scholarship Committee was first nominated by a sub-committee in one of these states, the name of the president of the state university was omitted, only to be reinstated by the wiser counsel of the committee of the whole. In this same state a governor, who was a trustee of a privately controlled college and ex officio a member of the state board of education, summoned to his office the presidents of the leading denominational colleges for consultation on a state program of higher education. After his plan had been outlined, three of the presidents in the conference opposed the governor's program on the ground that the representation was not sufficiently inclusive of the educational leaders of the state, and the plan never reached the public.

On the whole, these state associations of privately controlled institutions were weak and ineffective, and except in one or two states they gained no particular prestige. It was felt by many presidents of these institutions that constructive measures ought to be developed. It was out of this background that the idea was conceived of forming a national association of colleges. The time appeared to be ripe for such an effort in view of the additional fact that the land-grant colleges and the state universities already had such associations.

The Council of Church Boards of Education, representing what were then known as denominational colleges, authorized its vice-president, who was the president of such a college, to take steps looking toward that end, provided, upon investigation, the prospects seemed favorable. As an outgrowth of this assignment, presidents of ten denominational colleges met at St. Paul, Minnesota, in July 1914, in connection with the annual meeting of the National Education Association. They were unanimous in approving the idea of an association of colleges of national scope, and suggested the name, Association of American Colleges. They approved the issuance of a call to the first meeting to be held in

Chicago in January 1915. Without dissent, however, they were of the opinion that the association when and if formed should be in no sense organically related to any other agency. They were also of the opinion that the membership of the proposed association should not be confined to denominational colleges. General consent was given to the idea that it should be an organization of colleges of liberal arts and sciences, and that it should not include standardization as an objective. A sub-committee was appointed to draft a tentative constitution carrying among other things the proposals just mentioned. The first steps had been taken toward the organization of an association, nation-wide in extent, with a policy of "inclusiveness, not exclusiveness."

At the first meeting delegates from 160 institutions were present, representing Middle Western colleges for the most part. There were several declinations, particularly from colleges in New England and the South. The judgment was expressed that the colleges of the various sections of the country had no particular interests in common; that the problems of one section were not the problems of other sections, and that the administrative methods, the curricula, and the general outlook were so different as to indicate no need for such an organization. All of the institutions represented by these doubters eventually became members of the Association of American Colleges.

This Association, founded under the impulse of the spirit of cooperation and in the effort to make a more comprehensive interpretation of America's program of liberal education, soon removed its headquarters from Chicago to Washington, and in conjunction with the Emergency Council on Education became an agency of coordination between the colleges and the Federal Government in time of war. Neither the Association nor its colleges became permanently militaristic in spirit. They did what they could, on the educational side, in an unexpected emergency. After the armistice, the Association office was taken back to Chicago, but soon removed to New York as its permanent headquarters.

At the annual meeting of the Association in January 1916, a program for a nation-wide publicity and financial campaign was set forth on behalf of the Council of Church Boards of Education, which was approved by the Association "as a project of that Council." Another program was suggested for the Association itself by the president for that year, which in general terms the Association has followed, except for the interruption during the World War. This program recommended the discovery of the facts about the colleges, the free and open discussion of facts, programs and policies, the publicity of such discussions, and the absence of legislative or administrative power on the part of the Association itself. The principle of self-determination was implicit in the entire outline. The Association has addressed itself for a quarter of a century to the exposition of educational principles, programs, and strategy. It has distinctly avoided partisanship, sectionalism, propaganda. In it the cooperative spirit has been set free.

It is entirely in line with the trend of the philosophy of higher education in the United States that in the same year when the ten denominational college presidents met to consider the organization of an association dedicated to the fostering of what may be called the old line colleges, another group of presidents organized the Association of Urban Universities. Side by side, these two associations have developed, one devoted primarily to permanent values inherent in liberal education, the other conceived particularly to serve complex and often congested communities in any and all ways deemed helpful. Practically all of the members of the Urban Association have been active in the Association of American Colleges, with its more restricted objectives but more extended membership.

In the college world the face of nature has been changed; the spirit of cooperation has largely eliminated the narrow spirit of competition. The most glaring exception is in the field of recruiting. In many sectors, the larger values of competition and cooperation are functioning harmoniously. The numerous voluntary associations are now cooperating to raise the level of the nation's educational, social, and religious life. This is particularly true of those organizations devoted essentially to college and university problems which have permanent staffs—the American Council on Education, the American Association of University Professors, the American Association of University Women, the Association of American Colleges, the North Central Association.

There are numerous other agencies of voluntary cooperation concerned with special fields, such as the American Association of Teachers Colleges, the Association of Collegiate Schools of Architecture, the American Association of Collegiate Schools of Business, the National Association of Schools of Music, etc., etc.

Differing in purpose and methods, but nevertheless imbued with the spirit of cooperation, are the organizations of scholars. There are the American Bar Association, the American Institute of Chemical Engineers, the American Library Association, the American Medical Association, the Dental Council of America, etc. The National Research Council operates in the field of the physical and biological sciences. The Social Science Research Council is composed of representatives of the national societies in history, economics, political science, sociology, anthropology, psychology, and statistics. The American Council of Learned Societies includes the humanities—philosophy, languages, literature, archaeology, and several fields of the social sciences. Each Council carries on cooperative studies. They approach a given problem simultaneously by way of its many facets by the diverse disciplines. The American Association for the Advancement of Science, a superorganization with sections for the many specialties, is essentially an association of scholars rather than an organization of scholarship.

Indeed, the personal element is the strongest feature of all of these associations. The American Association of Uni-

versity Professors cuts across all subject areas in its membership, but each department has its own national and often
regional organization. To illustrate, there are the American
Association of Physics Teachers, the American Association of
Teachers of French, the American Association of University
Teachers of Insurance, the Association of Teachers of Mathematics of New England. There are said to be almost forty
national associations representing various interests of American biologists.

In like manner practically every phase of college and university administration has its organization. To mention but
a few, there are the Association of University and College
Business Officers, the American Alumni Council, the American College Publicity Association, the Association of College
and University Broadcasting Stations, the Association of
Superintendents of Buildings and Grounds of Universities
and Colleges, the National Association of Deans and of Advisers of Men, the National Association of Deans of Women,
the American Student Health Association, the American Association of Collegiate Registrars, and the Association of
College Admissions Counselors.

On various levels, then, from the individual institution to
the superorganization, we witness the process of cross fertilization. This is what is meant by the academic spirit on or
off the campus, always felt, never fully analyzed. A company
of English visitors spent some days on an American college
campus. Coeducation impressed them profoundly, but of
all the features of the college they were amazed most at the
atmosphere. They asked, How do you do it? No satisfactory
answer was forthcoming. President, then Dean, Ford of
Minnesota was quizzed in the same manner by a representative of a German university. "What makes your professors
work together?" "Oh," he replied, "they just naturally cooperate!" Does it take much stretch of the imagination, or
much resort to poetic license, to suggest that perhaps Emerson *was* a major prophet? May not all these be manifestations of the Oversoul?

We are indebted to an unknown colleague for the assertion that America, having set the stage for free individuals, finds these individuals entering into more combinations than any country with a will to regimentation has ever conceived.

CHAPTER X

FROM PROVINCIALISM TOWARD AN INTERNATIONAL MIND

MARCUS AURELIUS once wrote, "My nature is rational and social, and my city and country, so far as I am Antoninus, is Rome, but so far as I am an educated man, it is the world."

There is no more striking indication of the progress that has been made in the cooperative thinking and planning of American citizens than in the field of international relationships. The peace movement, thus broadly conceived, furnishes a demonstrable and on the whole a hopeful sign of the new era, even if it is as yet very largely a psychological phenomenon. Since the movement now includes the entire world in its compass, a brief adequate summary is well-nigh impossible. For the present purpose, a survey is attempted under two heads: (1) the non-academic, (2) the academic. Marked progress in each of these fields has been made within forty years; most of it since the World War. It is quite impossible to follow a rigid course under this or any other classification of events. Fortunately there has been a high degree of cooperation between the participating individuals and agencies. Nearly all agencies are led by college men and women.

It must be confessed that all this interest and progress has failed to lead the Federal Government to develop a comprehensive and continuous foreign policy. Except in the field of the Monroe Doctrine, foreign policy has been the football of politics, with a new goal set for each "change of sides." The structure and leadership of a foreign policy is yet to be achieved.

96

The American Peace Movement is well grounded. George Washington announced the fundamental principle of non-interference in European affairs. Hugo Grotius and Immanuel Kant have had sympathetic students ever since their works on peace and war appeared. The Monroe Doctrine, on the whole, has been an influence for peace. To dig deeper, the *New Testament* has been taken seriously by an increasing number of patriotic citizens.

Non-academic Developments

The American Peace Society has operated in this field for well over a century. It and other pioneer agencies marked the idealistic phase of the peace movement. It is an interesting fact, however, known to a few but never heralded abroad, that before the Czar of Russia issued the call to the nations of the earth for the first world peace conference an educational and religious leader of the American Society of Friends had been admitted to the Court of the Czar, who had listened attentively to his appeal for action in the cause of world peace.

The Red Cross is certainly one of the most remarkable manifestations of the spirit of good will. By implication, it was given status in international law in the international Treaty of Geneva in 1864, which designated as neutrals all hospitals, hospital officers, and all others attending the sick and wounded in war. It first became operative in Austria and Germany during the war of 1866. The American Red Cross, founded in 1881, now has the general confidence of mankind.

A different type of approach to the problem of better relationships, good in its purpose if often ineffective in results, is the American Tariff League, which has functioned since 1885 in informing its members of the development of tariffs in general and of foreign trade agreements in particular.

Just as the American Red Cross represents the attitude of benevolence and the American Tariff League the point of view of commerce and trade, the American Society of International Law since 1906 has fostered the study of that discipline, much abused in recent years, and has attempted to promote the establishment of international relations on the basis of law and justice.

Other contributions of greater or less effectiveness to the growing sense of oneness among men had been made before the World War: by the Carnegie Endowment for International Peace—"the pioneer body created to plan and encourage research in international relations"; the World Peace Foundation, founded and endowed by Edwin Ginn to educate the people of all nations to a full knowledge of the waste and destructiveness of war; the Rockefeller Foundation, one of whose three areas of concentration is in the field of international relations, and all of which certainly contribute to the welfare of mankind in peaceful pursuits; the Church Peace Union, financed from Carnegie funds since its founding in 1914, which acts as a policy-forming body and functions largely through subsidiary agencies. The Church Peace Union is controlled by representatives of the Catholic, Jewish and Protestant faiths. Its chief agent is the World Alliance for Friendship through the Churches. It has a committee on Religious Rights and Minorities, and another in conjunction with the Federal Council of Churches on the International Interchange of Preachers and Speakers.

After the World War a multitude of organizations in this general field came into existence. The following list illustrates their type and character: International Labor Organization, International Chamber of Commerce, International Institute of Agriculture, Institute of Current World Affairs, Organization for International Intellectual Cooperation of the League of Nations, League of Nations Association, Council of Foreign Relations, Foreign Policy Association, National Council for Prevention of War, National Committee on the Cause and Cure of War, International Federation of University Women, Women's International League for Peace and Freedom, Peace and Disarmament Committee of the

Women's International Organizations, National Peace Conference, American Youth Hostel Movement, World Federation of Education Associations, World Peaceways, The Fellowship of Reconciliation, the Catholic Association for International Peace.   44783

Then there are organizations not primarily concerned with international relations, but which have developed such as one phase of their activities as, for example, these: Association of American Universities, Social Science Research Council, American Council on Education, National Research Council, American Bar Association, American Library Association, Special Libraries Association, American Geographical Society, Chamber of Commerce of the United States, National Bureau of Economic Research, National Industrial Conference Board, American Medical Association, American Statistical Association, American Historical Association, American Economic Association, American Political Science Association, Academy of Political Science, American Academy of Social and Political Science, Rotary, Kiwanis, and Lions Clubs, and numerous scientific organizations.

Carnegie Endowment for International Peace. It would be difficult to overestimate the influence of the Carnegie Endowment for International Peace. It has stood steadfastly for the better understanding between nations. The income from its ten-million-dollar fund has been used wisely under the leadership of Elihu Root, the first president of its board of trustees, and Nicholas Murray Butler, who succeeded to this presidency in 1915. Its Division of Intercourse and Education has a remarkable record of achievement both within the academic and non-academic fields.* Its leaders have become world citizens of the first order. Among more recent developments have been the creation of (a) a joint committee of the Endowment and the International Chamber of Commerce which works in the field of international economic relations, and (b) the National Peace Conference for the better coordination of the various peace forces of the country and

* See References, p. 352.

the pooling of resources of agencies and individuals making
for peace, and (c) the Foreign Policy Association whose reports are uniformly given a very high rating.

The Rockefeller Foundation.   In addition to its remarkable achievements in human betterment through conquering
the ravages of disease throughout the world, the Rockefeller
Foundation has rendered assistance and guidance to government agencies, to special agencies of research, and to the
strengthening and binding together of major and secondary
centers of research and training in the social sciences.   Such
centers now operate cooperatively on a regional and national
basis.

The Federal Council of the Churches of Christ in America
has maintained for several years a Department of International Justice and Goodwill.   Its position is strategic because
of its very large institutional constituency, which is readily
accessible through thousands of cooperating church officials,
ministers, and individual associates; the state and local councils of churches, the numerous church conferences and con-
ventions, the Council's various publications, the denominational and independent press, and the Council's radio programs.

The American Legion pledges itself to work "to promote
peace and good will on earth."   To that end the Legion has
a standing committee on World Peace and Foreign Relations, which has for its general aim securing of world peace
through a better understanding among the nations.   In addition, the American Legion is a member from the United
States of FIDAC—*Fédération Interalliée des Anciens Com-
battants.*   As its representative the Legion conducts annually
a competition for three medals: one awarded to a university,
one to a college, and one either to a university or a college.
The awards are made on the basis of achievement by the university or college in promoting international good will and
understanding.   Recent resolutions passed by the American
Legion at its national convention show that it believes in

"adequate military and naval preparation for the defense of the United States as the best guarantee of peace."

The International Peace Campaign was established in 1936 with headquarters at Geneva. On the basis of organizations then holding membership, it claimed before the outbreak of the present European war 400,000,000 adherents. There were 250 affiliated organizations in Great Britain, a smaller number in the United States. Forty countries were represented, there being thirty-seven other international organizations as members. This campaign represents a heterogeneous mass of peace advocates—absolute pacifists, absolute world organizationalists, and many shades of pragmatists.

James T. Shotwell, Director of the Division of Economics and History of the Carnegie Endowment for International Peace, points out that the arts and letters constitute the voice of the intellectual life. The Organization for International Intellectual Cooperation of the League of Nations, despite the loss of prestige of much of the work of the League, stands forth as an instrument of lasting value and importance. Among its participants have been Madame Curie, M. Painleve, Professors Millikan, Einstein, Bergson, Nitobe, Anesaki, Gilbert Murray, Henri Bonnet. "These intellectual forces are not defeated."

The Director General of the Pan-American Union asserts that international differences between the United States and Latin America have been settled largely by the orderly processes of mediation, conciliation, and arbitration; that the assumption by all the Republics of America of responsibility to maintain the peace of the continent has been achieved, that there is absence of compulsion in dealing with inter-American problems; and that there are concerted efforts to remove artificial barriers to international trade. The total effect has been a stabilizing influence in world affairs. Improved facilities in transportation, banking, and other fields of activity have aided the processes of interchange of cultures. The United States is beginning to recognize the high cultural content of Latin American education and Latin American art. Latin Americans cherish their inherited European culture. For philosophy, art, music, they go to Europe, but Latin American students come to the United States in large numbers to prepare for careers in medicine, engineering, technical research, agriculture, journalism, education and social problems. The Pan-American interchange of students is now in its very beginning.

The latest important contribution to this group of agencies is the Division of Cultural Relations within the Department of State of the Federal Government. According to the Chief of the Division, it was created to coordinate and facilitate the activities of private agencies and institutions desiring to further cultural and intellectual interchange with other countries. Among the first projects to be undertaken is the implementation of the Convention for the Promotion of Inter-American Cultural Relations which calls for the annual exchange of two graduate students or teachers and one professor between the signatories. The exchange of books, periodicals and reviews, translations of the literature of the other American Republics into English and its dissemination in this country, as well as the translation of American works into foreign languages, are included in the program. Educational films to develop appreciation of and information about other countries, the encouragement of travel, the establishment of summer schools in the Caribbean and South American areas for American teachers and students, and the use of the radio for conveying understanding are among the other activities developed by the Division.

The Departments of State, Commerce, and Labor, and the Office of Education of the United States constantly publish material of value to the student and investigator in the field of international relations. The Office of Education cooperates with teachers of comparative education, arranges study programs, and aids college and university registrars in evaluating credentials of foreign students. It also seeks to develop an appreciation and understanding of foreign cultures through its radio program.

Among the Colleges and Universities

It is probable that the colleges related to the Society of Friends were in the lead in consistently and continuously inculcating the need for a peaceful settlement of international affairs. This was one of the cardinal principles of the Friends' "guarded education." They based their stand principally on moral and religious considerations and preached non-resistance, on the ground that this was the attitude and teaching of Jesus. In the early history of Pennsylvania, before others not of their faith gained the ascendancy in public affairs, they had been remarkably successful in their dealings with the Indians. In more recent years many Friends have participated in reading a profounder content into the term "pacifist." The pacifist now, if he follows the light of human experience, is not content merely to assume a negative attitude toward war. He is not satisfied with exemptions only on conscientious grounds which the Friends, Mennonites and Brethren have always had in this country. The Friends are not content even to confine their energies to forms of relief to the wounded and hungry during the time of war. They feel the responsibility of using their influence in the attempt to discover and remove the causes of war. At a recent World Conference of Friends held at Swarthmore and Haverford Colleges a report from a special committee on peace of the Philadelphia Yearly Meeting brought out very impressively this enlargement of the content of the term "pacifist," and formally set a new standard of thought for Friends. Positive meaning was thus put into a term which too often had been interpreted in negative terms.

The return of the Chinese indemnity by the United States Government and the reciprocal action of the Chinese Government in establishing the Indemnity Scholarships in 1909 was a striking illustration of a "better way" to handle international affairs than had usually prevailed. The movement of Chinese students to American institutions of learning, thus initiated, became a token and a cause of friendship between the two states. For many years the number of Chinese students in this country has far exceeded that from any other country.

The Rhodes Scholarships had antedated the Indemnity Scholarships. G. R. Parkin, the Executor of the Rhodes Trust, established in 1902, visited New York, Chicago, and other educational centers, and invited representatives of the colleges to assist in the selection of state committees to conduct the Oxford Entrance Examinations and make the selection of Scholars.

These two scholarship plans seemed at the time to be pointing the way to the millennium. They had a profound effect on American thought and feeling. They have certainly assisted in cementing permanent international friendships.

Events moved rapidly among the colleges. By 1920 the Association of American Colleges took a bird's-eye view of the entire scholarship situation as related to this country.

Already the Association had brought two groups of French girls to the United States to the total of more than three hundred, and the French Government had reciprocated by offering scholarships to American girls. Shortly, young invalided French soldiers were also awarded scholarships.

The Committee on Friendly Relations, although working under the auspices of the Young Men's Christian Association, did not feature that fact. It had no spirit of propaganda and its work, chiefly personnel in nature, was done with such devotion to the well-being of foreign students that it became a powerful instrument of good will. It will be observed in passing that just as the religious impulse was strong or even determinative in the early development of American colleges, so it operated in the early steps which were taken for the dissemination of better ideals of international relationships. This impulse operated distinctively on the principle that the left hand should not know what the right hand was doing.

The number of foreign students in the United States increased until 1931-32. After a short "recession," it has exceeded the 1931-32 figure. In 1938-39 it was 11,083; with Hawaiian and American born deducted, 7,948.

As early as 1920 the American Rhodes Scholarship Committee had placed appointments largely in the hands of ex-Rhodes Scholars. Oxford University had made changes in her regulations for the better adjustment of the plan to American conditions. Compulsory Greek for admission had been abolished, and the records of students were accepted in place of examination. Oxford had established the Ph.D. in research conforming to American practice. A movement had set in for more definite and severe standards of intellectual and personal distinction in American undergraduate education. There was noted a growing disposition for America and Great Britain to stand together in defense of their common heritage, and Rhodes' dream was recalled as to the day when all the English-speaking nations having come under the influence of these traditions would be united under one flag—perhaps the flag of the United States!

The American University Union in Europe had done remarkable work during the War. Some thirty-five thousand American college men had been served through the agencies of the Union's offices in Paris, London, and Rome. These men had represented 540 different colleges. Overseas they were learning under tragic conditions the lesson of cooperation. The foundations of closer intellectual relationships between the United States, England, France, and Italy were being laid. Common conceptions and ideals of learning and morals were being developed. Steps had been taken which led to the establishment of the *Cité Universitaire* in Paris, of which the culminating event, later, from the American standpoint, was the gift by John D. Rockefeller, Jr., of America's International House there. It was pointed out that "the soil of which France was unwilling to cede one inch to hostile aggressors, it now proposes to generously yield to the force of friendship."

The Institute of International Education proclaimed its aspiration to promote good will founded on knowledge. The Institute was then supplying the International Polity Clubs with bibliographies, syllabi, and books for a scientific and detached study of international relations. In conjunction with the American Council on Education it was concerned with stating equivalents of American and foreign degrees and setting standards of evaluation. It noted the increasing demand for American professors in Europe, and called attention to such facts as that the transportation cost of $800 to Constantinople and back, and of $1200 to Shanghai and back, was interfering with the extensive exchange of students. Less than twenty years later the Pan-American Airways is supplying free traveling scholarships from South America to the United States!

The American Council on Education had conducted the visits of the British and the French Missions to this country and had made its services available as a representative of the American colleges as a group whenever problems of world-wide scope were set for collaboration with other nations. It had not then entered upon its now well-defined program of dealing with large domestic problems, reference to which is made elsewhere.

The National Office of Universities and Schools of France reported that the students who had come to America on scholarships proffered by the Association of American Colleges had "taken the fresh air cure"; that they had found the system of guidance in American colleges of great value to them, and that they stood ready to cooperate in defending the principle "we must be free from every wind that blows."

The Universities' Bureau of the British Empire pledged itself to the cooperative development of intellectual accord and reported, significantly enough, that this Bureau had been organized as early as 1912 with an office in London as a clearing house of information between British universities and later as a central agency for cooperation with the American Council on Education and the American University Union.

Thus they hoped "to tie together all the threads relating to this international work."

Institutes

In 1921 the Institute of Politics was founded at Williamstown, Massachusetts. This Institute, held at the college which is famous for the student "Haystack Prayer Meeting," —out of which eventually grew the initial foreign missionary board—became the pioneer and model, as it was the most cosmopolitan, of the series of institutes which today touch directly or indirectly almost every educational center in the land. Six years later the Institute of World Affairs was organized at Riverside, California, through the leadership of the Mission Inn. For a number of years it has been under the management of college and university men and women. It claims to be the "oldest organization in the United States holding conferences for the discussion of international affairs." Since 1924 Institutes have been held regularly at the University of Chicago. In 1926, the Institute of Oriental Students for the Study of Human Relations, whose members are largely graduates and graduate students, was organized as a clinic for the examination of racial attitudes and cultural viewpoints, and as a social test tube. From the first it has held annual sessions and now has headquarters in Brent House, Chicago. The Earlham Institute of Foreign Affairs, at first under the name of the Institute of Polity, has met annually in Richmond, Indiana, since 1930.

The number of such institutions has rapidly increased in recent years. Edith Ware of the staff of the Carnegie Endowment for International Peace is authority for the statement that in 1933 there were thirty institutes and conferences on international questions held under academic auspices. Among the hosts of these organizations besides those already mentioned are Virginia, North Carolina, Georgia, Louisiana, Sarah Lawrence, Haverford, Wisconsin, Vanderbilt, California, Oberlin, Pennsylvania, Dartmouth, Atlanta, Vassar,

Smith, Reed, Mills, Whittier, Duke, Grinnell, Stanford, Swarthmore, Peabody, Cheyney State Teachers College, Wellesley, Bethel, North Central, Pennsylvania State, Lincoln University, Southern California, and Oklahoma.

Activities of Students

In somewhat more than twenty years, 696 (figures for 1938) International Relations Clubs have been organized in American colleges and universities through the Division of Intercourse and Education of the Carnegie Endowment for International Peace. Twice a year each club receives books from the Foundation to assist in the study of international relations. The Division itself prepares and distributes, especially to these clubs, the *Fortnightly Summary of International Events,* which carries no editorial comment; and from time to time the Foundation also supplies other publications. The college clubs in the United States and Canada meet in twelve regional conferences once a year.

College students are taking an active part in the peace movement. They not only cooperate with other agencies in promoting peace efforts, but through their own organizations set up peace programs.

American Friends Service Committee. Among the organizations which make a strong appeal to student interest is the American Friends Service Committee. Two features only of the remarkable work being done by their student peace service are mentioned here. This service each year sends hundreds of college students throughout the country for the purpose of discussing informally with individuals and groups the problem of war and peace. A more thoroughly organized project is that of its institutes on international relations. During the years 1930-1938 inclusive, it has given general direction to many such institutes and now conducts ten of them annually in different sections of the country, with the moral support of the Congregational-Christian Council for Social Action. It has furnished more than 340 highly equipped lecturers and conference leaders drawn from Switzerland, France, England, China, Germany, Japan, and most of the leading universities and colleges of the United States. More than a thousand participants per year pay the nominal fee. Living expenses are usually offered by the colleges. The "student body" is composed of school and college teachers and students, ministers, and other church leaders representing in the aggregate nearly all the leading occupations, and more than a score of religious denominations.

In the United States, within two years after its establishment by the American Friends Service Committee, the Emergency Peace Campaign announced that approximately 10,000 college students had participated actively and 413 had given their entire summer to peace education in rural areas. The National Intercollegiate Christian Conference, the American Student Union, and the National Student Federation are committed to the promotion of world peace and the protection of the democratic method of government. All three have voted to re-affiliate with the United States Peace Committee which sponsors the annual "strike against war" in the colleges.

The Intercollegiate Peace Association was organized at Earlham College more than thirty years ago and has since conducted hundreds of intercollegiate student oratorical contests on Peace and related subjects.

Other important student groups called for the consideration of international problems have met within the past few years at the University of Wisconsin, Sarah Lawrence College, Dartmouth College and the University of California. Six American-Japanese Institutes have been held alternately in Japan and America.

World Youth Congress. The first session was held in Geneva in 1936, under the auspices of the International Federation of League of Nations Societies. National committees of the Congress have been functioning in the countries represented to coordinate the activities of national youth organizations. Twenty-nine youth groups in this country are represented. The second conference was held during August 1938 at Vassar. In addition to national delegations, some fourteen international organizations appointed representatives.

At the International Youth Peace Conference held at Brussels in 1936, delegates and observers were present from 339 international and local organizations of various types, representing 14,000,000 members. This Conference condemned religious and political persecutions, anti-Semitic and other manifestations of race hatred.

The World's Student Christian Federation, founded in 1895 to promote Christian faith and to encourage friendly intercourse between students of all countries on a basis of Christian principles, has been an effective agency in the field of international relations. During the World War it undertook student relief, and since then has established international summer schools, camps, conferences, and student exchanges. It organizes clubs for foreign students, such as the Student Movement House in London and the *Foyer des Etudiantes* in Paris. It introduces foreign students to family life in the countries to which they come. It has organized a number of international discussion conferences and after the 1932 Conference, American Federation students returned to organize the Intercollegiate Council for Disarmament—the Council which sent the Yale student to Geneva, whose address before the Disarmament Conference there was described by Sir John Simon as one of the most impressive utterances on the disarmament question that he had heard.

It founded the European Student Relief in 1919, which in 1924 became the International Student Service, now operating as an independent organization. Its purpose is to express through material aid to students and professors, who are economic victims of war and oppression in Germany, Austria, the Central European and Far Eastern countries, the common solidarity of students and professors the world over—a fellowship of learning which has existed since the Middle Ages. The International Student Service in 1939 had national committees in fourteen countries and corresponding members in six others.   The Department of Cultural Cooperation arranges yearly for about one hundred American students to participate in European work camps.   It sponsors about a dozen small study conferences to which American students are invited, bringing together student leaders, professors, and writers.   It conducts special study tours to Europe for carefully selected American students.   Other active departments are University Research, Student Relief, Self-Help, and Social Service.

The Student Institute of Pacific Relations for a decade and a half has addressed itself to the effort of understanding the problems of the Pacific area.   Originating at San Francisco among the Bay region colleges and universities, it has developed into a group of earnest students loosely knit in form, unsalaried, and geographically widely scattered.   In their annual meetings held alternately on the Pacific Coast of the United States and in Japan, the twain do meet—the East and the West, the North and the South, Mexicans, Jews, Chinese, Hindus, Filipinos, Negroes, Japanese, and Americans for a single purpose: discussion and understanding.

Research and Training in International Relations

In addition to the institutes developed for the purpose of education of large and influential groups, there are the Institutes and Bureaus of Research and Training in International Relations.   At Harvard there may be named the Bureau of Economic Research in Latin America and the Council of Hispano-American Studies, as well as the Harvard-Yenching Institute and the Harvard-Radcliffe Bureau of International Research; at Teachers College of Columbia University, the International Institute; at California, the Bureau of International Relations; at Yale, the Institute of International Studies; at Chicago, the Oriental Institute; at Hawaii, the Oriental Institute; at Claremont, the Society for Oriental Studies; at Denver, the Foundation for the Advancement of the Social Sciences; at Tufts, the Fletcher School of Law and Diplomacy; at Florida, the Institute of Inter-American Affairs; at Johns Hopkins, the Walter Hines Page School of International Relations; the Middle American Research Institute at Tulane.

The Institute of Pacific Relations grew out of a conference of scholars in 1925 and was established to promote the co-operative study of the relations between countries in or interested in the Pacific area. Biennial conferences are held for the discussion of specific problems. The American Council of the Institute of Pacific Relations is devoted to the study of Pacific questions in the United States. It publishes material in this field and issues interpretative digests.

The American Coordinating Committee for International Studies, supported by the Rockefeller Foundation, was created in 1936 and attempts to do what the name implies. Its permanent membership includes the Council on Foreign Relations, the Institute of Pacific Relations, and the Foreign Policy Association. Six universities or institutes doing research in international relations are chosen by the Social Science Research Council to be represented on the Committee for periods of two years. The Committee organizes its own research committees.

Then there are numerous extra-curriculum plans of study, as at Dartmouth, where teachers and students join in explorations on the nature of war along its various "fronts"—political, propaganda, military, eugenic, etc.; the costs of war—economic, cultural, physical, and the means of preserving peace as related to the causes of war.

Foundations

Without attempting further to epitomize the work of the various agencies it may be noted that there are no fewer than seventy-five or eighty American Foundations, Councils, Societies, Unions, and Associations which function exclusively or partially in the field of cultural contacts and mutual understanding among men and nations. The best known of these were founded by or bear the names of Carnegie, Rockefeller, Ginn, Guggenheim, Davison, Woodrow Wilson, Russell Sage, Milbank, Carl Schurz, Rosenwald, Maurice and Laura Falk. In addition to these there are numerous international associations, scientific, educational, religious, benevolent, agricultural, or labor.

Libraries. Among the libraries especially equipped for the study of international relations are those of the Pan-American Union, the Carnegie Endowment, the Council of Foreign Relations, the Foreign Policy Association, the American Council of the Institute of Pacific Relations, the Hispanic Society of America, the American Geographical Society; the Woodrow Wilson Library, the Hoover War Library, and the Library of Congress.

International Relations Courses

Quite recently much consideration has been given to the statistical announcements that American college and university students appeared to be abandoning the study of the humanities and concentrating upon the study of the social sciences. The fact is not generally appreciated that one of the very important causes of this apparent shift is the increased interest of faculties and students in international relations. Such courses are usually classified under the head of the social sciences. There are, of course, mixed motives behind this significant shift. Among these motives are considerations of trade, involving tariffs, etc., diplomatic relations, involving a new structure of international law, and other practical considerations in the fields of history, political science, economics and technology.

A number of institutions provide vocational training in foreign affairs. George Washington University was among the first to offer courses in international relations. In 1898 it established the School of Comparative Jurisprudence and Diplomacy (now the School of Government), "to fit men" for the practice of international law and for positions in the diplomatic and consular service. Georgetown University has a School of Foreign Service. The Los Angeles University of International Relations, chartered in 1924, is closely connected with the University of Southern California, but has its own special courses on foreign lands, arranges for exchange of professors, and has scholarships and fellowships both for foreign students in the United States and for American students abroad.

The School of Public and International Affairs, established at Princeton in 1930, provides opportunity for concentration in the field of international relations, and is the principal agency for bringing to the University many special lecturers on foreign relations. The School of Public Affairs and Social Work at Wayne University, opened in 1935, gives courses in international relations. The Hall of Nations, a unit of the American University's Graduate School, through the medium of fellowships and professorships administered in cooperation with the Pan-American Union and the Institute of International Education, brings students to Washington for a year's study. They may enroll in any of the universities in Washington. Distinguished foreign scholars are invited to lectureships. A School of Pacific and Oriental Affairs is conducted during the summer at the University of Hawaii. It brings scholars from the Orient and the American mainland to Hawaii.

Carleton College received a gift of $500,000 from Frank B. Kellogg to establish a department for the study of international relations. The income is used for the salaries of such a department, for building up a library section in this field, for scholarships, and for the publication of monographs.

The Brookings Institution, an educational and research institution, has made a number of studies dealing with international relations.

According to the Ware report of 1937, a general characteristic of the present day is the constant reappearance of an urge to study courses involving the will to peace and a more intelligent understanding of international relationships with that end in view. While nominally in the realm of the social sciences, such courses are often permeated with a definitely altruistic motive.

Another very interesting development in the multiplication of these courses is that no discipline exercises exclusive jurisdiction and this phase of curriculum building, therefore, constitutes a marked illustration of the present synthetic tendency which is operating all along the line, strengthening the bonds of intellectual and spiritual unity.

The Ware study shows that there are between four and five hundred accredited colleges and universities which offer courses looking toward a better understanding of international relations. This development has come about practically since the World War.

These courses of study reveal that post-War international affairs have received increased attention throughout the last decade, and that the social sciences in particular are being synthesized for and in the study of international relations. A generation ago courses dealing in international affairs scarcely figured at all in undergraduate instruction in American colleges, while the graduate faculties which offered such courses could almost be counted on the fingers of one hand. During the last ten years it has not only become more and more possible for undergraduates to take their degrees with majors in some phase of international relations, but candidates for the doctorate have been able to concentrate in this field at Bryn Mawr, Chicago, Clark, Columbia, Cornell, Fletcher School at Tufts, Harvard, Illinois, Iowa, Michigan, Minnesota, Pennsylvania, Radcliffe, Stanford, University of Washington, Walter Hines Page School at Johns Hopkins, Wisconsin.

The University of Delaware inaugurated the "Junior Year Abroad," when its first group of students went to Paris in 1923 to gain a knowledge and appreciation of French culture, and at the same time to carry on studies equivalent to those of the junior year in their own university. Groups from other colleges soon followed. According to the record, over seven hundred students from 120 colleges have studied in France under this plan which has been adopted by Smith and other colleges. The idea was expanded so that it became possible to have a Junior Year in Germany, Italy, or Spain. Before the outbreak of the war in Spain, studies were transferred to Mexico City.

The Institute of International Education has greatly developed its work within recent years. The permanent formulation of its aim is: "To develop interest, understanding, good will and education through such activities as the exchange of professors, the establishment and administration of international fellowships and scholarships, the holding of conferences on problems of international education; and the publication of books and pamphlets on the opportunities for study in countries abroad."

It brings to this country distinguished scholars, educators, publicists and men of affairs from various parts of the world. They are circuited as lecturers among American colleges and universities. It assists American colleges and universities in procuring visiting professors and sends to its representatives in other countries a list of American professors who plan to spend some time in that country. It cooperates with regional groups of colleges and with some of the more remote institutions in sending foreign visitors who stay at least three days in each institution to lecture and conduct round-table discussions with students and faculty.

Probably the most important function of the Institute is the administration of fellowships and scholarships for American and foreign students. Under the various exchanges administered by the Institute there was an interchange between 1922 and 1936 of over 2500 students, representing 1193 American students abroad and 1363 foreign students in the United States. When the students arrive in the fall it conducts a school devoted to the process of orientation to American ways of life. It also organizes conferences from time to time to discuss practical problems of cooperation. One such held in 1933 resulted in the organization of the Emergency

Committee in Aid of Displaced Scholars. The Institute
maintains and administers the Paris and London offices of
the American University Union.

International Houses. In 1924 John D. Rockefeller, Jr.,
entered upon his project of developing well-equipped international houses with the erection of the building in New
York, near Columbia University. Its ultimate end was to
promote international understanding. A more immediate
purpose was fulfilled in providing a residence for those who
arrived in this country without homes or friends.

His second International House was opened in 1930 at
Berkeley, and two years later the third was dedicated at the
University of Chicago. Quite recently, as the fourth of the
series of Rockefeller creations has been the erection of the
Maison Internationale de Cité Universitaire, near the University of Paris. With the exception of the last, all maintain
dormitories, each having accommodations for some five hundred residents. Each house has both American and foreign
students. They have become significant centers of intellectual and social life.

The houses are controlled by governing boards which are
presided over by directors. The policy of administration is
very democratic and is adapted to the needs of the residents.
These needs are expressed by their own representatives
elected to membership in a student council. The house in
New York has the highest percentage of foreign residents.
At a dinner at International House, New York, in 1937, celebrating the first anniversary of the Alumni Association of the
International House, Mr. Rockefeller said: "If in this world
in miniature which we call International House, such an
atmosphere of fellowship can be developed, is it too difficult
to believe that the extension of the same tolerant spirit over
wide areas of the earth is beyond the purposeful intelligence
of mankind?"

There are other international houses. That at the University of Pennsylvania, sponsored by the Christian Association, which lodges about a dozen students serves as club head-

quarters for between three and four hundred from over fifty different countries. Others are located at the University of Oregon, at Iowa State College, at Ohio State University. In Washington, D. C., there are two—one connected with George Washington University, another sponsored by the American Friends Service Committee. There is one, Brent House, at Chicago, and another at Geneva, Switzerland.

The Rhodes Scholarships. Perhaps it may be asserted that the primary purpose Cecil Rhodes had in mind in founding his trust was to educate men for public service within the realm of political life. He manifestly had in mind the remarkable influence of Oxford men in what is now known as the English Commonwealth, and he hoped to extend this type of leadership and understanding among all English-speaking peoples as a productive basis of the first order for world fellowship.

The method Rhodes adopted for achieving the purposes he had in mind was to delegate to trustees the work of selecting young men of promise and bringing them together for three years at Oxford. The Scholars were to be selected on four grounds: (a) their literary and scholastic attainments; (b) their qualities of manhood, which he defined as truth, courage, devotion to duty, sympathy for and protection of the weak, kindliness, unselfishness, and fellowship; (c) their exhibition during school days of moral force of character and of instincts to lead and to take an interest in their schoolmates; and (d) their fondness for and success in manly outdoor sports such as cricket, football and the like. The key to the system lies in the instruction that the scholars be chosen from among those exhibiting moral character, leadership, and interest in their fellows, because "these latter attributes will be likely in after-life to guide them to esteem performance of public duties as their highest aim." He wrote once that he did not want "bookworms" but "the best man for the world's fight."

Certain things stand out among the accomplishments of ex-Rhodes Scholars:

1. They have enormously improved the competition for Rhodes Scholarships and the selection of Scholars.
2. They have been largely instrumental in bringing the most significant foreign contributions to American education that we have had since the influence of the German universities at the end of the last century.
3. The success of the Rhodes Scholarships has brought into existence reciprocal schemes bringing as many Englishmen to the United States each year for study as there are American Rhodes Scholars going to Oxford.

It is a fact well authenticated that in practically every college which has in recent years shown especial signs of intellectual vitality, one or more of the American Rhodes Scholars is to be found as a leader or a guide. This may not all be due to the spirit he has imbibed at Oxford. Much credit must be given to the system of selection which requires "distinction" either in scholarship or character, with athletic ability as secondary. The selections are based on sound educational philosophy.

In 1929 George Eastman contributed to the Association of American Rhodes Scholars a fund of $200,000 to establish the George Eastman Visiting Professorship at Oxford University, which was accepted by the authorities. Tenure is provided from one to five years to be held by an American citizen eminent in teaching or research in any branch of university study in which he will lecture or teach.

The Scholars upon returning home have not until quite recently gone into political life to any great extent. In this particular the plan has been disappointing. The conditions of American political life are far different from those of England, and indeed of the British Commonwealth. Eventually, it is hoped this aim of Rhodes may yet be more fully realized as conditions become more favorable in America for political leadership of high order. In *The Vision of Cecil Rhodes,* being the Marfleet Lectures which President Aydelotte, Director of the Institute for Advanced Study at Princeton, delivered at the University of Toronto in 1939, it is stated that with the increasing importance of political problems in

this country there is an increasing number of ex-Rhodes
Scholars entering government service and political life.
President Aydelotte asserts that while prior to 1918 only 17
per cent followed such careers, during the six year period
1930-36, 64 per cent entered this field, and a considerable
number of others have taken an active part in public life.

In the field of education and law the Scholars are making
a most commendable contribution to American life. This
is particularly true within the field of higher education. If
the Rhodes plan, or the scholarship and fellowship plans in
general are compared in the matter of results with many
efforts to achieve good fellowship through vast expenditures
of money, through the setting up of complicated international machinery, through the erection of impressive buildings as symbols of peace and good will, or through the efforts
of diplomacy, the conclusion emerges that the best investment is that in persons of character and capacity. We have
not yet found a rewarding substitute for the educative
process at its best.

CHAPTER XI

ACADEMIC FREEDOM AND ACADEMIC TENURE

SAID Milton in his *Areopagitica;* "Though all the winds of doctrine were let loose to play upon the earth, so truth be in the field, we do injuriously by licensing and prohibiting to misdoubt her strength. Let her and falsehood grapple; who ever knew truth put to the worse, in a free and open encounter?" The difficulty is that neither truth nor falsehood is usually found as a separate entity. The encounter therefore is seldom either free or open. The cases of academic freedom pure and undefiled before God and man are very rare. As President Gilmore remarked in his inaugural address in 1935, "Complete academic freedom may be merely an ideal never fully realized but it is the only ideal with which liberalism can hope to survive and to attain a reasonable measure of development of security. No university can compromise or surrender it." Like the idea of freedom from the slavery of the body, the idea of freedom from the slavery of the mind has had a slow and tortuous growth.

At the close of 1938, *The Annuals of the American Academy of Political and Social Sciences* presented a condensed story by Tyler and Cheyney of outstanding instances of insistence on the freedom of expression by college teachers and of opposition to it by superior authority.* Some of these may serve as a partial background of factual data for this discussion.

During the Abolitionist controversy three professors were forced to resign from Western Reserve College "be-

* See References, p. 356.

cause of their favorable attitude to Abolition." Another was dismissed from the University of North Carolina because of his support of the party considered to favor Abolition. In 1870 John Fiske, ranked as an infidel by certain groups, was refused reappointment by the Overseers of Harvard after a short term as instructor in history.

The publication of Darwin's *Origin of Species* had far-reaching effects on the freedom of teaching in the United States as well as in other countries. "A notable case on this basis was that of Professor James Woodrow who, as recently as 1888, was compelled to resign his chair in a Presbyterian seminary in South Carolina for advocating the theory of evolution."

The next invasion of significance was within the area of the social sciences. In 1897 President Andrews of Brown University, while not actually dismissed on account of his advocacy of bimetallism, was subjected to such criticism by his trustees that he felt it necessary to resign. On account of pressure from faculty members, alumni, colleagues in the economics field in other universities, and others, the trustees reversed their former position, disclaiming any intention to restrain the president's freedom of opinion or reasonable liberty of utterance and asking him to withdraw his resignation, which he did. Another notable case occurred at Stanford, when the founder, Mrs. Stanford, insisted on the resignation of Professor E. A. Ross. This case led to other resignations prompted by sympathy and resentment at interference with freedom of teaching.

The Scott Nearing Case at the University of Pennsylvania resulted in the adoption of a statute by which appointments, reappointments, and decisions not to reappoint, must be announced well before the end of the college year, and the responsibility for the removal of professors was placed almost entirely upon their faculty colleagues.

At the December 1913 meetings of the American Economics Association and the American Sociology Society a joint committee of nine was constituted to consider and report on the question of academic freedom and academic tenure so far as these affect university positions in these fields of study. Two years later the American Association of University Professors took up the problem of academic freedom in general and a committee of fifteen was authorized. The members of this committee represented the fields of economics, sociology, law, political science, Latin, education, history, zoology, philosophy, English, psychology. Within the year 1915 eleven complaints were laid before the chairman. In December of that year the committee submitted a report which contained (a) a declaration of principles relating to academic freedom, and (b) a group of practical proposals of procedure. The report concerned itself with the freedom of teaching within the institution, and freedom of extramural utterances and action. Because freedom of inquiry and research was "almost everywhere so safeguarded that dangers of its infringement are slight," the report disregarded it. The practical proposals were that a representative committee of the faculty should be a party to all reappointments, that tenure should be specifically defined, that a formulation of the grounds of dismissal should be required, and that judicial hearings should precede dismissal.

Soon after its organization in January 1915, the Association of American Colleges appointed a committee to formulate definitions of academic freedom and of academic tenure. This committee made two tentative reports and a final report, giving the matter, therefore, three years of study. The final report was approved by the Association, which, however, had no legislative power in so far as individual institutional members were concerned. Boards of trustees generally declined to commit themselves in advance either to the proposals of the Association of American Colleges or those of the American Association of University Professors. Later, a joint committee officially representing the two Associations

and the two points of view was constituted, and its delibera-
tions, particularly under chairmanships of Presidents Mc-
Conaughy and Wriston of the Association of American Colleges committee, have been very effective in creating an
atmosphere of understanding and good will.

It has been unanimously agreed that the American Association of University Professors should take the initiative in
receiving and considering complaints, that it should have
power to dismiss complaints after preliminary examinations,
that those complaints which seemed to require fuller examination should be referred through the office of the Association of American Colleges to that Association's committee,
and that joint conferences should be held, if deemed necessary, before a judicial investigation should be undertaken by
the American Association of University Professors. By these
means most difficulties, real or imaginary, have been ironed
out, and the number of formal investigations greatly reduced.
The record of complaints and their disposition indicate the
effectiveness of the procedure. Too much cannot be said in
praise of the earnest effort the members of this joint committee have made to pour oil on troubled waters and guarantee
safe voyages on academic seas. It is to be noted that the
Association of American Colleges has advisory power only in
all these negotiations. With the American Association of
University Professors is lodged an unusual combination of
powers: those of detective, sheriff, grand jury, prosecutor,
jury, judge and jailor. From the time it follows clues to the
time it places colleges on the black list, it is responsible for
the conduct of the cases. Cases may be reported at any time
by any individual member. At the January 1940 meeting of
the Association of American Colleges a redefinition of the
issues involved was approved without dissent by the Association. The text of this definition will be found in the Appendix (page 340).

It is worthy of note that indefinite teaching tenure developed at the same time that improvements were made in the
Civil Service. Most of the states which have either general

or restricted Civil Service laws also have indefinite tenure laws, but the menace of political influence has never been so great in the public schools as in other fields of government service. Much credit must be given to the National Education Association which began the study of tenure in 1881. Open advocacy of tenure by this Association began in 1915.

It is not surprising that the tremendous social impacts of the present century have put academic freedom on the rack. The surprising thing is not that there have been so many but rather that there have been so few instances in which the breaking point has been reached. The World War and its aftermath threw into the caldron of controversy a series of events not paralleled since the government began.

There were—

The draft, its appeal to loyalty to the state regardless of one's conception of loyalty to God, its partial revocation of the Bill of Rights, its concentration of power at Washington;

The startling and tragic downfall of democracies in Europe.

The proffered gifts to higher education by persons known to be sympathetic with the totalitarian systems of government, which were rejected here on the ground that such money was "tainted";

The appropriations by the "New Deal" Government for the benefit of college students;

The effects of the depression on the colleges, which intensified "class" feelings and led college officers and teachers to move either to the right through the inevitable caution produced by uncertainty, reduced income, unemployment—or to the left through resentment against the obvious abuses of the capitalist system;

The revival among the friends of the colleges of the truth that a good name is rather to be chosen than great riches;

The passage by several state legislatures of bills calling for oaths of allegiance to the country from teachers;

The awakening of American youth to a fuller appreciation of the responsibilities of citizenship;

The decisive resurgence among the people of the United States of the spirit of democracy, with conscious appreciation of constitutional and parliamentary government.

The democratic theory comprehends the existence of institutions committed to the maintenance of definite orthodoxies, political, social, or religious. In such, the initial contracts with professors must set forth the peculiar form of orthodoxy at stake, and the professors must respect the faith once delivered to the institution. This is assented to by both Associations officially concerned with complaints in the field of academic freedom. Of course, this procedure may pass over into unwise forms of indoctrination. The institution which fosters it deliberately delimits its area of freedom. By implication, if not in fact, it may hamper some or all forms of creative thought. It may consciously or unconsciously foster a certain imperviousness to the stimulative power of heretics, who often in human experience have become heralds of progress in thought and life. On all these points each college must stand on its record.

Perhaps the most heartening feature of this whole development has been the forthrightness with which certain representatives of the two points of view—that of justified indoctrination and that of creative thought, that of the executive and that of the teacher—have issued warnings to their professional confrères; or, in other words, the judicial rather than the partisan attitude which has permeated the discussions of the principles and practices involved. A strong case has been made for the teacher's point of view by certain executives, and an equally strong case for the institution by equally tolerant teachers.

In his paper on "The Responsibility of Boards of Trustees for the Preservation of Academic Freedom," Chancellor Samuel P. Capen, while admitting that "a few presidents have been among the most courageous and effective defenders of the citadel of scholarship," finds that, by and large, the record of the presidents in this matter is not good. "More often than not they, who should be the powerful champions of the faith, have joined the enemy or have weakly yielded to pressures exerted by board members or by outsiders." He points out that the records of board members are even less trustworthy. "The suppression of academic freedom is far more common than most casual observers are aware. Only the most spectacular instances of it come to publication, those instances in which there is a protesting victim. The suppression is more often brought about by a subtle form of terrorism, which is perfectly effective, but which produces no explosion. . . . Most boards of trustees either constantly employ this method of preventing discussion of controversial subjects or are believed to be disposed to employ it whenever occasion may arise."

This paper was read to trustees and was for trustees. It did not pretend to be a balanced statement of either theory or practice. Even if in some institutions forms of terrorism do appear, there is much experience to show that the scholar does not have to yield to it. In the end it is likely to be found that not all the wisdom is with one party to the controversy. There is the institutional as well as the individual point of view. Neither the institution nor all other members of the faculty are justified in granting to one of their colleagues the last word on all phases of scholarship. A courageous spirit and temper are required on both sides of the issue, if justice is ultimately to prevail.

In spite of the fact that no strings were tied to the Federal Emergency Relief Administration grants to students, several Eastern institutions declined to accept them and former President Dennett of Williams College went so far as to say: "If there is any professor here who approves the New Deal he is perfectly free to say so, but if he does not approve it, he at least does not have the embarrassment of knowing that when he teaches that Federal Emergency Relief Administration economics are bad, he is arguing against his salary."

In Relation to Tenure. The official reports of the American Association of University Professors clearly show that the majority of the cases which have been investigated are related to conditions of tenure and not to academic freedom.

But neither is tenure pure or undefiled. The late Dean M. E. Haggerty, in a study of fifty-six North Central institutions, discovered that definite tenure policies have become established rather through custom than through formal definition. These policies involve

> indefinite term for the instructional ranks of professor and associate professor; term appointments of one to five years for the lower ranks of assistant professor and instructor; promotion of instructors who have demonstrated their competence during a period of service in the lower ranks; termination of the tenure of less competent teachers at the end of a term appointment; termination of any appointment upon clear evidence of failing competence.

The 1935 report of Committee "A" of the American Association of University Professors contained this reasonable assertion, "The Association can hardly deny to administrators in times of genuine financial distress a reasonable discretionary power in choosing among their staffs those most fitted to remain." That in such times they will choose to retain those members who will contribute to stability, is simply to express the genius of the college function. The boat will stand more rocking during a calm than during a storm. The case cannot be ruled out of court, however, because of the presence of the element of tenure. Teachers cannot justly be required to take their lives in their hands. Most teachers cannot do themselves justice unless they have a reasonable degree of security.

This is one of the new ideas that are developing not only in the colleges but in society at large. It is implicit in unemployment insurance and in social security which, while they do not protect the worker in the job, do provide substitutes if required to replace the job. The colleges would offer protection in the security of the job itself because they recognize the equity which has been built up during the years of service. The colleges would go still further and guarantee some compensation to the emeritus officer or teacher. The ideal is accepted by all the colleges in spite of the difficulties involved, chiefly on the financial side.

The heart of the problem is found to be still more deeply imbedded. The question appears to be primarily concerned with the competence of the teacher. The weakest link in the chain of circumstances which eventuate in a formal complaint is that there is no adequate formula for determining competence. Nor, it must be acknowledged, is there much urgency on the part of the administration to discover such a formula. The desire for security on the part of teachers and for the stability of the institution on the part of administrators often ignores the danger of inflexibility. These desires tend to suppress the recognition of insincerity which too often lurks behind the chance of interference with the teacher's freedom, as well as the cumulative personal dislike which may have developed in the mind of the administration.

The situation requires periodic reappraisals of the teacher's competence. From such appraisals teachers are usually inclined to shrink, although in recent years the American Association of University Professors officials have distinctly disavowed any desire arbitrarily to require the maintenance in faculties of teachers of mediocrity or whose professional competence has declined to the point where it jeopardizes the service of the faculty to the students. There is no doubt that keen students are often able to detect staleness in the teacher. Student opinion may not always be infallible, but student insight confirms the need of some kind of evaluating process.

In Relation to Mass Psychology. Professor A. J. Carlson, who uttered the dictum, "Academic freedom is freedom to teach your field without suggestion or pressure from without," and who recently served with such distinction as president of the American Association of University Professors, has deplored the fact that not all teachers are exempt from the influence of mass psychology. He points out the responsibility of teachers to be exigent in this matter, particularly in times of general stress, anxiety and fear. The teacher cannot ignore the welfare of the larger public any more than he can ignore the welfare of the students. Pedagogical insight—to use a despised word in its original good sense—requires the teacher to preserve a balance of judgment which is consistent with his supposedly superior preparation and experience. Personal inhibitions should prevent wise teachers from following the crowds to and fro. It is, for illustration, a distinct credit to university authorities that they have been harboring professors who are—or were—convinced that the totalitarian form of government would usher in the millennium, but it is of no particular credit to the professors who so readily took up what Paul would call this "latest thing." Ideologies which in calmer periods would be relatively harmless are essentially harmful when the minds of men are surcharged with fear. God, we are told, is no respecter of times and seasons. Man has not yet reached so exalted a stature.

In Relation to Knowledge. Former Chancellor Charles W. Flint summed up an argument in the words, "The measure of the knowledge bounds the measure of the academic freedom."

A statement formulated by the American Association of University Professors is to the effect that "the liberty of the scholar within the university to set forth his conclusions, be they what they may, is conditioned by their being conclusions gained by a scholar's method and held in a scholar's spirit; that is to say, they must be fruits of competent and patient and sincere inquiry and they should be set forth with dignity, courtesy, and temperateness of language."

Knowledge undoubtedly should have the right of way but unfortunately it proceeds very slowly. Almost all economists in England and America since Adam Smith have advocated free trade. A remarkable appeal was made to the President by the nation's economists against the Smith-Hawley Tariff Bill. Economists pointed out at the time of the Treaty of Versailles and since, that war debts are uncollectable. Scholarship has rather hard sledding in the hands of "practical" men. This is in conformity with all human advance. In spite of this, definite principles of academic freedom are more generally held now than ever before. What is still more encouraging is that while the practice of academic freedom lags, it really does make gains.

In Relation to Status Quo. Again on both sides may be discovered an abhorrence of the unconventional. On the side of many teachers the "new thing," whether it is heralded as the product of political or social change or as the outcome of frontier intellectual investigation, is immediately suspect. The author recalls from his student days the remark of the teacher of psychology that he opposed the introduction of James and Wundt into the classroom for they were disturbers of the peace. He knew Porter's *Human Intellect,* paragraph by paragraph, and could outline each chapter in the book and do a perfect job of teaching! However, this human frailty is not monopolized by the reactionary. As this is being written, one of the most distinguished national leaders of a significant phase of progressive education is authoritatively reported as saying that all of his former students still hold to the philosophy he had propounded; not one had wandered away into forbidden paths.

On the administrative side there is the same urge to peace, where there is no peace, if the students are allowed to think. The successful business man on the board has difficulty in treating with respect innovations which may upset well-tested formulas of business or administrative procedure. There is a case authenticated by John Ise of a wealthy business man who wrote a letter to a university chancellor and who expressed indignation at something a teacher was reported as saying in class about President Coolidge. The letter closed with the warning, "I must insist that the professors absolutely desist from expressing views other than those generally held by us." The late Ogden Mills, wrote on one occasion to the Harvard University office,

> I recognize, of course, that by saying things which may shock public sentiment a professor can do great harm to the institution with which he is connected. However, good

taste, a sense of the proprieties and the influence of his colleagues can be relied upon to exercise a restraining influence. Should these fail, even so, I am sure that as compared with unfair and humiliating restrictions, and their inevitable consequences, the temporary embarrassment is the lesser of two evils.

In Relation to Neutrality. The ideal of the colleges is that they may be forums for the free presentation and discussion of controversial questions. The college will and must have a dominant philosophy of life, which is determined not so much by legal enactment or even by its stated objectives as by the influence and will-to-be of its dominant personalities. This grows out of its nature as a social institution. Such influences represent some of the many inevitable pressures that bear upon the organism. In order that the institution shall not succumb to such pressures, however valuable they may be considered as character forming influences, provision is made for the presentation of conflicting views. The main objective must not be lost sight of, that of furnishing fuel for student fires of thought. Thought must be substituted for pressure. But the device of having these diverse presentations made by the same professor, while it may be helpful in stimulating student thinking, nevertheless has its shortcomings. The human equation is ordinarily too strong to overcome the artificiality of such procedure. After all, the professor is entitled to his own point of view. He is a better teacher if he is an advocate of a point of view. His value is less than it should be, either if he preserves impartial neutrality, or if he becomes a mere salesman or propagandist. The students certainly have little respect for a teacher who is able always to maintain complete neutrality. A faculty composed of "yes men" would be neither serviceable nor inspiring. The ideal therefore, seldom achieved in most colleges, is that both sides of fundamental issues shall be presented by teachers who believe in them. Then the area of academic freedom will be extended, the student will be free tentatively to make up his own mind. Having "made it up" once, he may do so again and again.

A practicable device, in most colleges, for accomplishing this purpose is through the introduction into the faculty of a constant stream of younger and more recently trained teachers, drawn from a variety of graduate schools. Through their freshened imaginations and abounding energies they tend to vitalize the stream of academic thought. A certain flexibility of thought and practice in institutional life is thus guaranteed if not heralded to the public. One of the serious effects of the depression is that the younger men have been forced to go first, not having earned tenure, while those who remained have been impressed in the emergency with the need of unusual caution.

In Relation to Loyalties. The professor is not a free lance. He is a part of a group, every member of which possesses sensitivity. The group forms a corporation which, in the definition of federal law, has the rights and responsibilities of a person. He must look to his various loyalties—to himself, to be sure, but also to the professional group, to the church and to society of which he is a member, to the state of which he is a citizen. The National Catholic Educational Association, to select from many interested groups, made this contribution in 1936:

> Academic freedom is not academic license. It does not guarantee to any individual the right to teach whatever he pleases, nor to impose on the immature, the uncritical, the unwary, his own, untested intellectual idiosyncrasies. It is the state's function to see that adequate provisions are made for the education of all its citizens, and that in every field that is necessary for the common welfare.

S. A. Mitchell, in his retiring address as president of the American Association of University Professors, uttered the warning: "When we as professors have something on our chests that we must get off, I hope that we shall not forget that the title 'professor' brings a twofold responsibility, one to ourselves as individuals, the other to the college of which we are members."

*   *   *   *   *

When it comes to statistical data relating to cases during the past five years, there are grounds for different types of interpretation. These statistics will be found in the Appendix.

The largest number of cases were negotiated and adjustments were sought. In 1937, for example, 23 cases were settled through adjustment, and in 1938, 43 were sought to be adjusted.

There are those who interpret this record as indicating a concerted "assault upon the liberals." Such an attitude fails to comprehend all the facts, one of which, in addition to those previously set forth in this chapter, is that a new broom in the American Association of University Professors office is disposed to sweep clean.

President Wriston, who during the past few years has been chairman of the Committee on Academic Freedom and Academic Tenure of the Association of American Colleges, observes:

> Frankly, I do not believe that these figures show the state of health of academic freedom and tenure. It must be remembered that the Teachers Union has come into the picture; that their activities have stimulated a good many people to report difficulties who would previously not have reported, and it has also stimulated the American Association of University Professors to be more energetic in taking up cases. You will notice the very sharp drop in the number rejected or requiring little investigation, from 28 in 1934 to 2 in 1937.
> For those reasons I do not feel that there can be a statistical statement. I can give you, therefore, only a personal impression, which is that the situation at large is getting better in terms of freedom and more sensitive in terms of tenure. The famous Walsh-Sweezy case at Harvard was precisely like dozens and dozens of previous cases which had never attracted the slightest attention. The Davis case at Yale was a case of a discontinued appointment of a man on

limited tenure, but a new theory, which I call the acquisition of tenure by adverse possession, has gained currency during the last seven or eight years. The man's equity in his job, which arises because of continuing appointment, which arises because his salary was increased or his rank was changed—that is a new feature which has risen to great sensitiveness. It is merely a reflection in the academic world of that demand for security which is reflected in the economics and the politics of the United States. It is that which accounts for the recommendation in my report to the Association this (1939) January of a six-year probationary period, and which in the Harvard committee report on problems of personnel and tenure (the second volume of the Walsh-Sweezy case) leads the Harvard committee to urge a maximum probationary period of eight years.

That represents the emergence of a new principle which in its incidence is bound to cause a good deal of tension and which has produced and will continue to produce a number of "cases" in the immediate future. When it comes to academic freedom as against these problems of tenure I think genuine progress has been made. The principal difficulty arises from the fact that a certain academic timidity prevents people from saying what they think until they have bottled it up so long that they explode and say much more than they should. And, in the second place, in the name of freedom some people exercise license.

CHAPTER XII

PUBLICITY AND PROPAGANDA

THAT THE colleges have had some sort of publicity from the first cannot be questioned. The chief publicity agents who may be said to have been first organized for the task were clergymen. One of their important functions was to discover among their congregations promising candidates for the ministry. In so highly and compactly organized a system as that of the Methodist Church this remains a powerful influence both in recruiting students and in fund raising. In view of the fact that nearly all college students today claim church preference and that most of the gifts to colleges are made by members of the churches, the recruiting function remains inherent in the task of the minister. Now that the term "minister" has gained a more inclusive meaning and connotes the sense of obligation to serve mankind, all friends of the college assume similar responsibilities.

The presidents of the colleges have always assumed large responsibilities in the field of publicity both for students and funds, although these functions are now highly specialized. The presidents usually function today as the chief interpreters of the educational programs of the colleges.

In more recent years the printing press has become the chief implement of publicity, although it is now sharing this function with such recently developed devices as radio and the cinema. The extent to which the general magazines have considered it worth while to present discussions concerning the college enterprise was brought to light by the research department of the Association of American Colleges about a decade ago. It published annually the titles relating to higher education. In these lists it was demonstrated that

American higher education, in the judgment of magazine editors, ranked high in reader interest. During the latter part of the '20's and the early part of the '30's, these titles numbered from one hundred to two hundred per year.

There has been within the past two decades an amazing development of professional literature within the college field. Not only has the number of organizations dealing with college education exclusively or in part multiplied indefinitely, but almost every one of these organizations has developed a journal or bulletin devoted to the special problems of the agencies of which it is the organ.

The recent multiplication of books dealing with college problems is quite unprecedented in educational history. Many of these books are the outgrowth of extensive factual and interpretative surveys. A survey of surveys by W. C. Eells reported that more than two hundred such studies had been published within the last twenty-five years.*

That very different points of view had developed regarding desirable publicity at the time of the organization of the Association of American Colleges was illustrated by two addresses made at the second annual session, January 1916. One of these reflected the attitude of the Council of Church Boards of Education, the other the attitude of the college administrators. The first address outlined a definite campaign of publicity on a nationwide scale in behalf of the denominational colleges with special reference to the securing of financial support and of setting before the public the claims of Christian education.

The second address laid emphasis upon the necessity of factual investigations of the ideals, the programs, and achievements of the colleges; the elements of their strength and weakness, and the means of their possible improvement. It was assumed in this address that valuable publicity would be a by-product of such research and discussion. The effort was to be centered on improving the colleges, not on promotion *per se,* regardless of quality.

* See References, p. 355.

The proposed campaign for funds was approved by the Association "as a project for the Council." As for its own program, with the exception of the period during the participation of the United States in the World War, the Association has followed along the lines of the second address. It has placed educational achievement first, publicity second, and has frowned upon propaganda as at best a phase of indoctrination.

The Interchurch World Movement in 1919 afforded an opportunity for experimentation in the field of a nation-wide, high-pressure "publicity" campaign with special reference to securing financial support. This Movement was an attempt to capitalize the psychology of the World War period which had resulted in the subscription by the people of colossal sums of money for Liberty Loans. It is well known that the Movement failed of its primary purpose.

The most lasting constructive outcome of the Movement was the series of surveys which were developed in behalf of the multitude of organizations and agencies related to or affiliated with the churches and their work. Prominent among these surveys were those dealing with the various areas of American and foreign education. True to their purpose, the surveys were sometimes critical and were not considered by the promoters as so valuable for their publicity purposes.

Some years later the Liberal Arts College Movement was launched with a program very similar in purpose and method to that of the Interchurch World Movement. It continued in existence for a few years without attaining its primary objective. Soon afterward the National Conference of Church-Related Colleges was organized and drew into its membership a number of leaders who were not identified with the Liberal Arts College Movement. It holds an annual meeting in connection with that of the Council of Church Boards of Education, and conducts occasional regional conferences.

More recently some of the foundations have been impressed with the advantages of "good publicity" as contrasted with the usual survey report, and have assigned to gifted writers the task of interpreting the "scientific" survey to the public. This seems to promise publicity at its best. Such interpretations have a secure basis of fact and are expressed in readable English. Of course, this division of labor is not always necessary for some surveyors have the gift of clear and elegant composition.

The first annual report of the president of Harvard was published in 1825, but it was President Eliot who introduced in 1871-72 the detailed report of the activities of the institution, including the report of the college treasurer. Interestingly enough, the first alumni magazine was launched the year before at Cornell University, to be followed shortly by that of Earlham College. The influence of the alumni in their Alma Mater today would require a special dissertation, a chapter which should be written by an alumni secretary.

The distinct movement in behalf of college publicity began to develop about thirty years ago. Some investigators assert that publicity as a separate college activity arrived in 1902 when the Case School of Applied Science and James Millikin University began the circulation of publicity material. Harvard created a separate publicity department in 1910. In 1917 the Association of College News Bureaus was established which later became the American College Publicity Association. In 1938 this Association had 340 members representing the publicity departments of the most important colleges and universities in the country.

It is now the exception rather than the rule to find an institution of higher education without a publicity or press bureau, a director of public relations, or some person carrying on similar functions. Among the current publicity media are: president's reports and reports of other officers, catalogues and bulletins, student publications, the activities and publications of field representatives (financial and recruiting), alumni publications, articles in professional magazines, publicity bureaus, college view books, glee clubs, speakers' bureaus, publicity stunts, college movies and sound pictures, radio broadcasts, "college days," "alumni days," "parents' days," etc.

The last report of President W. A. Neilson of Smith College included the reports of the secretary for publicity, the college physician, the director of physical education, the librarian, the vocational secretary, the graduate school of architecture and landscape architecture, the school of social work, the summer school of music, etc., etc.

The secretary for publicity gave a detailed account of the increase in quantity of Smith College news in the local newspapers, in the coverage by wire syndicates, in the field of news and magazine articles and photography, by radio news commentators in the moving pictures, in exhibit books routed by the publicity office to alumnae in various cities, in talks at Smith College clubs, and paid tribute to the forty members of the Press Board.

For the purposes of this exposition a cross-section of general periodicals has been taken for the year 1929-30. Much of the material concerning the college was of a controversial nature. Controversy grew fiercer as the depression advanced but during all this bombardment of the colleges from the air as well as from underground there have been amazingly few fatalities. The effects of the depression on the colleges were belated as compared with most other areas of our national life.

Of the thirty-five or forty specific criticisms brought to light by this cross-section view of the magazines, considerably more than half have to do with the faculty, their scholarship, personality, and methods of teaching. Less than one-third of them attack or defend the organization of the college program, and frequently this is done with very little discrimination as between the college program and that of the university. Practically all of the other criticisms may be included under the general head of social life within the institutions and the alleged failure of the colleges to make adjustments to the larger social world, to business, public service, and the life of the people.

Another cross-section view of the magazines was taken in 1936-37. For both periods it may be remarked that the criticisms are in no sense all antagonistic, since upon almost every topic at least two points of view are urged. The criticisms of the second period, however, tended to be more fierce than those of the first, particularly in the area of vocational or prevocational education. Subsequent chapters of this book treat of the progress which is being made by the colleges within the various areas of attack.

It is worthy of note that during this extended period of controversy the colleges have shown the greatest degree of vitality.

Out of such controversy, and the still more rewarding discussions within the administrative and teaching groups, have developed programs of procedure which make of most colleges very different institutions from those of fifty or even ten years ago.

It might savor of unwarranted propaganda for the colleges to claim the application to their experience of the text, "Whom the Lord loveth He chasteneth." It does appear to be a plain statement of fact that the atmosphere has been somewhat clarified. The colleges have passed over lightly the confusion of mind of many of their adverse, and frequently uninformed or misunderstanding, critics. They have recognized the justness of the exposure of some of their weaknesses and difficulties, and they have been spurred to seek remedies for the ills that beset them. Repeatedly their own organizations have furnished platforms for the presentation of their shortcomings.

As illustrations of the responses of the colleges evoked in part by these processes of aeration may be mentioned the personnel movement, honors courses, tutorial and preceptorial plans, independent study, comprehensive examinations, survey courses, individualized curricula for talented as well as less gifted students, the various studies of youth by the Federal Government and the American Council on Education, placement tests, achievement tests as a substitute for course credits, reorganization and condensation of educational programs, cooperative integration and synthesis of studies, the inclusion and increase of offerings in the fine arts, music, dramatic art, citizenship, and public service.

It is by no means true that all publicity issued with the authority of the colleges themselves reflects a high degree of credit upon the college management. The wheat and tares, good and bad publicity and propaganda, grow up together.

Illustrations of the disposition of colleges to overemphasize the significance of the opportunities they offer may be found in numerous college publications. Like all motivated publicity this type has its good and its bad qualities. Some of it is excellent. Some mine-run samples are given in the Appendix on the theory that the thing itself is more informing than any amount of talk about it. It is left to the reader to distinguish the good from the bad.

A small group of metropolitan newspapers are setting a high standard of educational publicity. While it is said to be true that 80 per cent of all college newspaper linage is to be found on the sports page and that very seldom does educational news make the first page, such newspapers as the *New York Times* and the New York *Herald Tribune,* the *Christian Science Monitor,* the Springfield *Republican,* and the Boston *Transcript* are extending a fine degree of cooperation. In these papers thousands of linear inches of news exclusive of sports news and comment are appearing, covering hundreds of institutions in practically every State of the Union as well as in many foreign countries. It is the policy of the *New York Times* to submit unfavorable "news" to the institution concerned before its publication, with the purpose of presenting the college version at the same time. Very complete reports of annual meetings of presidents and faculties are presented with truth and understanding, particularly by the *Christian Science Monitor* among newspapers, and

School and Society among educational journals.   In the "Stanford School Press Relations Investigation" by R. F. Harlow, it was found that 5 per cent of the total news space in the forty-six newspapers studied was devoted to college and university news.

Many colleges now produce their own films.   Such forms of publicity are as yet in their infancy and much is yet to be learned.   Relatively superior results are being secured through radio and the broadcasting systems are cooperating in laudable fashion.   They employ directors of educational news of wisdom and experience and give them freedom to do highly constructive work.   The accomplishments of the United States Office of Education in this field are worthy of high praise.   But the movies and the radio have their distinct limitations.   Culture cannot be based on sound and sight alone, to be caught in a hurry or lost forever.   There must be something more ultimate than mechanical devices, however brilliant in their conception and operation.

Propaganda might well have been enumerated above as one of the inalienable rights for it is grounded in human nature and by implication it is incorporated into fundamental law.   So long as there is freedom of speech, of press, of worship, of assembly, there will be freedom of propaganda. It is inherent in democracy as it is an official implement of power in totalitarian states.   We cannot eliminate it from publicity, the best we can do is try to recognize it when we see it.   College men and women must learn to read between the lines.   At this we may succeed sometimes.

At first propaganda was an abbreviation from the Latin *de propaganda fide;* a congregation or department of the Roman Catholic Church charged with the management of missions.   Now it means any one or more of a variety of things: the spreading of a particular doctrine or system of principles; the extension of a doctrine that is considered as subversive; the expression of zeal without knowledge or regard for knowledge; putting the best foot forward; the result of pressure from government, from advertisers, from any organization or group; the spell of symbols, verbal formulas, stereotypes; deliberately misleading or misinforming the public to prevent, impede, or forestall the objective consideration of facts; to capitalize on fallacious habits of thought; to put something over, regardless of the means.

With new and highly developed means of communication, propaganda has become a world-wide activity—political, economic, pseudo-scientific, religious, racial. The propagandist does not take the oath to tell the truth, the whole truth, and nothing but the truth. Philip Guedalla's maxim has much meaning—"Any stigma is good enough to beat a dogma with."

Among specific agencies, besides some colleges which have been organized at least in part to combat the influence of evil propaganda, may be named: America's Town Meeting of the Air which goes on the theory that the best cure for democracy is more democracy; the public forum movement; private letters circulated by commercial and other agencies, the *Herald Tribune's* Annual Forum on Current Problems; the Foreign Policy Association; and various institutes, conferences, and round tables. Many clergymen, educators, and editors supplement the work of these special agencies.

In October 1937 the Institute for Propaganda Analysis was launched in New York. It was defined as "a non-profit corporation organized for scientific research in methods used by propagandists in influencing public opinion." Much of the material here used in exposition of the nature of propaganda is drawn from its publications. In the second issue of the bulletin seven common devices of propaganda were described:

1. Name Calling device—"to make us form a judgment without examining the evidence on which it should be based." The propagandist gives bad names to those individuals, colleges, groups, nations, races, policies, practices, beliefs and ideals which he would have us condemn and reject.

2. The Glittering Generalities device—identification of a

program with virtue by use of "virtue words." Appeals to our emotions of love, generosity, and brotherhood.

3. The Transfer device—carrying over the authority, sanction, and prestige of something we respect and revere to something the propagandist would have us accept.

4. The Testimonial device—would make us accept anything from a patent medicine to a program of national policy.

5. Plain Folks device—used by politicians, labor leaders, business men, ministers, and educators to win our confidence by appearing to be people like ourselves.

6. The Card Stacking device—one in which the propagandist employs all the arts of deception to win our support for himself, his belief or ideal, his group, nation, race, policy, practice. Stacks the cards against the truth; uses underemphasis and overemphasis to dodge issues and evade facts. Omits facts. Offers false testimony.

7. The Band Wagon device—to make us follow the crowd. Directs appeal to groups held together by common ties of nationality, religion, race environment, sex, vocation.

That much of the criticism has "news value," that it is pungent and eloquent and entertaining and some of it undoubtedly deserved is true. Among the adverse criticisms of the colleges and universities referred to on a previous page, it was said that they have surrendered themselves to every public whim; the trustees are controlled body and soul by Wall Street, the presidents are liars and hypocrites, faculty members weak, cringing creatures, half the seniors are illiterate, fraternities are hotbeds of smug self-complacency and snobbishness, college athletics are a monstrous cancer, students enter college as Christians and graduate as atheists or agnostics, the curriculum is a mass of inherited rubbish, the classroom is the tomb of curiosity, alumni are the major educational crime of this generation, in a half century the degeneration of the American college will be complete.

Professor George Boas of Johns Hopkins University rendered a public service a few years ago by publishing in

Harper's Magazine an analysis of the characteristics of the "Complete Scandalmonger." This analysis appears to be pertinent to the discussion of propaganda and publicity in the colleges. He called attention to the fact that the good scandalmonger will not worry so much about what is true as about what people like to believe. And one may therefore say at the outset that certain rules are applicable, other things being equal.

The first rule is that the familiar has greater probative force than the unfamiliar. The scandalous is in part unfamiliar, however, so that sensitiveness is needed as to just what degree of familiarity is required. Boas remarks that when "Faculty Wives" was printed in *Harper's,* originals for the purely imaginary ladies were found in two universities other than the one which had the misfortune to shelter its author. In one a professor of English with a penchant for satire was ostracized for many months since he alone could have known the women whom he was charged with maltreating.

Rule two may be stated: The greater the evil, the more easy to believe it. Debunking and denunciation are both more persuasive than eulogy or even fair-mindedness.

Rule three: The greater the charge, the greater the probative force.

Rule four: It is easier to attack a person's private life than his public life.

Rule five: The discreditable motive of an act is the real motive.

Rule six: The discreditable motive, if not apparent, or if denied, is unconscious.

That the colleges have suffered from the operation of the rules of procedure outlined by Professor Boas is strikingly illustrated in the indictments of the students which have been made largely on the basis of gossip, but to some extent in published articles and documents, concerning their radical tendencies, their habits in drinking and in sex relations. The excesses set forth by these critics of the colleges have very generally been denied by the college officials, many of whom are presumably in position to know at least some of the facts. It is an amazing phenomenon of current psychology that individuals in good standing in the community, who are quite unable to furnish concrete evidence, nevertheless are willing to refer to well known colleges and universities as "dens of vice."

Several significant and presumably impartial investigations have been made of these various charges. One published by the magazine *Fortune*, June 1936, resulted in the setting forth of certain conclusions regarding the outlook and disposition of present-day college students.

As to the alleged radicalism of college students, it found the campus is a very little to the left of the country as a whole, and because of this fact the Hearst newspapers have grown volubly excited about the Red "menace" in our colleges. According to the findings, the group of Reds is numerically negligible. There are fewer Fascists, and the conservatives are not quite as many as those vaguely interested in an ill-defined socialism. "Of bona fide collectivist radicalism in the colleges there is at the most but a chemical trace." In fact *Fortune* characterized the present college generation as "fatalistic, cautious, subdued, unadventurous. Security is the *summum bonum*." The students want a job guaranteed to be safe and permanent. Youth is "passive." "It is intellectually curious about the world. The undergraduate will turn to new leaders and is already doing so to some extent. This does not mean that the colleges are becoming radicalized. Unable to plot his future, the average undergraduate has turned to minor cultural and semicultural activities. Too passive to be atheist the undergraduate is vaguely deist. Liquor and sex used to be part of the great triumvirate of campus topics that included religion. Today economics is to the fore as bull session pabulum with religion playing a minor role."

According to a poll conducted a few years ago by the *Literary Digest,* drinking among college students had declined recently and it was estimated that 5 per cent would be a generous estimate of regular drinkers. While there was some drinking at the metropolitan universities it was not considered a problem. Dom Proface in his study found one dean who claimed there was more liquor consumed today but that its use was more widely diffused. Most authorities, however, regarded the problem as less acute in recent years.

In the matter of sex immorality, *Fortune* claims that "sex is no longer news, and while it is impossible to discover with any accuracy the actual sex habits of students, if the present day undergraduate indulges in intercourse before marriage with any frequency, he doesn't talk very much about it."

Another investigation was made by Mrs. Rita Halle Kleeman who during the past few years has written on various phases of college life. Independently she visited some two hundred colleges with a view to ascertaining the accuracy of various sensational charges against the students. She talked with students, teachers, townspeople, parents, and believes that while evils exist in varying degree, in practically no college do they constitute a menace to a reasonably decent boy or girl. Certain publications play up the few cases, and many of the stories are based on erroneous statements. Investigation indicated very few certified cases of sex immorality.

Mrs. Kleeman found some parents troubled at the loss of religion among college students. She claims that the students have substituted for the formal religion they brought from home standards and ideals that are clear and conscious, having reason rather than emotion as their basis.

Various other investigations have been made especially by newspaper writers. *Newsweek* is convinced that restraints formerly common in colleges have disappeared from all but a few coeducational schools (chiefly denominational) and some colleges for women. It is worthy of note that reports of such surveys necessarily are frequently sprinkled with such phrases as "it seems that," "the general idea seems to be," "the code seems to indicate," etc.

An illustration of a different kind indicating the disposition of certain newspapers and journals to emphasize the exciting or sensational story "regardless of the effect on public education" is found in the charges against Teachers College, Columbia University, following the retirement of Professor Kilpatrick, the dismissal of Associate Professor McDowell, the discontinuance of New College, and the policy of the College which resulted in the dismissal of four cafeteria workers. In view of these charges, the College selected representatives who have made an investigation and in a twelve-page statement have set forth the institution as a victim of sensational publicity and misrepresentation and have offered rebuttal to the assertion that the institution has become "arbitrary and reactionary."

Maurice S. Sheehy, writing in *The Commonweal*, testifies that in many ways the depression has been a blessing to the American college. He claims it has lessened the number of playboys who go to college to spend the excess income of their parents. It has compelled many or enabled a large number of students to see even before matriculation the real value in a college education. "Students seem to have a more serious purpose in coming to college and they seem to have a bit more vision in linking a study to the general purpose of education. In the Catholic University of America a greater proportion of students are concerned with liberal rather than vocational studies since the depression."

In a recent analysis Dean Gauss of Princeton has declared that "beyond question youth is moving rapidly toward new standards of wisdom and sobriety." This view is held also by Dr. Walter A. Jessup, President of the Carnegie Foundation for the Advancement of Teaching, who says: "The student on the campus is no longer the blasé sophisticate but a hardworking, serious-minded person who demands more of the college library, the laboratory, and the instructor than did his brother of a decade ago. It can almost be said that

the present college student is the person that the college professor was asking for a decade ago." Such a view conforms
to the estimate now made by most college authorities.

The insidious infection of the contemporary connotation
of propaganda is threatening, in greater or lesser degree, the
integrity of leaders in almost every realm of human activity.
It has become a more deadly weapon to sovereign states than
the explosive shells of war. Like termites, it is secretly eat-
ing away the foundation of democracies. It is pouring
hatred, suspicion and intolerance into the life stream of nations that have not yet fallen. It offers a new and unexpected
challenge to American education. Teachers in schools and
colleges, in churches and in the Fourth Estate are called to
take their places in the front line of defense. They must
recognize its danger, understand and point out its symptoms,
combat its encroachments, and guard as best they can the
health and happiness of our people. Most difficult of all,
they must be careful that the antidote they administer is
itself free from poison.

CHAPTER XIII

THE FINANCING OF COLLEGES

THE problem of the financial support of colleges has had a long history. It deals with one of the most interesting and complicated phases of college administration.

John Harvard gave a small collection of books to the struggling institution at Cambridge, and forever after the institution has borne his name. In acknowledgment of a gift of £800, the institution at New Haven became Yale University. Queen's College was designated Rutgers as the sequel to a gift from Colonel Henry Rutgers. Numerous institutions and a multitude of lesser items of plant and equipment in many colleges have, during the years, carried names of donors. Frequently this has been on the basis of relatively small gifts and in many cases such christenings have been accompanied by a lively anticipation of favors yet to come. Andrew Carnegie expressed the conviction that it was a disgrace for a man to die rich, a conviction upon which he eventually acted to a degree unprecedented among men of great wealth. This prompted him to become a pioneer in bestowing large gifts. He eventually became one of the most distinguished of all donors to higher education.

American colleges were founded upon philanthropy, and upon that foundation they still stand. No other people in the history of the world has voluntarily poured out money so lavishly for education. While some of the governments of Europe—Great Britain and France notably—have assumed large responsibility for various forms of social welfare, the United States continues to be distinguished for the great number and variety of its private endeavors. The colonial governments rendered important services to Harvard and William and Mary, to Yale, King's, and Dartmouth, but in no instance did they accept determinative responsibility. Outside of Massachusetts, Connecticut, Virginia, New Hampshire, and New York, aid from the state to higher education during the colonial period was unknown or quite incidental. Of the entire group of colonial institutions, only William and Mary became a state institution, and that not until 1906. Rutgers College still stands on its original foundation. Rutgers University has a contract with the New Jersey Board of Regents for the maintenance of agricultural, engineering, and woman's colleges, and an agricultural experiment station through funds appropriated by the state legislature.

Several special trends in financial support and administration developed during the colonial period.

One of these trends was the search for funds in England. Jesse B. Sears shows that during certain five-year periods from 1641 to 1775 the percentages of such gifts to the total gifts to Harvard were as high respectively as 90, 80, 78, 77, 63.* Later, colleges farther west and south found private benefactors, particularly in England and outside of their immediate fields in this country. A sense of reciprocal reasonableness now prompts Oxford to seek funds in the United States. One very large gift has already gone from America to the Oxford libraries.

It is worthy of note that most of the funds which have been secured have come through the solicitation of representatives of the institutions. While the majority of gifts are probably still for specific purposes, the college authorities often suggest the purposes for which the money is to be expended. Girard College, Philadelphia, is a notable example of a college whose founder laid down specific regulations. Speaking in the large, there has been relatively little effort on the part of donors to dictate the policies of the institutions. Gifts with hampering strings attached are less acceptable to the colleges. Occasionally such proffered gifts are

* See References, p. 358.

refused. William R. Harper announced early in his administration that no gift for a building would be accepted unless
provision were made also for its maintenance. In recent
years much has been done to educate college officials and the
public generally as to the undesirability of restricted gifts,
and of gifts inadequate for the purpose intended. The purposes of donations should be stated in more flexible terms,
or the power to make adjustments as social trends may require should be lodged with college financial boards. Many
instances could be cited of funds which have been tied up
for purposes now obsolete or worse than useless.

Equally as important as the gifts themselves are the responsibility borne, the unselfish service rendered, the time,
and most of all the experience and thought of men of affairs
put at the disposal of the colleges. Many of these are donors.
The best equipped men and women of the community are
nearly always available. Increasingly, men of large affairs,
regardless of location, serve on the various boards and committees of the colleges. Prominent men in public life, from
the presidents and their cabinets, the chief justices of the
Supreme Court and the associate justices, numerous leaders
in the legislative branch of the government, and the managers of big as well as little business, identify themselves with
the destinies of one or more colleges. This fact accounts in
part for the prestige of the institutions and their sound financial management. The loss of principal from the permanent
funds of colleges due to malfeasance or bad investments is
very exceptional, even during periods of financial distress.
Industry and business conducted with the profit motive have
nothing like so good a record. College trustees play safe.

Just as the impulse of religion usually furnished the leadership and the funds, as well as the students, for the colleges,
particularly until the outbreak of the Civil War, in the same
way it developed that the theological seminaries, first as departments in the colleges and later as separate schools, were
the gifts primarily of members of the churches. This sometimes made an additional contribution to the spirit of de-

nominationalism against which most of the enlightened leaders of the churches are now reacting unfavorably. At the
same time, the fact must be put into the record that it was
the protest of the Council of Church Boards of Education,
soon after its organization in 1913, that led the United States
Bureau of Education to abandon its classification of colleges
as "sectarian" and "non-sectarian." The representatives of
the churches convinced the United States Commissioner of
Education that this classification did not truly represent the
facts. The "denominational" colleges later began to call
themselves "church-related" colleges, also under the leadership of this Council, which was composed of practically all
the Protestant church boards of education of the country.
Now all high-grade colleges are recognized as public institutions even though privately controlled. The sectarian institution is the exception. Experience shows that colleges may
foster religion without being sectarian, and also even if they
are "secular."

Since the Civil War several new forms of philanthropy
have been introduced. Twelve or fifteen large fortunes have
contributed to the remarkable development of as many institutions. Chicago, Cornell, Vanderbilt, Tulane, Stanford,
Rochester, Duke, Rice Institute, Emory, Carnegie Institute
of Technology, Johns Hopkins, Peabody, Vassar, Bryn Mawr
are examples. Until recent years philanthropy has been almost solely responsible for the development of separate colleges for women.

Between 1893 and 1915, it was estimated by Sears, education received 43 per cent of all gifts in the United States of
$5,000 and over. Since the World War, colossal sums have
gone to some twenty institutions of higher learning—Harvard, Yale, and Chicago leading.

Indeed, as late as 1937, $600,000,000 was set aside for new
foundations—the contributions of Andrew W. Mellon and
Charles Hayden topping all others. Ernest V. Hollis finds
that "those who control the stable fortunes in aluminum,
coal, and other mining enterprises, in the automotive and

food-processing industries, and in the public utility, merchandising and banking fields are beginning to follow the 1912-14 example of the steel and oil magnates." Several notable gifts for philanthropic purposes have been made since 1937.

Outstanding among all these agencies of philanthropy are the great educational foundations. The best known of these are connected with the names of Carnegie and Rockefeller, although there is an increasing number of others in addition to the various boards established by the churches.

Hollis made the statement a few years ago—that of approximately $220,000,000 which have been given to American higher education by the foundations since the beginning of the century, a large proportion has been supplied by the Rockefeller and Carnegie trusts. Much of this has served as challenging proffers which have stimulated other gifts to endowment estimated at $660,000,000. Of the foundation gifts to higher education, Eastern schools were granted $133,000,000 between 1902 and 1934. The ten universities receiving the most during the 1902-34 period were in order: The University of Chicago, which received $46,240,767, the Carnegie Institute of Technology, Johns Hopkins, Columbia, Vanderbilt, Yale, Harvard, Cornell, Duke, and the California Institute of Technology with the smallest sum, $11,033,316.

The foundations have led in the development of businesslike techniques of philanthropy of immeasurable value. This accounts in considerable measure for the multiplication of such foundations. Historically, the General Education Board built upon the experience of the Baptist Education Society, which had been largely the benevolent agency of Mr. Rockefeller. This is indicated in one of its reports:

> The General Education Board is, on this side, an outgrowth of the Baptist Education Society. The Board adopted the main principles and practices of the Baptist Society and extended them, dropping the denominational and other limitations. It took over the conception of a system of higher education, comprehensive, mutually related

and supplemented in its parts, so expanded, however, as to cover institutions with and without denominational connections. The Board adopted, too, the manner in which the Baptist Society had made its contributions and even the precise form of pledge that had been employed.

During the present century the endowments of the colleges of the country have increased 1,000 per cent. The direct contribution of the General Education Board to this increase amounted to about $150,000,000. This sum is about equivalent to the total amount of endowment held by the colleges and universities in 1900. The 1938 report by President Raymond B. Fosdick of the General Education Board stated that the Board had expended toward the progress of education since its organization in 1902, $255,334,670. Raymond Rich Associates announced that in 1937, 243 leading foundations contributed more to medicine and public health than to education. Thus education dropped to second place.

In 1920 the practice was initiated by the General Education Board of spending from principal as well as income. Up to the end of 1937 appropriations from the principal were greater than those from the income. The president disclosed the full significance of this trend by asserting in the 1938 report that the funds of that Board had been reduced in round figures from $180,000,000 to the present level of $24,000,000. More recently, part of this program has been abandoned.

In the few years of life that remain to the General Education Board its resources are being concentrated largely in connection with three types of activity: first, the continuance of the existing program in the Southern States; second, the support of research and experimentation in relation to the problems presented in the field of general education, i.e., the secondary school through the junior college level; and third, a program in child growth and development.*

According to the latest biennial report of the Rosenwald Fund, three-fourths of the original endowment of $20,000,000

*Italics the author's.

has now been disbursed. The donor stipulated that the entire fund was to be spent within twenty-five years. The present capital is reported as $5,000,000, which must be spent by 1957.

Notwithstanding the generous support which education has received from private sources, much of the recent pioneering, particularly in vocational and mass education, has been supported by and under the auspices of the state, the city, and to some extent of the Federal Government. The 1935-36 Biennial Statistical Report of the United States Office of Education reveals some significant developments. It shows that in the Western States which are largely dependent upon publicly controlled institutions, $20 to $30 per youth of 18 to 21 years of age is contributed by the states for the support of higher education. On the other hand, in states where there are strong privately controlled institutions, for example, Connecticut, New York, Pennsylvania, Massachusetts, and New Jersey, the corresponding figures are from $5.28 to $8.49 per capita. In an analysis of receipts for current expenses in publicly controlled institutions, it is shown that whereas the Federal Government contributed in 1925-26 but 8.7 per cent of such income, in 1935-36 the corresponding figure was 16.2 per cent, an increase within a decade of approximately 100 per cent.

The same source reports the receipts from private gifts and grants as $54,945,828 in 1933-34, the bottom of the depression for the colleges, and as $84,153,788 in 1935-36. When this increase of 53.2 per cent is broken down into the purposes for which the gifts and grants were made, the percentages of increase in 1935-36 over 1933-34 were: for current and plant extension, 35.1; for endowment funds, 71.3.

In 1929-30 the publicly controlled institutions received 6.3 per cent of all private gifts and grants reported. In 1935-36 their share was 16.9 per cent of such gifts, an increase of almost 300 per cent. Of the receipts in 1935-36 intended for increase of endowment and other permanent funds, 22.1 per cent went to publicly controlled, and 77.9 per cent to privately controlled higher institutions. While today the privately controlled institutions hold nine-tenths of the endowments, the tables are certainly being turned.

Other sources of gifts, to which favorable reference must be made, are the alumni funds and the special campaigns, some of which have been directed by the institutions themselves and others by professional agencies. Of the alumni funds, the first of which was established by the Yale alumni in 1890, there are now somewhere between eighty and one hundred in existence, all based on collecting annual cash contributions. Director Felix A. Grisette of the Alumni Loyalty Fund of the University of North Carolina states that 15 per cent of the cost of higher education in the United States is paid by the small annual gifts of alumni. A custom at Harvard is that each class on its twenty-fifth anniversary gives at least $100,000 for unrestricted purposes.

The first campaign for a large alumni fund was conducted in 1904 under the leadership of Bishop William A. Lawrence, then president of the Harvard Alumni Association. The effort resulted in the raising of $2,400,000. Bishop Lawrence announced a rule for securing money: "The way to get it is to go out and get it." In 1927 Yale conducted a financial campaign which resulted in an addition of $21,000,-000 to her resources. There are few colleges now that have not attempted one or more such campaigns. Sometimes these have failed of their purpose, and this is particularly true of cooperative ventures.

In the spring of 1938 a professional money-raising agency assured the public that "the universities and colleges did not suffer greatly from a decline in gifts and bequests made to higher education during the 'seven lean years.' An analysis of forty-nine leading institutions reveals a yearly average of $45,573,053 in gifts and bequests for the fiscal years 1920-21 through 1928-29, as against a yearly average of $45,094,512 for 1929-30 through 1936-37." The reader must understand, however, that such gratifying figures are likely to be wrongly interpreted. After a small number of exceedingly fortunate institutions have been excluded, a very marked decline is apparent. Mr. Trevor Arnett and Professor W. C. Eells point out that one-fourth of the privately controlled institutions hold 88.8 per cent of the total endowment, and twenty of them—3 per cent of the number—hold over 50 per cent of the total. On this point it may be noted that of 1,200 institutions of higher learning, only 453 have received a grant of any kind from a foundation.

All this is the more significant when contrasted with the policy of Daniel K. Pearsons, one of the trail blazers among systematic contributors, who adhered to the plan of giving to "poor" and undernourished colleges. Some colleges of the better sort, but far from adequately provided for, got the surprise of their lives by being refused assistance by Mr. Pearsons on the ground that they were too rich! When the great foundations were established, they reversed this order of procedure and have now verified the doctrine that to him that hath shall be given. Naturally, the foundations believe the strong colleges have a better chance to survive.

In a letter from one of the professional agencies, dated May 24, 1938, the following observations are made:

> You will probably agree that in the general run of college giving, alumni loyalties still count heavily—loyalties to Alma Mater, to locality, and to sections, loyalties even to what the giver may regard as a proper atmosphere, point of view, or doctrine.
>
> If we look beyond these basic motives, we may discern today a tendency among larger givers to waive the merits of appeals which rely on a preservation—even a fear—impulse. Individuals of means are, we believe, increasingly open to conviction:
>
> (1) That their gifts will help to maintain the independence and integrity of education, to protect it from the vagaries of public thought or the dubious impulses of political control.
>
> (2) That "after all, some of the good things must be saved."

(3) That liberal arts colleges are a bulwark against loose, uninformed thinking; that in them lies—more than ever—the hope of an intelligent, balanced democracy. . . .

(4) That one's funds will be devoted to more efficient, constructive use if given to a college than if paid in income or inheritance taxes to government.

The large majority of the privately controlled colleges get only crumbs of comfort from the rich men's tables. The vast totals which have been reported from time to time have swelled neither their permanent funds nor their budgets. Reluctantly they are realizing that the foundations are not now giving large sums to colleges except in rare cases. These smaller institutions are learning to face the facts.

Some of the elements of the total situation which confront the private institutions follow. These are taken from a summary by Mr. Arnett with a few adaptations and additions.

(a) There is a diminishing return from endowment funds; the funds themselves are increasing very slowly, if at all; accumulated reserves in some institutions fortunate enough to have them are rapidly being worn down.

(b) There is a shrinkage in gifts and bequests, because donors are disturbed by the uncertainties of business and taxation; an increasing proportion of gifts is going to tax-supported institutions.

(c) There is a similar shrinkage of gifts from the large foundations, except for research, not only for the reasons just cited, but for the more significant reason of the reversal or the modification of policy in the matter of giving to colleges. Some of the foundations are rapidly liquidating their principal.

(d) There is increasing competition from tax-supported institutions, which now surpass those privately controlled in total enrollment, in immediate service rendered to the mass of the citizens; in funds for building operations, largely from government grants; and in other forms of expansion.

(e) There is insistent need of greater compensation, that able faculties may be retained and attracted. The

average salary in state universities now exceeds that in
privately controlled universities.

To meet this situation, what consolations does this majority group of colleges have?

First of all, there is the manner in which the colleges have
worked their way thus far through the winds and waves of
the depression. While their experiences have varied, there
is one invaluable lesson all have learned, namely, that the
Lord helps those who help themselves. They have increased
their initiative: they have become less dependent, more resourceful. Working upon this principle, a very considerable
number of them have repeatedly reported balanced budgets
with salaries paid in full and no current indebtedness. A
larger group has been obliged to cut salaries, but the range
of these cuts has usually not been above 25 per cent, and in
some cases less than 10 per cent.

Scarcely one of these colleges was guilty of doubtful
methods of financing or took what are known to be great
risks. Remarkable as it may seem, many who could not quite
stem every tide, nevertheless did succeed in righting their
barks and actually in decreasing or completely liquidating
standing indebtedness. They refused to draw upon their
endowments for current operations, building projects, or any
other purpose. They did not allow their desire for expansion to go beyond their assured resources. They did not
count annuity funds at their book value; indeed, they seldom
counted them at all. They did not include pledges or other
prospects as though they were cash. They did pursue a
sound, conservative financial policy. They did build up a
technique of college financing. They did demonstrate that
college administrators, using the term in a comprehensive
sense, are among our best American financiers. Cooperatively, the acumen, training, devotion, and industry of the
presidents, treasurers, business managers, the members of the
finance committees, the entire board of directors, and—be it
said to their honor—the members of the faculty who in emer-
gencies not only cheerfully accepted cuts in salary, but even

volunteered temporary reductions, overcame financial difficulties without seriously interfering with the educational
program of the institution. The officers and faculties saved
the colleges from disaster. The colleges for the most part
have preserved their integrity, financially, culturally, mor-
ally. A picture of his institution's morale was unconsciously
drawn in the words of the president—"The economic conditions in our state are extremely bad. We have had in succession in the last four years a most destructive flood, a great
drought, bank failures, and the depression. This leaves the
purchasing power in our state very low. The college itself,
however, is getting along quite well."

A further analysis discloses trustworthy bases of faith in
the future. These facts and hypotheses are furnished by a
professional agency.

> The motive for voluntary giving to the institutions through-
> out the country is, in my opinion, about 90 per cent reli-
> gious. We are now giving about a billion and a half dollars
> each year. Very little of this money comes from persons
> without a religious connection or a religious background of
> family training. The appeal for a particular college has to
> be made to that fundamental motive, made in terms of
> service to man and God.

This psychological basis of support is of immeasurable value.
Contributions to colleges become adventures in faith.

Several months before the same agency treated the case historically:

> Simple plus and minus arithmetic evidently does not
> afford a calibration of philanthropy, for, strangely enough,
> every expansion of government in these fields has been
> accompanied by a similar expansion of philanthropy in the
> same or new fields. We have noted how the Land-Grant Act
> in President Lincoln's administration brought into being
> the modern tax-supported state university in the 1860's. . . .
> Did this lessen philanthropy's interest in higher education?
> On the contrary, philanthropy's voluntary gifts to our pri-
> vate colleges and universities have sometimes in recent days
> totaled as much in one year as they totaled in all the two
> hundred years of collegiate history prior to that Act. Dur-

ing the year 1870 the total private gifts to education in America equaled $8,593,740; during the year 1930, they equaled $139,508,920!

It is pointed out that President Nicholas Murray Butler's prophecy that in the future more of the nation's income will flow to millions of persons in the lower income brackets need not cause alarm, since these millions are already providing two-thirds of the annual support of our philanthropies out of their meager incomes.   Dr. Butler's forecast of a wider distribution of income should be interpreted as a harbinger of good news rather than a foreboding of disaster.

Other considerations are: the base for giving to colleges is being broadened; means are being discovered by a few institutions by which those who are able to do so may and will pay more adequately for their college education; there is a distinct and measurable rise in relative income from tuition funds.   Many men and women of wealth have given little or nothing as yet.   Few who do give have given to their limit. Gifts for such purposes, deductible under the 15 per cent exemption clause of the Federal Government, amount to less than 3 per cent of reported income.

Add to all this certain subtle influences now at work: a distinct gain is taking place in intellectual, religious, cultural and public service interest; educational programs are being pruned without loss of effectiveness, often with great gain; vigilance in the administration of the budget is creating a more wholesome atmosphere; the cost of higher education has been rather definitely computed—colleges need not fly blind; the increase in applications for admission points toward greater appreciation of college opportunities—the awareness of need of the liberal arts tradition has been augmented rather than dissipated; the total income of the majority group of colleges, as well as of the more favored ones, is indicated by a rising curve; the need is being recognized for a more definite statement of individual as well as group objectives; the general cooperative trend of the college is in the opposite direction from that of either present government financing or cut-throat competition.

The good colleges recognize that all of them, working together, cannot adequately serve America's aspiring youth.

Cooperative gestures between colleges and attorneys, trust companies, and insurance companies stimulated some years ago jointly by the Council of Church Boards of Education and the Association of American Colleges, known as "The Campaign of Perseverance," although checked by recent financial disturbances, are likely to be renewed with greater assurance of success if and when the Federal Government and business discover a basis of cooperation for the public welfare.

"The Campaign of Perseverance" above referred to was of distinct educational value. It had definite achievements to its credit, while its intangible influences continue to operate in spite of the depression. As samples illustrative of these achievements and influences may be mentioned the establishment in the Old Colony Trust Company of Boston of the Woman's College Foundation for Maine and New Hampshire; an unpublicized campaign under the auspices of the University of Oregon for bequests, which was reported by its director as highly successful; the organization by the Cornellian Council of a Committee on Bequests composed of nearly one thousand graduates of the Cornell Law School and other alumni to seek bequests for Cornell University. In 1938 the Executive Secretary of the Cornellian Council wrote that since the establishment of Cornell's bequest program more than $7,000,000 had come to the institution in testamentary gifts. He also asserted that "a survey of the present status of fund-raising activities in American colleges and universities reveals that at the present time at least thirty institutions have formal bequest programs in operation and many more have similar undertakings in contemplation." A study of recent additions to college endowments through bequests disclosed a decided upturn during the depression period among the institutions included in the study. According to statistics compiled by a well-trusted authority for

forty-six institutions during the six-year period 1930-36, out
of a total of $244,812,968 received by these institutions,
$90,478,375 came from bequests.

As the *New York Times* has asked:

> . . . but what of rising income taxes, the heavy duties
> levied on estates, the threat of inheritance taxes? The
> research departments of some universities are already pat-
> enting inventions and discoveries and using royalties to con-
> duct more research. And lastly there was the ominous will
> of the late Jesse Straus, a generous giver in his lifetime, in
> which it was plainly stated that since so large a part of his
> fortune would be sacrificed in taxes, it was no more than
> just that the Government should assume the burden of
> philanthropy. Indeed, there is some evidence that the foun-
> dations themselves are of a similar mind. A few of the
> largest may ultimately be liquidated and their functions
> taken over by the Government.

If all these things should eventuate, the funds will be
routed away from the privately controlled institutions.
However, the policy of the government to exempt gifts from
taxation up to 15 per cent of income would serve to mitigate
this threatened outcome.

An interesting phase of college financing is found in the
contributed services that make possible the existence of most
of the 170 Catholic colleges listed by the National Catholic
Welfare Conference. Although the exact figures are not
available, it is estimated that the total value of these contributed services is equivalent to the income on over two hundred million dollars.

Owing to the continuity of the Religious order and its
ability to provide for an oncoming supply of teachers, contributed services in a Catholic college are of a permanent
nature, more stable in their value than mortgages, bonds, or
stocks, which fluctuate both as to principal and income under
prevailing economic conditions. To consider them as continuing grants or aids similar to funds received by some colleges from public or private sources is not to do full justice
to the case. These services result from a capital investment

made by the order in defraying the expenses of education and personal support for the men and women who have dedicated themselves to the work of the order. In this way there has been established a real "living endowment" for higher education. The secret of the remarkable stability of Catholic educational institutions in times of financial stress is found in this "living endowment"—a phrase which stands for great devotion and personal sacrifice to the cause of Christian education on the part of thousands of men and women who have consecrated themselves to the Religious teaching orders of the Church.

After the most favorable report which is true to the known facts has been made, it must be said that there is a group of small colleges, usually though not uniformly related to Protestant churches, which have been on the decline financially for a series of years. This has been brought out statistically by Dean Baugher of Elizabethtown College, who has recently completed a study of colleges related to these churches. The income of this small group is consistently decreasing from year to year. These institutions are special cases requiring special treatment. This chapter cannot go into that matter. One consideration may be pointed out: colleges whose graduates largely become teachers, ministers, social workers, cannot expect large contributions from their own sons and daughters, no matter how much affection they may have for Alma Mater. In general, however, for some 150 church-related colleges cooperating in Dean Baugher's study, he reports the following trends:

> Since 1900 the source of financial support of church-related colleges has shifted to agencies outside of the church. The following facts indicate this change: (1) the percentage of the annual operating income derived from contributions from individual congregations of the related church has decreased; (2) income from denominational sources in proportion to the income from non-denominational sources has decreased; (3) the percentage of the annual operating income from student fees has increased; (4) the percentage of

the annual operating income from the alumni of the college has increased; and (5) the local college communities have gradually assumed greater responsibility for the financial support of the college.

The increases in the percentages of operating income from student fees, in those from the alumni of the college, and in those from the local college communities, seem to point the way to the new era in college financing.

Some of the great urban universities are pathfinders in the matter of financing colleges chiefly through student fees. For a number of years the proportion of the total income from such fees at Boston, Southern California, and New York Universities has ranged from 82 per cent to over 90 per cent. The income from student fees is not only much larger but it is more dependable than the income from permanent funds. In the report for the 1939 spring quarter of the University of Chicago, one of the most heavily endowed universities in this country and in the world, the information was given that while in 1928 the general budget was dependent on student fees to the extent of 22 per cent, it is now 44 per cent dependent. At Chicago in 1930-31, the rate of return on investments was 6 per cent; now it is 3.6 per cent. The statistical summary of the United States Office of Education for institutions of learning of the entire country for the year 1935-36 shows an increase in student fees since 1931-32. The endowment income was slightly less in 1935-36 than in 1931-32. The income from the federal, state and local governments increased slightly. All other incomes for educational purposes— (a) private gifts and grants, (b) sales and services, (c) miscellaneous receipts, have increased. Private gifts and grants have increased approximately 25 per cent.

Trevor Arnett in *Occasional Papers, No. 11* of the General Education Board verifies these general trends:

> The average fee in state universities in 1936-37 was $76, while in private universities it was about four times as much, $306.

In all types of institutions, and in all areas, the average fee was higher in 1936-37 than it was in 1928-29.

The number of institutions making increases each year was approximately five times as great as the number making decreases. The average percentage of institutions making increases per year was 15.7, and the average percentage of institutions making decreases each year was 2.9.

In a majority of the institutions in which the tuition fees were increased $10 or more, the enrollment increased.

The increases in fees in arts, literature, and science were usually accompanied by increases in loans to students and increases in scholarships and student aid, but not invariably. In some cases loans and other forms of aid were reduced. The private universities naturally were more generous with loans and scholarships and student aid than the state institutions.

To mitigate the effects of increases in tuition during the depression, the institutions of higher learning increased the amount granted for loans in 1936-37 nearly 50 per cent over that granted in 1928-29. . . .

The students in these 200 institutions were granted loans of over twenty-seven million dollars during the nine-year period under review. . . . The record of repayment of loans in the period is impressive when one considers the circumstances of the borrowers. We find that $19,365,911 was repaid. . . .

. . . The executives of the majority of the state institutions and of private colleges felt that fees should not be increased, but the executives of the majority of the private universities felt they could be. The increase suggested ranged from 10 to 30 per cent. . . .

The sentiment in favor of charging students financially able the cost of education appears to be growing. The executives of more than half of the private colleges and nearly one-half of those of the private universities expressed a favorable opinion. Many, however, expressed their approval with qualifications, mentioning particularly the difficulties which might be encountered in its administration. Consciously or not, the private institutions are approaching that objective by constantly increasing fees, thereby requiring the student to pay a greater part of the cost.

When the increases in income from students, from alumni, and from the immediate community are considered in terms of the distinct evidence of enrollment recovery in independent colleges, the silver lining to the threatened cloud becomes visible.

CHAPTER XIV

THE DEVELOPMENT OF THE INDIVIDUAL STUDENT

THE serious effort to develop the theory and practice of individualization in education has been carried on largely during the last fifty years. The greatest development has been made during the last ten years. The effort has in no sense been confined to colleges. It has affected all phases of American education. It has been a cooperative movement in industry and a protective one in the army. It affords a striking illustration of the operation of a principle of social control, with interchanges and adaptations between frequently diverse fields of endeavor. The theory has run counter to the prevailing political theory and its practice has been more striking in education than elsewhere.

Revolts from the standardized uniformity of the colonial college curriculum have been indicated here and there almost from the beginning of our history. These revolts were at first too feeble to be effective. The courageous Eliot, when he finally crossed the academic Rubicon, was impelled by the cumulative momentum of these early efforts and the scientific method.

When in 1826 the Amherst faculty called for the modification of systems of study and the creation of such facilities as would meet the need for improvement in the liberal education of their sons, a member of the faculty is reported as saying if they did not do this other institutions would! There was eventually some gain. Amherst made Greek elective.

The Development of the Theory. The year before Amherst made her pronouncement (1825), two students of Jahn and the German system of gymnastics set up at Harvard the first college gymnasium in this country. It was a break with tradition, although according to Dean F. Smiley, medical adviser at Cornell, it marked the origin of the "delusion" among colleges and universities that physical exercise is the guarantor of students' health. That most colleges fell a prey to this delusion is well known. Later, Amherst made another suggestion. In 1860 the first college department of physical education was inaugurated there. Vassar and a few other colleges early saw the light. When Harper came to the University of Chicago early in the '90's to found "another kind of a university," he brought Amos Alonzo Stagg along and made physical education and health, as well as traditional subjects, a component part of the curriculum. By the beginning of the second decade of the twentieth century several institutions were maintaining full-rounded health programs, based upon individual diagnosis and prescription. The appointment by President Hoover of his Committee of Fifty on College Hygiene led several hundred colleges to agree to a minimum set of principles for a college hygiene program.

This reference to physical education is submitted for purposes of illustration. The early dissatisfaction of Vassar and Amherst, and that of Harvard under Eliot's leadership had philosophical, physiological, and psychological justification, at the time, to be sure, not so fully understood as today.

The English investigator, Galton, announced in 1883 results of studies which led to the recognition among psychologists of marked individual differences in imagery. This formed a solid, if partial, basis for the theory and practice of individualization. Dewey developed his philosophy of education from the instincts, the impulses, the play of infants to the permanent interests of adults, and pointed out the progressive development in the processes of physical, intellectual, and social growth. He built, of course, upon the stimulating suggestions of other modern philosophers and especially of Rousseau, who in *Emile* (1762) had advocated a child-centered school. Dewey had available in the city of Chicago the

practical educational program of Colonel Francis Wayland
Parker, who fifteen years before had started in Quincy,
Massachusetts, the first progressive school system in this coun-
try.   There was also available the stimulating example of
Felix Adler, the dominating spirit of the Ethical Culture
School in New York.

By means of Dewey's books, some of the principles of
which were being verified in his laboratory schools at the
University of Chicago, he and his colleagues in the Department of Philosophy and Education applied the methods of
the pragmatic philosophy to educational growth.

The leading tenets of Dewey's philosophy as thus early announced still form the core of progressive education: that
children should be treated as individuals; the child's interests
and needs should shape the curriculum; children should
learn by doing—that is, taking trips, building, painting;
should practice democracy, should learn to solve the same
kind of problems they will meet after school.   He taught that
individualization and social control develop together, since
the individual also and always has social impulses.

This idea may be dated back to Aristotle, if you like, who
declared that man is a political being.   Because of this inherent and vital relationship, it is a part of himself that responds
to like impulses in others.   Because of this twofold endowment individuals readily merge into society.   It is not an
arbitrary procedure.   If there are few people in the world
who can truthfully say concerning a social experience, "All
of which I saw," there are many who feel, if they do not say,
"Part of which I was."   It is because of this corporate structure of the one and the many, now belatedly being recognized by college authorities, that the various forms of extra-
curricular activities are often more highly motivated and
more fruitful in results than the dry and formal methods of
ordinary classroom teaching.

Tests and Measurements.   While the developments just
mentioned were occurring at Chicago, Cattell was organizing
at Columbia a series of tests designed to discover the traits

of individuals and to measure the differences between them. He seems to have been the Samuel Adams, so to speak, on the psychological side of the measurement movement.

His most brilliant student, E. L. Thorndike, progressed much farther in demonstrating that individual differences are significant for education and for the placement of people in the professional and industrial world. It was not until 1905 that Binet devised his scale for the determination of the general intelligence of school children. To Goddard and Terman American education is indebted for the adaptation of the Binet Scale to uses on this side of the Atlantic.

President Harper predicted in 1899 that this total process of student diagnosis "will fifty years hence prevail as widely as it is now lacking." * The fulfillment of the prediction has been achieved through contributions by a multitude of workers. Among others who have participated in this co-operative movement are Yerkes and Bridges at Harvard, Otis as well as Terman at Stanford, Pintner and Patterson at Ohio State, Scott at Northwestern, and Thurstone at Chicago. Scott carried on tests in a practical way in the selection of personnel in large organizations. In 1916-17 the Bureau of Salesmanship at Carnegie Institute of Technology made studies with tests in thirty of the leading business organizations of America. Yerkes headed the work of mental testing in the United States Army during the World War, according to a letter to the author from President W. D. Scott whose name was associated with this work by the late Secretary of War Newton D. Baker. The widespread publicity given to the startling results of these investigations among the men drafted for the army, particularly since the stage was already set for the dramatic, gave the measurement movement a tremendous impulse.

Experimentation and Implementation. The urge to these developments came from research workers, teachers, and administrators, who were students and friends of youth, as well as loyal citizens of the state. They were guided by

* See References, p. 358.

accumulated knowledge and they had creative minds. Some of them were interested chiefly in theory, others in practice, many in both theory and practice. They all had the courage of pioneers.

The development of individualization, therefore, has had three phases: research, application, organization. Roughly, these phases correspond to pure science, applied science, the creation of overhead machinery. In so far as objective measurements are mathematically accurate, they belong to pure science; experimentation in the educational process may be considered as a phase of applied science; the organization phase represents the area of super-administration.

Never, perhaps, have the colleges shown so much vitality as during this era of experimentation. The efforts to implement the theory of individualization are like the sands of the sea— they have never been counted. Among them are included: the free elective system which reached its apotheosis during the last two decades of the last century, and which has now been superseded by the conditional elective: specialization, now veering toward a broader basis; a multitude of devices for securing higher achievement on the part of students, not only in the intellectual realm but in all phases of student experience. Many of these devices are of English origin but in all cases attempts have been made to adapt them to conditions in America. There may be listed: reading for honors, free reading periods, freedom in class attendance, the increased significance of the library, tutorial and preceptorial plans, independent study, comprehensive examinations, the conference plan, differentiation between the lower and upper divisions of the college experience, improved forms of housing students, institutional cooperation—indeed, the total content of the personnel undertaking. When the *Thirty-first Yearbook* of the National Society for the Study of Education was issued in 1932, thirty-two of the seventy-five colleges which reported experiments were making fifty different adjustments in curriculum or teaching procedures that were judged to contribute to individualization. They were manifesting their sense of responsibility to minister not only to the intellectual growth of students, but to growth in character, physical life, religious life, vocational plans, manners, appreciation of financial and family problems.

The leadership in the field of tests and measurements has been taken very largely in more recent years by the men and women who have cooperated under the joint auspices of the American Council on Education, the Cooperative Test Service, and the Educational Records Bureau. These organizations have brought workers together annually in New York for the presentation and discussion of phases both of the theories and the practices involved in this growing area of educational procedure. They have been largely responsible for the distribution and application of tests and measurements in a multitude of institutions.

Administrative Machinery. The agencies just referred to are representative of the third era in the development of individualization—that of administrative machinery. Within this group are included, true to the American way, a confusing multitude of alphabetically designated organizations and agencies with diverse functions and motives. Perhaps the most militant of these is the Progressive Education Association. It was formed in 1918 upon the initiation of Stanwood Cobb, an instructor in that bulwark of traditionalism, the United States Naval Academy. It has been and is a powerful, because a well organized, factor in the development of the personnel movement which has now reached a position of dominance in many elementary and secondary schools.

Both measurement and guidance activities have been highly professionalized and in some areas commercialized. Only the experts can speak or understand the language, electrified as it is by "batteries" and more or less well insulated wires. These activities are pushing individualization to its logical conclusion. They represent, both in theoretical and practical developments, the present-day fruition of Galton's idea. In the judgment of many critics they do not represent the total message of psychology to the educational process. The pendulum has swung too far when it ignores the lessons of long experience and of common sense. The perfectly good hobby horse is in danger of being ridden to death.

The most highly praised examples of progressive education are now found in certain private schools of the elementary and secondary grades, and more particularly in the suburbs of several of the larger cities. Several of the junior colleges with large enrollments have intricately developed personnel departments or divisions.

Among those competent to speak who are issuing words of warning is Charles H. Judd. He has pointed out that "our generation has been led to accept the doctrine that a thousand individuals exhibit a thousand different degrees of brightness and dullness, and with each individual there are a thousand or more distinct primary traits, each of which must be trained separately and by a distinct form of discipline."

Thus the pendulum has swung from uniformity of program to an atomistic program. Apparently the next step will be, by high pressures, to break the atom into its component parts. Then, in our search for individual differences, forgetting that racial likenesses are the substratum of all biological manifestations, we will become very "scientific," and will forget that teaching is also and principally an art.

As a group, the colleges are more conservative. They are calling a halt in this mad rush. They are recognizing in many ways the values of synthesis. Institutions like Bennington and Sarah Lawrence are certainly justifying their existence whether judged by their own programs and merits or as wisely conducted deviations from generally accepted patterns. They represent in a laudable way the application of the principle of individualization to corporate college programs. They recognize and accentuate the need for variety in college objectives and methods, a phase of development to which attention is given in another connection.

Ideas which might be labeled "progressive" are enriching the life of many of the colleges which prefer not to identify themselves with a "movement" which is in danger of becoming an "ism." The best colleges are addressing themselves to the total concept of personality and are attempting to improve the total and complicated process of learning. It may be recalled that Dewey once referred to the enterprise of education as "the most complex, intricate and subtle of human enterprises." A boy or girl is of more value than any one of the thousand traits which he may exhibit. Indeed, the wisest of the devotees of current testing and measuring frankly confess that they cannot say the last word on the achievement of students. So much of achievement depends on disposition. The wisest personnel workers know their business is merely to prime the pump—if and when it needs it. Tests and measurements help in student diagnosis; guidance likewise helps; but neither diagnosis nor guidance, nor both together, will make a perfect man: the unpredictable and evasive experience of self-propulsion lies deeper than either, and the struggles of the race form a necessary background. Instincts and appetites are racial, not individual alone. Impulses are social in composition, not entirely egoistic.

The exposition of the meaning of individualization in some of the most recent books which treat of the subject appears to the writer to leave something to be desired.

(a) By some, individualization is made to require in each instance an outline of different subject matter, and it is properly objected that this is entirely impracticable; there is not enough available subject matter to go around. But individualization is not to be achieved on the basis of subject matter alone or chiefly. It implies challenges to an increasing degree of self-determination. It implies an internal, not an external, expression of effort. The curriculum is to be constructed not in terms of peculiar subject matter but to meet the actual needs of students.

(b) It is objected that the interests of students are constantly changing, that capacities are often more apparent than real, and that interests and capacities, therefore, are unsafe guides for an educational program.

The interpretation of interests and capacities requires the insight of gifted teachers who can discover potentialities as well as apparent actualities. This is what the college is primarily for. The transfer of more power to the student enlarges the necessity for a wider and therefore for an overlapping rather than a narrow outline of subject matter. This is particularly true during the student's period of exploration. The wise teacher knows that one of the needs of students is basic subject matter dealing with health, recreation, home life, citizenship, expression, and communication. The entire personnel movement means, if it means anything, that a partnership is to be established between teachers and students. The college is not student-centered or teacher-centered. If a mathematical figure of speech is to be used, the relationship is represented not by a circle but by an ellipse with two foci. The figure cannot be drawn if either focus is absent. If both are present a community of interest is inherent in the process.

Free election has already become practically obsolete. It was an extreme reaction to an extreme uniformity. At Black Mountain, it is announced that "the student is the curriculum." On the other hand, at Columbia College freshmen and sophomores take required courses and like it—in Contemporary Civilization and Science, and in Humanities. In the degree to which they like it there is inner individualization in an apparently objective assignment.

The conditional elective capitalizes the student interest and the teacher's ability as a midwife, to use Socrates's well worn expression. Some might call this a new form of prescription; so be it; at least it ceases to be arbitrary in so far as details are concerned; it grows out of a careful diagnosis and it allows plenty of latitude for student follow-up. Eventually, during the college course, it is to be hoped potential interests or apparently real ones, as the case may be, may

assume a degree of permanence in the life of the student.
Certainly the two years of the lower division are none too
long for this period of experimentation.   Perhaps this is
what Dewey meant by referring to teaching as the most subtle
of all processes.

(c) It is claimed that small classes are necessary for successful individualization because the student must be kept in
constant and intimate touch with his teacher.

This again appears to assume that the forming power is
to proceed from without rather than from within the student.
It assumes that in his formal instruction, at least, the student
must forever be tied to pedagogical apron strings.   The student who is to proceed toward individualization, on the other
hand, will progressively cut loose from all forms of indoctrination.   If he is to become a man, he must put away childish
things.   That he may become a man is the *summum bonum*
of individualization.   The process applies to muscle as well
as to mind, and to the social mind in process of expansion.
In practice, therefore, there may be large classes without
any inconsistency in the program of procedure.   If such
classes, chiefly perhaps in the form of lecture courses, supply
the general needs of students, they must be supplemented in
one way or another by opportunities for the development
of individual needs.   If it happens that a divine question is
lodged in the mind of the student, the chief service which
the college can render him is to afford him the time and
opportunity to pursue the ramifications which the question
involves.   Individualization means the opportunity under
such guidance as may be necessary or available for the student to cultivate individual power of propulsion.   Its unique-
ness in a given case depends chiefly on the student, not on
the assignment.   Will the student "take the message to
Garcia"?

CHAPTER XV

THE USES AND ABUSES OF EXPERIMENTATION

IN THE first place, it may be observed, experimentation has suffered from many educational physicians. The term is manifestly borrowed from the vocabulary of science. The effort is made to emulate the acknowledged excellence of scientific technique. Thus educational planning, it is believed, will be trailing clouds of glory.

Science has developed instruments of precision, by means of which materials of study are isolated, weighed and measured. An experiment conducted under fully known conditions may be repeated and will produce similar results. Unfortunately the exact repetition of an educational experiment is practically an unknown phenomenon. Imponderables are usually, if not always, lurking within the "material." They vitiate or evade the experiment. Education remains primarily an art.

During the earlier part of the special era of planning which has been an increasingly striking feature of college activity for some thirty-five or forty years, unwarranted pretentions were made. College specialists liked to be called "scientific." They made "scientific" surveys. They demonstrated educational principles "scientifically." Thus it was "proved" that teaching in large classes is just as effective as teaching in small classes. As a matter of fact this may or may not be true. The chief elements in the problem are the art of the lecturer or teacher and the nature and disposition of the individual students. They are predominantly subjective and evasive.

Great expectations of finality were aroused in the early announcements of psychological tests and measurements. Now the claims of most specialists in these fields are more cautiously made. The application of scientific technique to educational procedure is undoubtedly serviceable.

More recently the work of the measurement specialists has been supplemented by the contributions of a multitude of student advisers. A complicated personnel system has been developing for more than a quarter of a century. The multiplication of specialized deans of men, of women, of students; the appointment of chaplains, hostesses, psychiatrists, placement officers, and other guides to educational health and social programs constitute a typically American development. It may easily be overdone; sometimes it degenerates into coddling the student.

Experimentation, within or without its legitimate bounds, has been abused because of the disposition of one college to emulate other colleges. This sometimes leads to fads which follow each other in rapid succession. What one college does, another attempts to do, it may be many years after. The developments of honors courses and of comprehensive examinations are cases in point. Such experiments carried on with inadequate equipment and personnel retard progress. Successful honors courses and comprehensive examinations in American colleges, while having models elsewhere, are uniformly adaptations. They are not slavish imitations. The greatest threat of danger comes from their uncritical friends. A lecturer to a college faculty set forth the procedures along various lines of several other institutions. The president of the college then asked, "Do you think our faculty should have a plan?"

One may be impressed from newspaper reading alone that plans and experiments are raging like wild fire over the face of the college world. Metropolitan newspapers maintain special education editors who give pages of space to what new things the colleges are doing. It may be that in not a few instances the mention of the experiment in the *New*

York Times of itself brings to the college a sufficient measure of reward. It is certainly true that many colleges without concern for wide publicity are doing more constructive work than some that get this free advertising.

Whatever the motive may be which prompts the alleged experiment, it must be admitted that much of such activity is in the realm of form and not of spirit. It often degenerates into mechanical tinkering. This is true particularly within the realm of curriculum structure. There is no end to the slight modifications of this or that part of the curriculum. Many a curriculum sprawls out all over the lot like a Mediterranean house, but not with any degree of order because it is made a piece at a time as a new need seems to appear. Many curricula are formed by accretion. One of the blessings of the depression is that it has somewhat arrested the process of these forms of curriculum building which are without unifying aim.

Kathryn McHale, Director of the American Association of University Women, reported, in 1932, 128 outstanding experiments and changes in 75 colleges and universities.* There has probably been no cessation of such changes since that time, though many of the changes, perforce, have been in the direction of desirable compactness of program. That confusion has arisen in the minds of some was to be expected. It is not surprising that a distinguished critic has declared in his haste that "unmitigated empiricism is the curse of modern life," and has proposed a relatively simple substitute.

An analysis of the multitude of cases reported, which approach infinity in number and variety, shows much repetition and relatively few areas of change. In behalf of the changes it may be said that many faculties are showing a spirit of discontent with present achievements. They are becoming aroused from the inertia of *laissez faire*. They are seeking to clarify their objectives, to improve their methods, to give a reassuring account of their stewardship. They are breaking up the treadmill of routine, they are introducing

* See References, p. 359.

manifold devices of aeration. Above all, perhaps, they are making rediscoveries if not discoveries. What boots it that many other faculties have done essentially the same thing, if this faculty is impelled by a new spirit of understanding? Some very valuable goods come in by freight. Several million students also have learned the same old multiplication table. To many this has been a brand new adventure; to all it has turned out to be a good investment. A number of colleges that have courageously entered new fields have already demonstrated the security of the ground upon which they stand.

Most of these trends in college program making may be classified either as structural or functional changes. Three of these are concerned with the curriculum approach:

(1) There is the effort to break down barriers of mechanization, and to substitute more flexible arrangements of curriculum material. Among the substitutions are the various and sundry divisional organizations in place of extreme departmentalization, and the numerous devices for correlation and integration in place of narrow specialization.

(2) There is the effort to return to the classical tradition of a uniform curriculum.

(3) Curricula are being built on the basis of major fields of knowledge.

Three trends are approaches along functional lines:

(a) There are college programs emphasizing the need of more vital methods and devices of teaching.

(b) Efforts are being made to build upon the interests, capacities and needs of individual students.

(c) There are programs being developed upon present day cultures and current tendencies within the social order.

There has been some disposition to classify these several trends under the head of developing "patterns" of liberal curricula. Few colleges, however, are content to adopt the one or the other trend as an exclusive or even a dominant basis of procedure. Some good is found in each of them. Few colleges are ready to announce a final synthesis.

Behind each one of the six trends just outlined there are values which are becoming more apparent as they are being put to the test of experience.

A. As the curriculum is made more flexible through the integration of subject matter, the possible unity of the world of knowledge is becoming more manifest. While it is impossible in four years entirely to capture the secrets of this unity, justifiable rewards come to students who devote even two years to exploration, under guidance, of the general fields of knowledge, and two additional years to selected subjects in line with expanding interests.

A majority of the colleges of the country still operate on the basis of a four year unit. They have not adopted a bifurcated curriculum.

Out of the emphasis on a synthesis of bits of scholarship come challenges to the creative powers of students. Thus unsolved problems may develop to which a lifetime of study may be devoted, either as a vocation or an avocation. A teacher of Jusserand said to him at the Sorbonne, "Select a vast intellectual task to which you may devote your life." He did so and always pursued it as an aside to his profession as a diplomat. While professionally he dealt with dynamic problems of the moment, avocationally he kept his anchorage to a previous century.

B. The student who confines himself to the classics—ancient and modern—makes contacts with the world of thought and action of a selected number of creative authors. The books of the authors have become great because they have had a very general appeal to mankind. They are remarkable pictures from various angles of human understanding at its best. Since the method has but one approach, through reading, it tends to overemphasize one function of the mind at the expense of other functions. It appeals primarily to the book-minded. It encourages a receptive attitude on the part of the student. He is successful as he thinks the thoughts of others. He may not be stimulated to try his own wings. He is held captive in a world which is not his own.

This curriculum is based on the philosophy of scholasticism somewhat broadened in scope and extended in time. It serves the same purpose as did the curriculum of the colonial colleges. It preserves much of the intellectual but not necessarily the spiritual excellency of the past. The social element in life is largely omitted. The nature of science is subject to misunderstanding in that the method of science cannot be caught alone from books even if supplemented by an occasional repetition of a classical experiment. The plan tends to conserve a knowledge of much of the best thought of the past. It was better adapted to the homogeneous population of colonial times than to the present day melting pot of democracy.

C. The attempt to build a curriculum around the major fields of human knowledge is apt to adopt the survey course as the chief instrument of progress. The survey courses are predigested. They are based upon syllabi which become another kind of textbook. Such syllabi represent the abstract and sometimes mechanical procedure of specialists. These specialists themselves in many cases are unable to grasp the total view. The chief virtue of the survey from the air, lies in its integrating method, likely to be accompanied however by lack of clarity of vision. The student is confronted with a synthesis of what to him is the unknown. The syllabi must be administered by masters in the art of teaching. The successful outcome is "knowledge," measured by examinations. The student hands back what is given him. The challenge to the thinking power of the student is apt to be submerged. Breadth is emphasized at the expense of depth. The genetic order of discovery by the individual student is largely ignored. The pursuit of knowledge, not to say of truth, which characterizes all creative work, is swallowed up in possession. The assumption is that knowledge is power. Let the student be fitted to the ready-made machinery of life.

By common consent, the survey courses, in rare instances, have led students to discover specialized aptitudes.

D. An entire chapter of this book is devoted to better teaching in colleges. The interest in better college teaching has been a distinctive feature of the last few decades. A large array of devices and methods has been introduced. The ultimate ideal has been to transfer initiative to the student. The motive of all devices and procedures is to set free the student's power of self-propulsion. Free reading periods and independent study are among the means used; individual and social resourcefulness are ends sought. The teacher, at his best, becomes more concerned in stimulating in the student the process of learning than in his own instruction. In such a process, subject matter becomes a means of great importance but not the ultimate end.

E. Closely associated with the improvements in teaching is the recognition of the interests, capacities, and needs of students. The theory and practice are subject to many possibilities of error. The plan is based upon student curiosity without which there can be no advance. It frequently falls into the pitfall of recognising only immediate interests, apparent capacities, conscious needs, and of losing sight of student potentialities. The discovery of permanent interests and needs must ordinarily be a cooperative enterprise. The student at times must follow the superior wisdom of the teacher. The process of education becomes a partnership in which the big brother furnishes much of the experience. The educable student becomes amenable to suggestion and guidance. Coercion, if the ideal is realized, passes from the picture. Student and teacher join in promoting the private as well as the public welfare.

The remarkable assumption is sometimes made by critics of the plan that each student must be furnished subject matter which differs from that of all other students. But most students have a complexity of social as well as individual interests as native endowments. Neither the individual nor the social program is statable entirely in terms of subject matter. The program is individual because the centre of gravity has passed over from the teacher to the student, and the student makes the program his own. Since practically all students have many of the same approaches to the educational process, obviously much work may be done in groups, classes, seminars and lecture courses. The plan is subject to great variation and does not involve a schedule different in every detail or even in most details for each student.

F. In the recently devised "General College" the emphasis is upon current developments within the social order. It undertakes to respond to a "new age." It would make young people "at home in their complex modern world." It would set forth "the wholeness of human life instead of leading them deep into microscopy." It would "let them acquire a sense of values in the many phases of adult living outside the strictly vocational."

The emphasis is on contemporary living; "to catch the student where he is and build a fire under him." The effort is to "fit the garment to the student." MacLean of the University of Minnesota says, "We are trying in the General College to devise a general education that may underlie specialization."

But the General College would not rest content in the modern world. It would eventually have the students look backward and forward. It is an application within the college field of the old principle of going from the known to the unknown. It therefore has two essential problems. First, to interpret the current scene as a preparation for and point of departure from the immediate to the more remote and presumably permanent values of life. It represents a swing on the side of the subject matter to the area of the social sciences which are among the newest and least developed of human disciplines. Within itself it would fit the exposition of modern living to the comprehension of the students.

The Curriculum or the Functional Approach?

There is a conviction very generally held by the friends of the liberal college that the curriculum approach and the functional approach are mutually exclusive. You must take the one or the other. This will be true so long as the partisans of the one and the other insist upon the generally accepted rigidity of meaning of the two methods of approach. The writer holds to the view that the two approaches are means not ends and are not irreconcilable. It is the problem of the primacy of the egg or the hen. A clergyman told one of his parishioners the subject of his next Sunday's sermon; the parishioner asked, "What is the object of the sermon?" Either approach followed far enough will coalesce with the other. Each has certain advantages: they both have the same end in view.

The functional approach to the education of children and youth, which, it may be pointed out, is the one generally prevailing in the education of adults, is based on the nature of the *genus homo*. The most remarkable and enduring basis of our educational procedure is the wonder, the curiosity inherent in the nature of the child. When we say that youth are educable we mean that they preserve some of this dynamic principle of wonder. Neither the teacher nor the curriculum nor the school furnishes this. Boys and girls are made that way. You cannot dam up the flood of questions. It holds them to inquiry as the needle to the pole. It is central in the nature of the child. The mortality here, of course, as in all biological processes, is a matter of common knowledge.

With his curiosity as the inner urge, the task of the school is to guide the student into the rewarding fields of subject matter. The school must recognize that, at a given moment, interests and capacities are potential as well as apparent, that they are social and ethical as well as egoistic, and therefore that guidance is inherent in the enterprise. The child cannot understand his needs perhaps as well as his teachers can.   That was an exceptionally wise boy who said since he wished to become a scientist he wished to study Greek, "because scientific nomenclature is based on the Greek language."   The functional impetus leads into curriculum material.   Together, they lead to the versatility of the mental texture, not merely the intellectual texture, be it noted, which is the end of education.

The curriculum approach is made from another direction. It is the older approach and its techniques are based on long and often successful teaching experience.   It is more factual, less problematical.   After all, most of the basic educational needs are common to all students.   All students need to acquire the tools of learning—the trivium is ready made for the purpose, and for purposes of enrichment the quadrivium is added.   There is an acknowledged need for a set of well defined values growing out of the experience of the race. These should guide the process of intelligent participation in domestic, civic, and social affairs.   All these needs and many others, the well selected curriculum furnishes.   A reliable and reasonably comprehensive beginning is thus afforded.   The conquest of the curriculum is in response to challenges.   In the hands of a wise teacher it leads to the same end as that of the functional approach.

The most important feature of the educative process involves more than a choice between these two approaches. In either event, there is a subject and an object, and they are reciprocally helpful.   The most important thing is the disposition of the student and the stimulating influence of the teacher.   The desideratum in either case is the texture of the mind that may be developed in the process, the enlargement of the mind and spirit, the enrichment of the personality.

Summary

The names of individual experiments have not been mentioned in this exposition.   There is a vast literature on the subject.

No single experiment holds exclusively to one of these six approaches. Numerous experiments emphasize one rather than the others. Other approaches could be named.

Educational experiments are not purely scientific, since education is primarily an art. They may appropriate in some features the scientific method. They may appeal to experience as well as to reason.

While there are abuses discovered in adventures into such experimentation, the uses outweigh them in value.

The approaches may be classified roughly as curriculum or functional. As means they may be distinct one from the other. As ends, in the hands of superior teachers, they are complementary. There can be no permanent chasm between them. They represent the subject-object relationship. Their disposition is to coalesce. For purposes of concrete illustration two institutions may be selected from a multitude.

Reed College began an experiment a quarter of a century ago. It was frankly functional in point of view. Specifically it was student-centered. The free elective system was adopted. The lecture was taboo. The ordinary class recitation was eliminated. The program was quite self-contained.

There was, however, a superior faculty, alert and unified in purpose. As the experiment progressed, the conditional elective supplanted the free elective. The values of selected subject matter became more apparent. The social obligation emerged. The community became a laboratory. The movement was from the left toward the center.

Reed is no longer an "experiment." The college has found its general course. It would introduce students to themselves and to society. It would discover the secrets of life.

The Assistant Chancellor of the University of Buffalo is responsible for the assertion that "in 1922 the curriculum of the College of Arts and Sciences of the University was the typical rigid, prescribed curriculum of American colleges of arts and sciences of that day." The requirements provided small opportunity for the functional point of view. The college viewed its problem from the right.

The faculty proceeded to reduce the number of prescribed subjects. The "honors system" was offered to a small group of superior students who worked under the direct supervision of members of the staff. After seven years' trial the entire upper division was placed on an honors basis, that is, in Buffalo's terminology, a tutorial basis. The point of departure is the student's specific interests and abilities.

But the courses and the departments of the curriculum are maintained. While the requirements in any particular course are abolished, the curriculum sounding-board stands. The pendulum has not swung back to the old elective system. "Departmental requirements and comprehensive examinations guarantee penetration into some field of knowledge fairly deeply," as Dr. Earl McGrath has put it. At the same time, excessive specialization is not allowed to supplant a unified program. With a particular student the swing has been not from the right to the left but from the right to the center.

The functional approach in the hands of resourceful teachers requires the use of the curriculum and leads into the social order.

The curriculum approach in the hands of resourceful teachers is vitalized by the recognition of student interest and capacities.

The greatest means in the world of education is the resourceful teacher. The greatest end is the resourceful student.

The most important feature of educational experimentation is not the fact that experiments are being made, but is the insight of some of the experimenters. This is the essence of the present argument.

CHAPTER XVI

ON THE INTELLECTUAL FRONTIER

AFTER the World War a number of plans were introduced to discover exceptional students and to provide for them especial opportunities for intellectual achievement. These plans immediately revived and intensified discussion as to the real objectives of the liberal colleges. The proponents of liberal education soon began to identify themselves with diverse schools of thought. They became advocates either of the curriculum approach, usually identified with the philosophical approach, buttressed by the theory of discipline, or of the functional approach responding to the interests and capacities of students. More specifically, they grouped themselves either into the party that advocates "the development of the intellect," or the party which stands for a broader synthesis of human values.

A committee of the American Association of University Professors rendered a valuable service by reporting from time to time the nature and progress of the most significant experiments which were being tried out. Woodrow Wilson, before the World War, had greatly stimulated the thought of students of the American college by his attempted reforms at Princeton. He deplored the influence and popularity of the side shows of the college, recalled the students to the "main tent," and, in effect, identified himself with the curriculum party and the party of the intellectuals.

Following the War, Princeton became one of the intellectual leaders on the outskirts of the undergraduate mind, and maintains that leadership today. Harvard assumed the same type of leadership, largely through the influence of

President Lowell, who, during his entire presidency, without neglecting the other units of the university, gave especial attention to the progress of the college. At the time of the inauguration of Frank Aydelotte as President of Swarthmore, he launched his new college program, the unusual feature of which was the plan of reading for honors. Shortly he held a conference at Iowa City, to which a hundred colleges reported that they were adopting this plan. The plan was in danger of developing too rapidly.

On the other hand, for the year 1925-26 it was reported that Swarthmore had fifty-two honors students, twenty-five candidates for honors degrees, eighteen of whom were granted such degrees. Two of these, however, were in the "fourth class," such degrees being equal to ordinary degrees without honors, called frankly by Swarthmore "pass degrees." Today the honors work at each of the three pioneer institutions just named, as well as at some others, has made marked advance. It now enrolls a large proportion of the upper classmen in a limited number of colleges. Such watchwords of this movement as "independent study," "study for honors," "tutorial instruction," "comprehensive examinations," and the like, are signs marking progress in those institutions which are adequately supplied with material and personnel equipment. In 1933 the Association of American Colleges produced the first of a series of studies of comprehensive examinations under the editorship of Edward S. Jones.* At that time Dr. Jones reported that some sixty colleges, usually the smaller ones, were then using terminal examinations in two or more departments, and he set forth an outline of certain distinctive contributions made by colleges having considerable experience with such examinations.

In 1924 the Dartmouth Report appeared. Leon B. Richardson, head of the Department of Chemistry and therefore presumably far removed from the atmosphere of traditional "pedagogy," had been released from his usual duties for a semester's study of the liberal college. He made a first-

* See References, p. 359.

hand study of colleges in this country and abroad and summed up his report to the president of Dartmouth in these words:

> After all, we come back to the idea of the development of the intellect as the conscious purpose of the college; other results may be gained and will be gained, but they must be "by-products" and not the direct aims of the institution.

He led up to this conclusion by emphasizing intellectual training and observed:

> Our aim may therefore be stated as the stimulation and development of those gifts of intellect with which nature has endowed the student, so that he becomes, first, a better companion to himself through life, and second, a more efficient force in his contacts with his fellow men.

In thus setting up the "development of the intellect" as the one conscious objective of the colleges and relegating all other possible aims to the status of by-products and of indirect and fortuitous significance, he appeared to ally himself with a doctrine of aristocratic intellectualism. This high aim was modified, however, by his exposition of the concrete means of attaining the stated objective:

(1) So far as possible to detect the pedant and to make it no longer possible for him through a mistaken system of college grading to pose as a success in his academic career.

(2) To search out, encourage, and sympathetically to assist the man of capacity to whom the scholarly career appeals.

(3) To raise in the great body of students interests and ideals which will make them, not scholars in the technical sense, but men to whom the intellectual appeal strikes a responsive note and insures an understanding and sympathetic response.

This is what is meant by scholarship.

For the attainment of these ends Professor Richardson approved certain established features of current practice and several suggestions which were being tried out in a number of institutions. "Concentration," which together with "distribution" was being stressed by Harvard and other colleges, was the nucleus of the course which the Dartmouth Report recommended.

Along by the side of these declarations should be placed the report made the same year to President Hopkins by a group of twelve undergraduates who had been invited to consider educational problems and policies at Dartmouth and to make a statement of conclusions. The students recommended:

1. The fullest possible development of the individual and adequate training for membership in society.
2. A faculty that will subordinate their function as relayers of information to their office as guides to independent thinking and inspirers to an intellectual life; that more responsibility and independence be given the individual student.
3. The development of scholarship only in so far as it can have meaning in the life of the individual.
4. The admission of only those men whose capacities will enable them to further the purposes of the college.
5. Relatively strict application to required work during the first two years, and in the last two years—especially for outstanding students—relative freedom for the individual in his own development; reduction of required courses.
6. Shifting of emphasis from the passing of a number of more or less related courses in the major study to a responsible mastery of subject tested by a general comprehensive examination.

"The Experimental College" of Alexander Meiklejohn appeared at the University of Wisconsin some years later. It was in operation there from 1927 to 1932. In discovering the dominating principle of the new liberal education, Dr. Meiklejohn threw aside all activities which may be included under the head of vocational, and also "those special investigations, those limited and partial studies, which we sum up under the term 'scholarship.' . . . Liberal education is not training in technical skill; nor is it instruction in knowledge." The positive term which Meiklejohn used in the attempt to fix the aim of education was "intelligence,"—a much more comprehensive term than "intellect," pointing to the freer and more natural activity of the mind. He interprets intelligence as meaning "all the creative activities, whether or not consciously directed, by which men strive to raise the quality of human experience." He says:

> It is clear that into the meaning of the term there enter moral and aesthetic elements as well as intellectual. It is evident, too, that the idea implies unity of understanding as against the unrelatedness of scattered bits of knowledge. ... The function of intelligence is to serve men in the creation and maintenance of the social order, a scheme of individual and group living which will meet the human demands for beauty, strength, justice, generosity, and the like. . . .
>
> To put the matter quite bluntly, the college is as much interested in the making of scholars as it is in the making of bankers, legislators, grocers, or the followers of any other specialized occupation or profession.

Meiklejohn's objection to knowledge as an end of liberal education may also best be expressed in his own words:

> The trades, the professions, the various branches of learned investigations are "special" because they concern themselves with limited fields, with limited ranges of investigation, with limited departments of knowledge and experience.

A course of study was worked out on the basis of these and similar principles using two civilizations as materials— that of Athens in or about the Age of Pericles, and that of America in the nineteenth century. After acquaintance was made with the two civilizations, comparisons and contrasts would aid in an understanding of what a civilization is:

> At the beginning of the experiment it was decided that the greater part of the freshman year should be given to a study of the Athenian civilization in or about the Age of Pericles; that the tutorial method of teaching would at first predominate. It had been arranged that the students of the first class would live in certain sections of one of the dormitories. Modifications were made as the plan developed.
> . . . In the original notion, the sophomore year was to be,

like the freshman, preparatory. The student, having seen one civilization far in time and circumstance from the present, was to study another near to the present, so that by the comparison and contrast of these two he might then move on to the interpretation of his own present world. But in the sophomore year, as now conceived, preparation is over; the student is at work upon the final and permanent intellectual task. This is the last year of his formal liberal training. The time has come for him to ask for and to take self-direction in an actual world. He must therefore study now the modern, the American mind at work upon the situation in the midst of which he is to live. . . . Human problems must now become local and contemporary and specific issues. . . . The student will face the necessity of knowing what the sciences of the modern world are doing, what are the current and developing processes of industry and commerce, how the agencies of government operate and change, how the activities of modern men come into being, etc., etc.

As a by-product of the experiment he later announced:

The purpose of the College will be to formulate and to test under experimental conditions suggestions for the improvement of the methods of teaching, the content of study, and the determining conditions of undergraduate liberal education.

A summary of the results by MacLean, Little, and Works is quoted from *General Education in the American College:*

On the positive side, the Experimental College showed clearly that the trend of general education must be towards synthesis and unity of materials and curricula, and therefore away from the cancerous cell-division growth that has been common to most of our present courses and curriculum building. It demonstrated the importance of presenting to students whole pictures. . . . It demonstrated the difficulties of presenting such whole pictures, the need for teachers who themselves can either see such whole pictures, or who, starting with the general education point of view, are able to grow to see wholes and who are able to interpret as well as analyze, to give life and meaning instead of searching out nothing but facts and detail. On the negative side, it showed how fatal it may be to understress wide-ranging personnel studies of the students subjected to the new curricu-

lum and to fail to set up every possible means of evaluation
to determine and make known the results of such an educational experiment. It indicated further the present impos-
sibility, because of lack of teachers, materials, and costly
space, of giving general education to large numbers solely by
means of small classes, conference methods, and similar
devices demanding prolonged individual contact of teacher
and student.

The publication in 1930 of Flexner's *Universities, American, English, German,* created a sensation within and without
educational circles.   The cries of rebuttal indicated many
points of sensitivity.   Flexner's diatribe against modern
universities, and American universities in particular, was
inspired by the hope that by holding up to criticism and ridicule what in them is "silly, misdirected, and short-sighted,"
they would undertake to develop the good and cast off the
bad. Flexner said that there is in this country no university
in the real sense of the term—"no institution, no seat of learning devoted to higher teaching and research. Everywhere
the pressure of undergraduates and vocational activities
hampers the serious objects for which universities exist."
He enumerated four major concerns of a university:

> The conservation of knowledge and ideas; the interpre-
> tation of knowledge and ideas; the search for truth; the
> training of students who will practice and 'carry on.' . . .
> The pursuit of science and scholarship belong to the uni-
> versity. Assuredly, neither secondary, technical, vocational,
> nor popular education.

A university, he contended, cannot successfully combine
graduate and undergraduate teaching.   Not only does the
number of students become unwieldy, but the faculty is dis-
tracted with the responsibility of "teaching boys and educating men."   Colleges, he held, do not properly belong to
the university.

In this "bargain-counter period," the college student finds
almost every imaginable article, and after "nibbling" four
months at this and a few weeks at that, he can eventually

accumulate the credits necessary for the Bachelor's degree. "Instead of training broadly and deeply typical minds like the humanistic mind or the scientific mind, the colleges create departments and give courses which enable the students to do highly specific things such as washing and feeding babies or selling insurance."

For certain of the professions—law and medicine, Dr. Flexner can find a clear case in the university concept, but not for denominational religion, business, journalism, domestic science, or library science. "Hardly perhaps for education." The "learned professions" he would admit "because they have their roots deep in cultural and idealistic soil." . . . They derive "their essential character from intelligence." They are primarily objective, intellectual, and altruistic in their purposes. There is a place for training teachers, journalists, optometrists, librarians, etc., but it is not in the university.

He concedes the necessity for adjustment to genuine needs and pressures of life, but contends that American universities have lost their sense of values, and in yielding to transient and whimsical demands have "cheapened, vulgarized, and mechanized themselves." While they offer facilities and opportunities for the highest quality of scholarly and scientific study, especially in their graduate schools, at the same time they are engaged in the claptrap of home study courses, extension courses, and every miscellaneous activity.

> If, indeed, "university" is to mean . . . a "public service institution," then the university has become a different thing, a thing which may have its uses, but is assuredly no longer a university.

Manifestly Flexner was pleased with the German type of university, devoted as it was to "higher teaching and research." It is certain now, a decade later, that the German university could not preserve the Germany which was once the admiration of the people of all enlightened nations. The development of the intellect alone has had a tragic fall.

In his familiar talk to the members of the Association of American Colleges in their annual meeting at Louisville, in January 1939, Sir William David Ross, Provost of Oriel College, Oxford University, said:

> Many of you perhaps read, as I did, with great interest, Abraham Flexner's book on *Universities, American, English, German.* My general impression was it was rather entertaining and informative, but it was rather severe on the American system. He seemed to me to lay too much stress on errors which seemed to be the natural things in a university system relatively younger than the English or German. Many of the things he was severe on seem to me to be the natural expressions of young and vigorous life. I thought, further, that the book had one more error, among its many excellencies, that he rather narrowed down the idea of a university by restricting it solely as a place for training researchers.
>
> If we were to regard our universities simply in that light it would have the effect in our British universities that we would have to drop 19/20ths of our students. I venture to say, of the students that pass through our own universities, not more than one in twenty has the kind of very high quality of intellect and also the same set of interests which will make the really fine and successful original researcher.
>
> I believe in America the proportion of the population which passes through universities—not the number but the proportion—is something like ten times as great as in England, and if we were to drop 19/20ths, I think you would have to drop 199/200ths. I think that would be a great loss. I think perhaps if Abraham Flexner were writing the book today he might think that the concentration on research which he describes as characteristic of the German university has not been altogether good for those universities. If, besides doing the great work in training researchers, they had also devoted themselves to training men to be free citizens in a free country, they would have done something the present universities in Germany have failed to do.

The most extreme manifestation of a tendency "toward the right" appeared in the chapter on "General Education" of Hutchins' *The Higher Learning in America.* This raised the curriculum-philosophic-disciplinary theory of the college to the *nth* power. It advocated a curriculum composed of

the trivium—grammar, rhetoric, logic, with Euclid's contributions to the science of mathematics, and the classics, mainly
those of ancient and medieval vintage. After four years
devoted to the reading of "metaphysics," the last two years
of the high school and the first two years of college, the student will possess a solid knowledge of the foundations of
intellectual discipline. The curriculum just outlined must
be the instrument for intriguing the "intellects" of students,
not only from the usual processes of life, but from the other
functions of the mind and spirit. This certainly was not
only on the frontier of the mind but it was up in the intellectual stratosphere. Such a position of eminence could be
attained, however, by throwing overboard much excess bag-
gage that now encumbers the college program. This, the
author of *The Higher Learning in America* rather ruthlessly
proceeded to do. Out must go consideration of time and
place and environment on the part of curriculum builders,
for "the elements of our common human nature are the
same at all times and in all places." Overboard also must go
current political, social and economic studies for "the heart
of any course of study designated for the whole people will
be, if education is really understood, the same under any
political, social or economic conditions." The curriculum
builders need not be concerned for the body, for character,
for social grace, for utilitarian skill, for these are not essential
factors of pure thought. The present marked emphasis on
the sciences and the scientific method, and manifestly their
means of implementation—observation, experimentation,
laboratories, museums, observatories—must be eliminated for
"unmitigated empiricism is the curse of modern life."

Out must go especial concern for music and art and religion except as they may be approached through books. The
interests and capacities of individual students are dismissed:
"We are interested in the attributes of the race, not the
accidents of individuals." It is not necessary to include
ancient and modern foreign languages, for the classics have
good English translations. During the college course the

value of experience in the educative process—learning to do by doing, for instance, is unrecognized, for "We may wisely leave experience to life." "We may leave experience to other institutions and influences." All this appears to mean that our present college faculties are unsuited to their tasks, for few of them profess to be able to distinguish between "certain" and problematical or relative truth.

Having in these and other ways isolated the reliable subject matter, the colleges will be in position to grind the intellects of students to a sharp edge by formal discipline. The two-thirds of the American youth who are educable must be taught to read, to write, and to dispute—reading, writing and disputation constitute the straight and narrow path to the higher learning. At the age of twenty or thereabouts, the student will complete his general education by passing an examination.

While the theory as thus originally propounded has received much modification as the result of criticism, further reflection on the part of the author, and the attempt to put it into practice, the essential feature still stands—a college curriculum composed of a list of a hundred classic books. Such a list of books has often been recommended, of course, in the history of American higher education. Indeed, an officer of St. John's asserts that the "new" program is but "the restoration of an ancient and vital tradition." Such a list for students of literature is certainly to be preferred to the lists of current books which are now furnished teachers of English in several of the "progressive" high schools.

The effort is now being made at St. John's College, Annapolis, to demonstrate the soundness of the theory, not by disputation but by the laboratory, that is, the empirical method. A faculty has been brought together whose officers and spokesmen are sympathetic with the ideals set forth. This faculty is working in close cooperation with President Hutchins, who is a member of the governing board. The plan is being tried out with a small group of students drawn from the towns and the country districts. The claim is made that they are not exceptionally gifted students and that they are demonstrating the applicability of the plan, therefore, to the general run of college students.

After one year of operation the president of the college made public through the *New York Times* a number of facts as to progress and further plans. Twenty students had chosen to follow the plan; the second year there would be no option for entering freshmen. In a few years the elective system, with its departmental organization, will disappear. The students had been drilled in small classes on the basis of English translations in the whole of Euclid and in Greek. It was claimed that "for the first time possibly in fifteen hundred years a group of college students had read Euclid's *Elements* through," and also all but one of Plato's *Dialogues*. They had also performed certain scientific experiments which the Greeks devised, the instruments the Greeks used having been reproduced at St. John's for the purpose. The students were taught the Greek language, "not to make them fluent Greek scholars, but to give them a sense of language and to enable them to consult original texts in difficult passages." The second year there will be small classes in Latin. The president announced that Catholic educators have denounced the list for including Marx and Freud along with St. Augustine and St. Thomas. He also advised that opponents of the plan had called it authoritarian and Fascist because the student is not allowed to choose what he will study and what he will ignore. The claim was made that an earnestness on the part of students was developed and an intellectual interest discovered "which the elective system has all but destroyed in our colleges."

Columbia College, Columbia University, is also trying out the plan, not as a comprehensive college program as at St. John's, but as a possible means of developing one of the coordinate divisions of the college program—the division of the humanities. The dean of Columbia has not yet publicly evaluated the experiment. It is interesting to note that General Order Number 106, of the United States Navy

Department prescribes a reading course for officers of the line of the Navy, serving under revocable commissions. The Order is administered by the United States Naval Academy. The course itself follows in considerable degree the type of program outlined by St. John's College.

All of these and other devotees of concentration on intellectual pursuits have contributed immensely to the general theory and practice of American college education. In calling attention to a feature of college experience which bade fair to be underemphasized, if not forgotten, in certain institutions, they have rendered a public service. That their suggestions, in the drastic forms in which some of them were presented, have not appealed either to the theorists or the administrators as practicable, much less as cure-alls, does not discredit their efforts. They have helped to clarify the well-formed purpose of many college administrators to discover serviceable objectives for the college adventure.

CHAPTER XVII

A WORKING HYPOTHESIS FOR THE LIBERAL COLLEGE

STANFORD UNIVERSITY recently held a centennial celebration of the discovery that cells are the basic units of all living tissue. Among the sixteen distinguished men of science who came to do honor to Schleiden and Schwann as the first to postulate the cell as a fundamental unit of life was Edwin Grant Conklin of Ohio Wesleyan and Princeton, who made his contribution to the symposium by pointing out that Hooke, many years before Schleiden and Schwann, had seen, named, described, and pictured living cells; that he seems to have been the first to do so, and that the theory of cell development is the product of many scientific minds.

Scientific discovery and educational discovery have at least one trait in common. Their achievements, as a rule, are the product of many investigators, with varying qualities of observation and insight, each making his important contribution to developing knowledge.

The liberal college as well as science has its hypothesis. Now the hypothesis always has an open mind. It is not dogmatic. It is established or overthrown by reason interacting with the experience of the one or the many. The liberal college rests its case on experience and the interpretations of experience. This being true, if it is liberal in fact as well as in name, it gladly listens to suggestions. It recognizes that education is principally a matter of artistry.

There may be discovered a measure of validity in a multitude of apparently conflicting points of view. This accounts not only for the present-day liberal college; it accounts for the great variety of liberal colleges. All of these colleges strive to be serviceable instruments of democracy. The liberal college knows no final "pattern." Like the biological cell, it is a unit of the expanding life. It is as new as television. It is as old as the Garden of Eden. Its fundamental process is growth.

The colleges have listened attentively to the wisdom of metaphysicians and philosophers, devotees of religion, psychologists, scientists, sociologists, physicians, humanitarians, artists, musicians, professional men, business men, students, alumni, cobblers. Some of them have listened to politicians, interested as well as disinterested donors, boards of directors with ways of their own, and even feature-writers in the newspapers. They have learned much and they have discarded more. Above all things, they have learned both by means of theory and practice, carefully to scrutinize the gifts which the Greeks would bring. In the continuous reconstruction of the liberal college program it is fortunate that there have been so many vital sources of wisdom and strength from which to draw.

It is worthy of note that the metaphysicians and philosophers have not always agreed among themselves. Iron has always sharpened iron. They do not recognize universal and final bodies of truth. They question the claims of absolute and universal criteria. Indeed, they now distinctly revolt from an attempt at a complete systematization. The old conflicts arising early among the Greek metaphysicians between Being and Becoming, and between the One and the Many are still fundamental conflicts of metaphysical thought. The theory of their relationships has assumed as many forms as there have been major metaphysicians. Indeed, neither metaphysics nor philosophy has ever been interested primarily in the possession of truth, but in the search for truth. Metaphysicians and philosophers are always ready to incorporate new data into their thinking and they believe that the discovery of new data is a never-ending process. The metaphysicians of all peoples and in all times cannot operate on one track. Men must still be free to think.

Neither has there been absolute agreement among the devotees of religion. It is a generally accepted verdict of history that some of the world's worst wars have been wars over religion. The much maligned Jefferson wrote more than one hundred years ago:

> I have never permitted myself to meditate a specified creed. These formulas have been the bane and ruin of the Christian church, its own fatal invention which, thro' so many ages, made of Christendom a slaughter house, and at this day divides it into casts of inextinguishable hatred to one another. . . . The religions of antiquity had no particular formulas of creed, those of the modern world none; except those of the religionists calling themselves Christians.*

This may seem to be an overstatement to many devoted men. Yet the movement toward church unity which recently has found expression in the proposed World Council of Churches has deep historical roots. It has been growing for more than a century. During the decade 1927-37, according to Paul Douglass, there have been two cases of mutual recognition and intercommunion, two cases of federal union, and thirteen cases of corporate union. Since 1937 the number of such cases, including those of organic union, has rapidly multiplied in England and France as well as in the United States. Here as everywhere the bases of functional unity— of "Life and Work" are easier to discover than those concerned with "Faith and Order." Churches can work together if they do not think together.

There is no college or university in the United States which is officially uncordial to the teachings of the Ten Commandments of the Hebrews or the Way of Life of Jesus of Nazareth. Most institutions definitely provide directly or indirectly for the cultivation of the religious life of their members. Many institutions commit themselves officially to the inclusion of religion as fundamental in their program.

* See References, p. 359.

The world now witnesses the effect of the elimination of religion from institutions of learning.

Many important lessons likewise may be drawn from the area of the psychological disciplines. Psychologists know that it is futile to arrange a hierarchy of mental functions. Those who have sensitive viscera know the body is concerned, likewise. The mind simply does not play on one string, that is, under normal conditions. There has been the Age of Reason, the Age of the Human Intellect, of Physiological Psychology, of Dominant Will, and men have been told that the greatest thing in the world is Love. Psychologists have discovered that despite the variations in mental structure the whole mind is concerned in thinking, in feeling, and in volition. The intellectual function may guide, but the emotions must furnish the motive power. The I.Q., as such, does not go far and may go in the wrong direction. J. Edgar Hoover has furnished a striking illustration of this fact by his statement that behind every great crime is to be found as counsel a keenly equipped practitioner of law. Elihu Root was called by Theodore Roosevelt the greatest mind of his period, but Elihu Root made the assertion, "The greatest quality of statesmanship is patience," a function which certainly cannot be measured accurately by the instruments which measure the achievements of the intellect. The intellectual and the emotional functions must proceed together.

Psychology does recognize individual differences and this fact is one of the bases of present-day college teaching. Observers also recognize that youth is interested in great problems, but not so much as universal principles as for their own personal relationships to them. How can they meet them? How can they reform the world? The mind and body, in any event, do not constitute merely an intellectual machine for registering knowledge.

Those who have a right to speak for the humanities point out that the humanitarian way of life is the basis of Western culture. In this way the Greek ideal of intellectual honesty, the ideal of life guided by reason; the Christian ideal of love, sacrifice for the common good, the Golden Rule; the scientific faith in disinterestedness, objectivity; democracy's faith in the common as well as the uncommon man—all have been initiated and have made progress, driving back superstition and fear, developing personality, contributing to man's happiness. That is to say, philosophy, Christianity, science, and democracy have entered upon an informal, invisible, and indissoluble program to set men's bodies and spirits free. Matthew Arnold's definition has not been improved upon, "Civilization is the humanization of man in society." The colleges must help to bridge the gap that has developed between the physical and the spiritual world.

In the same fashion, the effort to isolate adolescents in a democracy from the stirring events of the time in which they live would prove futile, and, if it succeeded, would prove disastrous. While the various social sciences are still new and are in the stage of infancy as compared with certain other phases of human development, they contribute vitality to student life as to the life of all other members of the community. The greatest achievement of our modern educational theory and practice has been not to remove life from the colleges and consider college experience merely as a preparation for life, but to keep life in the colleges and recognize that the colleges are social institutions. As Conklin has said, "From amoeba to man, from reflexes to intelligence, from the solitary individual to the social organism." Why should not students be allowed to develop attitudes, even if of a tentative nature, toward work, leisure, class, race, the mores of sex, marriage, family, business, industry, property, wealth, government, law, and so on through the gamut of sociological studies? A better question is, "How can they be prevented from doing so?"

The testimony of the teachers must be heeded. They are not in the twilight zone of the educational process. They are down where things happen. The experience of a California junior college, which has operated for ten years on a four-year basis, emphasizes the value of the psychological approach. In this college, syllabi carefully organized by the methods of logic, with major and minor concepts heading the divisions of the text, have been abandoned, and for them have been substituted outlines which definitely provide for the biological approach. The conceptual plan was helpful to teachers, but students preferred the approach in terms of their present habits of thought. It might be reasonable to suppose that literature written for adolescents in the language of adolescents—literature which has stood the test of years, from Thackeray to Tarkington, from *Pendennis* to *Penrod,* might open the door to still richer treasures.

Nor can the suggestions of the cobblers be despised. They would pour into the crucible the rare wisdom of common sense—that enduring quality of mind and spirit which Edmund Burke called the common sense of mankind, which Abraham Lincoln trusted, which manifests itself in the recurring crises of America's turbulent life. When the late Will Rogers was asked, "What is wrong with the world?" he replied, "Well, I dunno, I guess it's people." Sooner or later, as Aldous Huxley says, this common sense becomes aware of exaggerations, then wearies of them, and finally revolts against them. President Park has emphasized this point of view in a recent issue of the *Alumnae Bulletin* of her institution. "The great number of students at Bryn Mawr . . . are able, serious, delightful, plodding, superficial thorns in the Dean's side. . . . What can formal, intellectual training do for this company of coming voters, givers, wives, mothers, captains and privates? . . . Research is not, nor can ever be, Bryn Mawr's final claim to value."

At the University of Chicago the college faculty has declared in formal resolution:

> The University, and especially that part of it which constitutes the College, has sought to deal educationally with the whole person—with men and women as knowers and doers and appreciators. This concern with the good, the true, and the beautiful points to the University's basic objectives:—to produce well-rounded men and women,

equipped with accurate knowledge and sound methods of
investigation and reflection, appreciative of the best that has
been produced in the various fields of human endeavor,
and concerned with the understanding and enrichment of
twentieth century human life in all its phases. This threefold expansion of a single aim, to be accompanied by whatever educational means may prove effective, clearly must
encourage the initiative, the resourcefulness, and the responsibility of students. . . . For over forty years the University
has led a distinguished existence without being officially
committed to any single system of metaphysics, psychology,
logic, religion, politics, economics, art or scientific method.

These selected examples of points of view indicate the
need for the liberal colleges to postulate the human spirit
as the basis of their work. Call it, if you like, "the coeducation of mind and body," as L. P. Jacks does; "symmetrical
education," or "the education of the whole man," as many
colleges do. How may the colleges discover, and if possible
help to guide, the irresistible energies of human behavior?

If the hypothesis of the liberal college involves a great
variety of functional approaches, these are but preliminary
to profounder syntheses. How can the colleges contribute
to the present halting movement toward forms of intelligent
synthesis of knowledge and experience—interdepartmental,
intercollegiate, intercommunity, interstate, interparliamentary, interracial, international? To make some contribution
is becoming their monumental, apparently unsolvable problem.

The liberal college must deal with far-reaching syntheses
in the world of events. It can do this only if it contributes in
some measure to like syntheses in the realm of body and
mind and spirit. Within that realm the objective has been
held up of "a scientific mind," or "a philosophical mind,"
or "a social mind." A world compressed in space and time
needs more than these, if human adjustments are to be made.
The scientist who has never gained the capacity to appreciate
philosophical or spiritual values may block rather than promote human progress. The theologian who knows nothing

of the scientific method is the very frequent product of the programs of the theological seminaries. The college trained man or woman who confines his studies to one type of discipline, even one type of self-discipline, does not make the most of his college course, either for himself or for the social order. The greatest disciple of the world's greatest teacher enjoined his co-laborers to have "the mind of Christ." He admitted that he himself had not yet attained, but he pressed forward to the goal. With such an injunction in our ears from such a source, it should not be thought presumptuous that the student with scientific interests should be asked to develop some understanding at least of the philosophical and other methods of thought required by the various offerings of the curriculum. That many scientists are striving to attain this larger synthesis is one of the hopeful signs of a better day. They attribute the present woes of the world not to the advances in science but to the weaknesses of human nature. If ever the colleges and the social order needed this higher type of mind, that time is now.

That the undergraduate college may become cordial to such a program only lays the foundation for the further reaches of synthesis in the graduate schools and the post-graduate schools which are forming here and there throughout the country. Conspicuous examples are the New York School for Social Research, the Institute for Advanced Study at Princeton, the Brookings Institution at Washington, Yale's Institute of Human Relations, the Pendle Hill Center near Philadelphia for the study of socio-religious problems.

Dr. Carrel has just proposed institutes of psycho-biology in which to develop leaders intelligent in proportion to the growing complexity of world life. "Specialists," he says, "can't deal with the difficulties of man as a whole: it will take minds capable of approaching our problems from different angles."

The scientists are attaining the larger synthesis by venturing into the forms of thought used by the philosophers: forms of thought concerned with imponderables and intangibles.

Equally is it true that the philosophers need the intellectual antidote furnished by scientific precision. The social scientists teach that a sense of social responsibility must be realized, but in order to do this they strive to develop the power of intellectual penetration.

The discipline of philosophic thinking is enriched by that of scientific thinking, and vice versa; both types of thinking are enriched by social thinking and vice versa; and still greater excellence is attained through the cross fertilization of theory and practice.

The upshot of all this is that the colleges will make no effort even to formulate a uniform and closed system of educational procedure. They are content to follow some such broad formula as the Preamble to the Constitution of the United States. They glory in unity in the midst of variety. They would treat each other as persons and not as things, and they would develop a spirit of camaraderie both corporately and among individual teachers and students. Each college or group of colleges, as the administrative arrangements may require, will define its own objectives, and will be judged by its fruits.

The disciplines in thought offered by these various types of subject matter and these interacting contacts will tend to counteract the inevitable "set of mind" and egoistic outlook to which "scholarship" alone, that favorite objective of the colleges, leads.

The shift will come in the process of college education only as John and Mary, carefully admitted to college work, take the place in the center of interest now usually occupied by curriculum material; only as motivation, interpreted in generous terms, is substituted for uniform prescription, guidance is proffered by wise and sympathetic teachers, and time is allowed for growth. If the college is to be a social institution, it will have its windows open in every direction. There are many facets to human intelligence. There are many worthy objectives in a democracy for the attainment of which intelligence, thus broadly defined, is needed. The necessary transformations in the nervous system and in the mind and heart to attain these ends are not made in a hurry.

For the accomplishment of this task other great unifying subjects must be introduced into the liberal arts curriculum, notably music and art. There is a glory of color and form and sound and of the book and the test tube, as well as of "the starry heavens above and the moral law within." Nor can these newer disciplines be required to conform to processes of logical thought. All must be free to pursue their several courses in the ways inherent in their purposes and materials.

The fact that art and music do not as yet have full academic status affords them an opportunity in some measure to transform college work and life. These disciplines must not be fettered. The artist must be free to follow the history and tradition of art, its uses for the individual or for public education, wise types of provincialism in its expression, soft or hard harmonies and colors, practicum and craftsmanship. Art must remain prophetic. The philosophy of the art group is not the same as that of some other disciplines already with status in the college program. The artist must be allowed to resist the tendency to make the work abstract, over-refined, meticulous, remote from its own spirit. Appreciation and performance of art—including the art of living—must permeate all life. Art is less preoccupied, at least in its early stages, with subject matter than with personality. It cannot abandon its procedure in order to conform to pre-conceived tests by which later it is to be measured. A study of the art departments of numerous colleges in 1932, by the Association of American Colleges, disclosed the fact, according to the surveyor, that most of the artists have personal magnetism, stamped with industry and self-discipline. They are fulfilled as personalities. As in the case of music, all concerned appear to be happy.

As a boy on a western Indiana farm, I was told of a pioneer farmer in whose hog-lot a hollow tree had fallen in such position that one end of the tree projected over a brook.

The pigs would crowd into the land end and finally Pig No. 1, urged on by his comrades in crime, would be forced to tumble out at the other end and splash into the water, only to come up and restart the process of perpetual motion. In the past, a good deal of pig psychology has gone into the construction of the college curriculum. For a long time the philosophical and classical litters were unmolested. But in time the natural sciences litter nosed itself in, to be followed by that of the social sciences. Philosophy and Greek and Christian Evidences each had its cold bath; then Latin, and now the modern languages, we are told, are close to the yawning chasm. By some such process the "enrichment of the curriculum" has been pushed *ad absurdum*.

Now we have found a better way. The newest comers—music and art—are pointing it out. With the new way, the pig simile and the pig psychology are abandoned. The new method is orchestration. We need the sweet sounds of all the instruments for perfect harmony. Music and art come as unifiers and permeators of all the work of the colleges, and philosophy and religion at their best would serve the same functions. The details of this better method are being worked out cooperatively by many profoundly interested faculties across the continent.

The liberal colleges of America in increasing numbers are becoming stirring centers of fearless and constructive thinking. Such reflections must stimulate to the fuller and more stubborn use of their minds the members of all colleges which aspire to identify themselves with the great oncoming achievements of the intelligent human will.

We no longer expect an Aristotle to assemble and classify all knowledge. We rely rather on the high-power human engineer, by the processes of selection, to show us the path to simplified practice. This he is doing by pointing out to us that within all human endeavor, however complex, there are a few definite and common functional operations, whether in the city or the country, among the rich or the poor, the high or the low. We must have gentlemanliness and sportsmanship if we are to be crowded together. We must preserve open spaces as the complement to subways, if for no other reason. We must have domestic loyalty and virtue. We must preserve and develop literature, science, the fine arts, an educated democracy as well as an intellectual elite. We must have a religion that is free from hypocrisy and intolerance. These are some of the conditions—not all of them, of course—of human unity, which is a huge and over-whelming goal as yet unachieved, but, some men dream, achievable.

At this moment the most vital problem which is being considered in some of the colleges is the problem of personnel; how to integrate and coordinate the now forcibly severed parts of educational subject matter into a unity which shall envisage the whole of life and shall foster a unified person, a unified society; how specifically to attain an effective plan of student housing; how to maintain the residential and other advantages of the smaller institution without sacrificing the peculiar advantages of the larger. The watchword of the American liberal college is no longer analysis; it is synthesis, such synthesis as is achieved simply in a well ordered home. Here begins the contribution of the colleges to the social order.

The American liberal college after nearly 300 years of experience thinks it has discovered some of the golden threads that run through all wholesome cooperative endeavor. Whatsoever things are true, in science and philosophy and religion, it would think on these things; whatsoever things are good, in human relationships, in things domestic, ethical, civic, social, without discrimination as to sex or race or nation or time or place of habitation, it would think on these things; whatsoever things are beautiful in God's creation and in human character—the joint product of God and man—and whatsoever things have been made beautiful by the rare gift of man's artistic touch, it would also think on these things. Few colleges have discovered all these golden threads that make up the warp and woof of human life—that bring human

contentment. Some of them have failed even yet to learn
that the temptations of beauty do not menace character building more than the perils of ugliness.

Thus the college disciplines are breaking down dividing
barriers. Our physicists of the first order are metaphysicians,
our metaphysicians recognize and may use the scientific
method, our astronomers and theologians, who once were in
mortal conflict, are vying with each other in attempts to
comprehend the infinite; our students of nature have discovered the existence of human nature; our students of
human nature find in their own souls the evidence of God.

All this gives the liberal college renewed strength and
courage to persevere in the colossal effort to build a new
civilization on physical, intellectual, and spiritual foundations. The appeal of Daniel Webster, effective in his day,
for "liberty and union, now and forever one and inseparable," may now be made on still higher ground for education
and religion. To this end the individualist must strive cooperatively, the nationalist must develop the international
mind, the man with the planetary mind, as the astronomers
discover new planets and new systems of planets, must stretch
his imagination to include the universe. All must weigh the
present against the past. Some at least, even though the
"flames are at our doors," must, as President Conant says,
"germinate new ideas which may bear fruit decades hence."

CHAPTER XVIII

THE JUNIOR COLLEGES, COMPETITORS OR ALLIES?

THE present junior college movement had its inception at the University of Chicago almost fifty years ago. At that time President William Rainey Harper provided for the division of the University College into a junior college and a senior college. His conception of the junior college, however, was far removed from that which is held by its leading sponsors today. He realized that many students who entered college were incompetent, or unfit, or financially unable to pursue to the end the program which the four-year college outlined. From the standpoint of the college of liberal arts and sciences, at least as then organized, many of these students were uneducable. The tremendous mortality prevailing throughout the entire country among freshmen and sophomores was sufficient indication of this fact. President Harper's idea, therefore, was that, since a large number of students would be sure to drop out about or before the middle of the college course, it might serve as an incentive to them to provide for a certificate which he named "Associate in Arts" at the end of the sophomore year, so that thereafter they would be in possession of a formal statement that they had done two years' work in college. It was no part of his plan to modify, much less weaken, the program of the freshman and sophomore years. He was not interested in providing vocational or other types of education in place of education in the liberal arts and sciences. He did recognize that during the period of orientation of the student coming from the usual high school and entering into the broader college

218

life, particularly when the college was dominated by the complex organization of a great university, there should be some variation in the types of teaching for the junior college and senior college students. Harper's formulation is the Magna Charta of the junior college.*

Comparisons are sometimes made between the development of the four-year college during a period of three hundred years up to the point where there are approximately one thousand such institutions and a total of over a million students, and the rapid development of the junior college during a period of a few decades. The deduction is frequently made that the four-year college is now tending toward obsolescence, and that the junior college is bound to take its place in American education and life. When the president of Stanford University became Mr. Hoover's Secretary of the Interior, and the State Commissioner of Education in California became the United States Commissioner of Education, they entered with considerable vigor upon a speaking campaign in the East, the purpose of which was understood to be to bring the country to an acceptance of this point of view. That effort, of course, is no longer a part of the program of the United States Office of Education.

During the half century which has passed since Chicago provided for her junior college, many unexpected things have happened. President Harper had listed among the menaces of the college, the high school and the junior college. He could not foresee, as no one could foresee, what was involved in that prophecy. It is now well known to every student of American education that the development of the high school has been one of the most remarkable phenomena of education in this or any country. The American people have poured out their money lavishly for this unit of our educational work, and the young people have, in rapidly increasing numbers, taken advantage of the opportunities afforded them. Not only has the traditional type of high school been maintained, but there have been striking developments of

* See References, p. 358.

various kinds in the area of vocational education, in the technical high schools in their various manifestations. During the successive decades of the fifty-year period from 1880 to 1930, high school attendance increased respectively—84 per cent, 370 per cent, 729 per cent, 1894 per cent, 3849 per cent. It is now estimated that the total increase has been 4,000 per cent. During this same period the population of the United States increased 150 per cent. The number of high school students has increased from 200,000 to 6,000,000.

Long ago most colleges of liberal arts and sciences gave up the idea, if they ever entertained it, as certainly a few of them did, that all high school graduates should go to college. This was a most unreasonable assumption from the point of view of the educability of the students themselves, the teachers, the programs, the budgets, the material equipment of the colleges. Nothing could have proved more disastrous to the colleges than for all of the high school graduates to knock at their doors for admission. The state universities, in particular, were placed in a most embarrassing position, for they were required by law in practically all of the states to admit every graduate of a high school who might apply.

On the other hand, many of the privately controlled institutions, fully realizing the significance of the situation, began a process of selective admission, and that process today has achieved remarkable developments. Too many high school graduates were seeking to enter our best colleges, not too few. The result was that particularly in the tax-supported institutions thousands of students were dropped at the end of the first term or semester. It was the only way in which such institutions could conform to law and at the same time carry out their purpose of maintaining educational standards. In the eyes of many, this relentless elimination of students during their freshman year developed into the proportions of a scandal. The institutions were severely criticized for their ruthless and heartless methods. When it was announced in the newspapers at Christmas one year that 3,000 freshmen had been dropped from the college of a Mid-West University, a great storm of disapproval broke forth. Such slaughter of the innocents outraged the people.

Now, this attitude was not a case of man's inhumanity to man—fathers and mothers included as well as adolescents. Whatever the totality of causes which led to the dropping of so many students so early in their course—and no doubt the university should take part of the blame—it at least served to dramatize a most undesirable, a really intolerable situation.

Successive tidal waves washed in to the shore line between secondary and college education vast multitudes of young people, many of whom were anxious to continue their educational work. A veritable crisis in American education was the result. It was at this juncture that the junior college idea was revived, and the proposal was made that this problem, which could not be solved by the liberal colleges, might be solved by speeding the development of the junior colleges so that opportunities might be multiplied for aspiring students to continue their education.

The most powerful promoters of the junior college idea in many instances were the authorities of the universities and colleges. The raw material was at hand for the new unit of education. Something must be done and the rapid progress of the junior college is due in very large measure to this quite remarkable situation in the development of American education. Never had any other unit of our educational program confronted at the same time such a challenge and such an opportunity. It is not strange that the junior colleges have multiplied rapidly, particularly in the younger states. It would have been very strange if they had not done so. And yet, even now, to the disappointment of many, this same type of mortality, which was a feature of the period before the junior college began aggressive action, persists. The junior colleges often report relatively large, although varying, percentages of withdrawals before graduation.

Assuming, of course, that they would have intelligent administration, the place of the junior college was won before their rapid increase in numbers began. The urgent question now confronting them is not what are the best methods of propaganda or how may they be reduced to a state of uniformity through processes of standardization, but, rather, what are they to do with the opportunity, the challenge, which now presents itself.

To this very vital question there is almost an infinite variety of superficial answers. In this respect the junior colleges are following right along in the footsteps of the liberal colleges. No two junior colleges are alike, just as no two liberal colleges are alike, but it is being recognized in both areas of educational procedure that there should be important principles of unity.

Not many years ago, in reply to a question submitted by the Association of American Colleges, 60 per cent of the junior colleges of the United States declared that they looked forward to becoming four-year institutions. While this is not true now, the results of surveys made independently by Taylor, Webb, and Eells do show that most junior college students plan to enter a liberal college. Eells reports, however, that only "28 per cent actually enter."

In certain sections of the country not a few of these colleges are continuations of institutions founded sometime before the Civil War as finishing schools or as military academies. In some of the states, practically all of them are private institutions. Not infrequently, they are organized for sectarian purposes to promote the interests of the supporting denomination. In a few of the states, notably in California, much progress has been made toward a systematization of these colleges. In Georgia, there are two junior colleges organically connected with the state university and under the general supervision of the chancellor. An important objective in these institutions is military training.

In Illinois, where the numbers break about even between the state-controlled and the privately controlled institutions, there are two junior colleges of the coeducational type organized with the cordial support of the state university, the University of Chicago, and other universities, in order that the pressure upon the university colleges in the freshman and sophomore classes might be relieved.   There is also a definite advisory relationship with the North Central Association of Colleges and Secondary Schools.   This North Central relationship is also an important feature in the development of a great junior college in Missouri, which has received a million dollar gift from one foundation.

In the State of California the junior colleges present a multitude of offerings varying with individual, and with diverse community and regional needs, but the majority of them can be classified under one or another of three objectives: (1) the academic, first in order of time, but not of significance; (2) the definitely vocational objective; (3) an objective variously named, but practically a combination of the liberal and the vocational.   The last type does not look forward consciously toward higher institutions; it does not look forward to a specialized job.   It is terminal so far as formal education is concerned, and it strives to familiarize the student with some of the cultural ideals of the race, and at the same time with some of the practical means of living.   In some of the large colleges, it appeals to more students than either of the other objectives.

Mere mention can be made here of the same type of development in the colleges of liberal arts more than fifty years ago when the old cultural ideals were being supplanted in part by the introduction of the study of science.   In this particular, and in numerous other particulars, history is repeating itself, and no doubt an adjustment will sooner or later be made in which each unit of our educational work—the high school, the junior college, and the liberal college—will find its place.   It is certainly true that all three of these agencies put together and all of the other agencies which may be resuscitated or invented, cannot soon perform the task of affording first-class educational opportunities to the millions of boys and girls of our American democracy.   That there should be permanent antagonism between one unit and the other units is not in accord with the spirit of American education. In some of the older states—New York, Pennsylvania, and Ohio—where many colleges are already established, it will be the part of wise statesmanship to modify some of the existing institutions rather than to launch a multitude of new enterprises. Excessive duplication is suicidal.

The junior colleges are contributing much to our educational progress as a nation. They are furnishing opportunities for further education to thousands of our boys and girls whose circumstances prevent them from leaving home.

They are making modifications in their offerings which cannot be made so successfully by established institutions with programs already well developed.

They are relieving the colleges from an embarrassing influx of that large majority of students who are looking forward to early vocational pursuits.

Some of them are leading in the development of student advisory service.

They are stimulating the colleges to a careful study of their fields, constituencies, objectives.

They are demonstrating certain advantages in the lower-upper, the junior-senior organization of the college curriculum.

They are turning over to the colleges many students with tested qualifications for further study.

They are helping liberal colleges to strengthen their upper divisions. In some of these colleges the senior class is as large as the freshman class.

They are teaching colleges not equipped for the successful continuance of their present programs how to make program adjustments to new social conditions.

They are developing vital centers of the democratic spirit.

What should be the most profound concern of the leaders of this unit of our education? Certainly not the concern for propaganda or the concern for systematization which has always been the peril of regimentation, but the concern to serve our American youth. The junior college seems to have come to the aid of our American education for just such a day as this. It now meets a tremendous challenge in American life, by which the high school and the liberal college are also confronted, to help to preserve and maintain our American democracy. The leaders of our high schools, our junior colleges, and our liberal colleges should join hands in restating and applying to contemporary life the greatest conception of human relationships that has ever developed in the mind of man, the conception of democracy. The present generation of students must face, once more, "the ultimate issues of human destiny."

All of which once more raises the question, "What is democracy?" Not long ago there was a discussion at a Town Meeting of the Air the purpose of which was to define democracy. No one of the persons who participated in this discussion was labeled with the exception of the communist who insisted he was a democrat. The others presented the points of view respectively of socialism, of the New Deal, of capitalism, of democracy of the Declaration of Independence, the Constitution, the Bill of Rights, and the Gettysburg Address.

At the end of the discussion a summary was made of four points on which all of the speakers had agreed. (1) Democracy has respect for the individual; (2) democracy trusts majority rule; (3) democracy insists upon the protection of the minority; (4) democracy stands for freedom of thought. These four principles, with their implications, constitute a great philosophy of education, and to these four principles was added by common consent a fifth principle. Democracy is the thing which, in that discussion, was being exemplified by the Town Meeting of the Air. Perhaps the fifth point is the most important of all, for it is rather useless to teach the principles of democracy in an institution which is not governed by the spirit of democracy.

Doubtless educators agree that along with freedom of thought there should be freedom of speech, freedom of assembly, freedom of the press, freedom of worship, and freedom for individual initiative.

In any event, here is the supreme task which is set before

American education, and it comes with peculiar force to the junior college. One of the present important trends of junior college development is in this direction. It is certain that we will never maintain our democracy unless we preserve and develop it in our local communities. Here is the supreme task of the junior college. The junior college, barring a few exceptions, is a community institution. It is equipped for making a contribution in this field which cannot be made so successfully by those liberal colleges which are, or are aspiring to become, institutions with national appeal.

The junior colleges are developing their programs in terms of the immediate needs of the people, and in doing this they are beginning to work out horizontally among all the people into adult education, forum work, and other forms of extension. We can have a nation unified by the principles of democracy if we can have our communities unified by the principles of democracy. Democracy was born in the community. It will function there or not at all. The junior college is challenged to work out in the crucible of experience this philosophy of education.

This statement of dual objectives—the welfare of the individual and the welfare of the community—certainly offers sufficiently vital principles of motivation for any educational program. Both objectives are needed for the promotion of the general welfare.

For the performance of such a task the junior colleges must tighten their belts. Some of them, as has been said, have organized their personnel work in a remarkable way. It ties the students into the life of the community, it enriches their outlook, it instructs them in the practical means of making a living. The majority have yet far to go in realizing the full fruitage of the six important steps now outlined in this total clinical procedure: analysis, synthesis, diagnosis, prognosis, treatment, and follow-up.

Again, in the field of instruction there is much progress to be made. The most important discrimination which the junior colleges must make is as to whether the instructional methods and the type of teachers to be found in the high school are to carry over into the college, or whether there shall be a greater disposition to throw the students upon their own responsibility and to encourage them to develop self-discipline and self-direction. The question to be solved in each institution in the light of its own situation is whether the students are reaching the stage of development where they can begin to put away childish things. The junior college, because of the age limits of its students, is in danger of myopia. One junior college has announced the apparently laudable enterprise of "fitting the college to the student, fitting the student to the college, and fitting both to life in a changing society." For some students there is great danger in attempting too snug a fit. Even reptiles in the swamp cast off their skins. In every community there are some boys and girls who are destined to help change the environment of their day and generation. This is what has been done by exceptional people—from Adam and Eve to Walt Disney. The emphasis of education should not be upon something that the management is going to do for the student. The emphasis sooner or later should be upon what the students are going to do for themselves and for the community.

For the attainment of such ends as these there must be a more carefully outlined plan of library development, library administration, and the adjustment of that administration to the teaching program of the college, than is found in most junior colleges. When the representatives of the Carnegie Corporation recently visited selected junior college libraries in California, twelve of the forty-nine were designated for grants for the purchase of books ranging from $1,500 to $6,000. How can the leaders of the educational and personnel program be induced to make greater use of the libraries in their guidance of the student's work? How can the library better contribute to the educational program?

To make but one other suggestion, junior college teachers— for some junior colleges enroll 5,000 or 6,000 students—are in peril of the monotony of teaching. With too heavy a load, this outcome is inevitable. They should be afforded time for individual study and investigation. The adventurous ones should be encouraged to pursue special projects for their own improvement which go beyond the immediate horizons of the institution. This means, specifically, types of research work to be carried on individually or in groups. In one junior college in California such projects were being pursued as these: first, the history of the theater in the Southwest; secondly, the 250 brightest stars; third, the practical application of the rigorous evaporation equations; fourth, the art of the ancient Peruvian civilization. One thing is certain, such teachers as these are expanding their own horizons, are adding stimulus to the same process on the part of their students, and they may be expanding the boundaries of knowledge. That such expansion is characteristic of a number of junior colleges is one of the most promising indications of their development.

The junior colleges of America are called to a great task. It doth not yet appear what shall be, but from the multitude of investigations now being made into the nature of adolescence, it is to be hoped and expected that this area of our educational endeavors will be greatly enriched.

Since the junior college is essentially a community institution, it will be more and more a terminal institution for the great mass of its students. Within this mass there will always be a group who will reach out for extra community objectives. Such students must not, and cannot, be hedged about with predetermined restrictions. They will go on for further educational work as their horizons enlarge. But the institution itself will serve its day and generation best which devotes itself primarily to leading students into the realization of their own powers in the light of their own community interests and problems.

CHAPTER XIX

THE GROWING INFLUENCE OF THE ARTS

JOHN ADAMS once asserted that he would not give a sixpence for a Raphael. He rejoiced with Puritan fervor that the age of painting and sculpture had not arrived to corrupt our beloved country. He was one of those Brahmins residing mostly in Massachusetts and Virginia who performed the epoch-making task of translating the Constitution into a working government and of determining the course of one of the strongest currents of our national life. The arts, not only painting and sculpture, but music, dramatics, dancing, and all the rest of them, had stubbornly to fight their way to recognition. Jefferson, of course, was an outstanding exception to the rule among these Brahmins. He attempted to create "an architectural style expressive of the lofty ideals of the new republic." The University of Virginia led all other American universities in a consistent architectural design. But artists of the first rank were not to be found in the South or elsewhere to carry on the Jeffersonian tradition. The almost universal prejudice expressed so summarily by Adams continued to stigmatize beauty of sound and form and color and movement until a very recent time, and does so even to this day among a very considerable proportion of our population. It was not until two hundred and thirty-three years after Harvard had been founded that the bold step was taken of making Charles Eliot Norton professor of the history of art.

At the same time there were, almost from the first, manifestations of unconscious traditions in some forms of art

229

which had been carried over from the mother countries. Striking examples of this are found in the colonial architecture of New England, New York, New Jersey, Maryland, Virginia and some other parts of the South, and in the regions occupied by the Spanish and the French in the West and the Southwest. These architectural forms were more than unconscious traditions; they came in response to personal religious and civic needs; they were homes, plantation centers, churches and missions, and centers for the expression of civic life. Today, by the thousands, we make pilgrimages to these objects of art.

Indeed, ironically enough, John Adams in a moment of weakness granted a sitting to Gilbert Stuart, yielded to his spell, and declared that he "would be glad to sit for him from one year's end to the other." It was this foible in human nature that made possible the Golden Age of portraiture, which began when the German Holbein came to England in the sixteenth century to make a living by painting portraits. The stimulus of it there, and later here, was the vanity of its patrons. Boston, for the most part, remained artistically torpid, while the art of Stuart and West and Copley prospered. These artists reflected the individualistic, the egoistic spirit of the time. Stuart adapted himself to this social temperament—and was buried in the potter's field. They loved not the artist, with all his charm, but themselves.

The Spanish and French who came to America had a background of artistic appreciation of certain forms. Early in the history of the European occupancy of the continent the Spanish monks had located the missions across the Southwest. Their knowledge of architectural form and substance impresses every sensitive visitor. Before the Revolution also, the French contributed to the diffusion of art objects and artistic appreciation. Consciously, these early settlers were interpreting art as a part of the living present. The Huguenot craftsmen contributed to artistic appreciation. The South supported "itinerant wood-carvers, silversmiths, cabinetmakers, and an occasional third-rate portrait painter."

When the State of Virginia wished to give Washington a tangible proof of its admiration, it followed the advice of Jefferson and Franklin and entrusted to Houdon of Versailles the honor of making the well-known statue of the president.   Franklin conducted Houdon to the American shore.   It took us more than a century even to begin to catch up with Franklin and Jefferson.

After the Revolutionary and Napoleonic periods hundreds of refugees came to America.   From Texas to Upper New York "they planted vineyards, painted exquisite miniatures, erected cotton mills, and founded academies of the liberal arts—all to the diversification and enrichment of American living."

Joseph Bonaparte, brother of the Emperor, lived for fifteen years at "Point Breeze," an eighteen hundred acre estate near Philadelphia.   There he entertained Henry Clay, Daniel Webster, John Quincy Adams, Stephen Girard, and many other distinguished Americans.   There came also many French marshals and generals, refugees after the defeat of Waterloo.   "Point Breeze" offered the guests the atmosphere of a Parisian salon.   W. Francklyn Paris says, "No gallery or museum in the United States possessed the artistic wealth which awaited Bonaparte's visitors: works of Titian, Van Dyke, Rubens, Murillo, Da Vinci, Velasquez, Raphael, Corregio, Veronese, Jules Romain, Teniers, Salvator Rosa." *

If the influence of France in early American art was small, it was especially notable.   The plan of the City of Washington and the designs for the first and the succeeding New York City Hall were drawn by French architects.   French architects worked under the limitations of colonial material in Detroit and about New Orleans.   French influence reached a high mark in 1886 when Bartholdi's Statue of Liberty was securely placed in the greatest of all the gateways to the Western world.

The World's Columbian Exposition in Chicago in 1893, which was derived from the work of French students com-

* See References, p. 362.

peting for the *Prix de Rome,* had much to contribute. By
the late '90's most ambitious and talented students of architecture were studying in France. With the Beaux Arts Institute of Design many of the leading American universities,
as well as the principal ateliers, are now associated.

To do full justice to the passengers on the *Mayflower,* and
especially to their proud descendants, it must be said that
they did develop the art of public speech—of elocution, disputation, oratory. This was a natural development. It was
part of their English heritage. England excelled in the art of
speech, written and spoken, rather than in what have usually
been called the fine arts. Speech was a natural and necessary
means of expression for the "learned ministry," which the
fathers wished to perpetuate. The ministers in the churches
must be graceful rhetoricians. Recently there has come to
the attention of the writer the funeral oration in honor of
Alexander Hamilton delivered by Hamilton's pastor, Eliph-
alet Nott, who was President of Union College from 1804 to
1865. In this pronouncement, "How Are the Mighty
Fallen!" are found a clarity of expression and a beauty of
diction which deserve to rank with the best of English composition. The new America believed with Cicero and
Demosthenes that while liberty was the parent of eloquence,
eloquence was the stay of liberty. If it were needed properly
to portray in the churches the "fiery depths of Calvinism,"
certainly without eloquence Faneuil Hall could never have
become the "cradle of liberty." Such talent gave Jonathan
Edwards and Daniel Webster secure places among the im-
mortals.

But the expression of art in the churches was not confined
to the highly educated ministers. There were the American
beginnings of psalms and white spirituals for which we now
have profound respect. In the fortunate revolt which has
expressed itself in recent years against the Moody and Sankey
type of evangelistic propaganda, a high standard of church
hymns has been set for the most part by college writers.
Outside the churches there was the tradition of square dances

—in the mountains and the country villages, and a revival of these is a feature of our time. It is one of the ironies of our development as a people that while much widely diffused art, sampling forms of which have just been enumerated, was taken for granted, the cultivation of other forms of art was considered a waste of time if not a manifestation of the devil. This tendency is paralleled in the disposition of the pioneers, having found liberty to deny it to others. At any rate, the arts of which we have been conscious have gained admission to the colleges only after many rebuffs.

Yale, following the example of Harvard, appointed a professor of art in 1870, and later there were added the names of Marquand at Princeton, Rice at Williams, Mather at Amherst, Tappan and Frieze at Michigan, as pioneer teachers. If history is the matrix of art, it is not to be marveled at that the beginnings of conscious artistic creation and appreciation in America were greatly delayed.

There was no widespread interest among the colleges in the teaching of the fine arts, however, until after the World War. This may be said despite the fact that for the first two decades of this century the fine arts generally, and music in particular, made much headway as a factor in the life of the American people.

Leading up to the present era, we quote from Emerson H. Swift, Professor of Art at Columbia:

In the decades which followed the Civil War American culture reached its lowest ebb. Stagnation in the South, boom times in the northern and central states, the opening up of the West, railroads marching across the continent scattering mushroom towns in their wake, an exclusive preoccupation with practical affairs and internal commercial development,—all were fatal to the interests of art and served effectually to cut off the country from the thin streams of culture which had hitherto trickled in from Europe. The results endure to this day in the architectural monstrosities of the '80's. Yet, as the deepest darkness falls before the dawn, so a glimmer of light lit the threshold of the '90's and burned to a glow in the World's Fair at Chicago.

The Columbian Exposition was indeed a milestone in our artistic progress, since there for the first time Americans became aware of the existence of art. It was nothing short of a revelation. . . . The leaven had been working and its results were beginning to appear. Already our would-be architects, sculptors, and painters had taken to going to Paris for their years of apprenticeship, and had returned with a knowledge of design, a technical skill, and a breadth and sureness of execution which compared not unfavorably with that of their Gallic fellows. Their attainments were made manifest at the Fair, and thousands of substantial citizens from all parts of the country traveled back to their respective Main Streets filled with admiration—though perhaps not always understanding—of the homely strength and idealism of Saint Gaudens' "Lincoln," the pensive charm of French's "Death and the Sculptor," and the sweeping beauty of Atwood's magnificent classic colonnades.

A new day had dawned, and with it a growing popular interest in the fine arts. At the turn of the century and thereafter national prosperity was steadily on the increase, providing for an ever larger number of the liberally educated the means of foreign travel.

Immediately after the World War, in 1919, the Association of American Colleges took an aggressive step in the field of the arts. It definitely committed itself to the effort to improve college architecture and appointed a committee to have this project in hand. This committee associated itself with the Commission on Education of the American Institute of Architects. The next year the Association accepted their suggestion that the colleges represented in the Association be asked to consider seriously as something of vital importance the introduction of courses in the appreciation of art —broadly defined—in the curricula of our colleges, to give amplification and further emphasis to courses already offered on art subjects and art appreciation, and to make art values dynamic in subjects in which such values were then merely potential.

During the years between 1919 and 1924 progress was made by the Association in formulating its program relative to the Arts. In this effort the colleges were buttressed by the independent establishment of schools of art and design, by national and international expositions, the development of art in advertising and manufacturing and commercial enterprises. The Association's Committee on Architecture was superseded by a permanent Commission on Architecture and the Fine Arts, including music.

Music first came into the colleges under severe handicaps. It was considered an extra and called for an extra fee. It was found to be a money maker, adding funds for the budget. The teachers worked on commissions, and turned over the balance to the treasurer. Music was not incorporated into the curriculum, much less encouraged officially as a means of diffusing culture. The standards either of appreciation or of performance could not be high. It would have been bad enough if its influence under such untoward conditions had been kept on the campus. But the wandering Glee Clubs, often sent forth with the blessing of the colleges, because they were good recruiting agencies, were often a travesty on the art they professed to represent.

In the judgment of many present-day teachers of college music, the introduction of Glee Club contests added little or nothing to the dissemination of high standards. Such teachers are convinced that the competitive motive mars rather than promotes high excellence. It presupposes the inability of music to reach high attainment without the use of artificial stimuli. In more recent years some of the colleges have demonstrated that music can win appreciation on its merits, largely following the successful pioneering of Harvard.

In 1924 the Carnegie Corporation issued a challenge to the colleges to share in and contribute to the movement to make this country more appreciative of the values of art. Said President Keppel, "There is great need of the refreshment and relief which the fine arts provide." The Commission entered upon its long period of active service in behalf of art education. Through the office of the Association it made contacts with the Metropolitan and other Museums of Art, and the National Commission of Fine Arts, and enlisted the active cooperation of some fifty or more of our distinguished architects, painters, sculptors, actors, musicians, critics, and teachers of the arts. They have served on committees and commissions as advisers and as speakers at the annual and regional meetings of the Association. Among these advisers, in addition to those drawn from the colleges and universities, have been Frederick P. Keppel, President of the Carnegie Corporation, Edward Robinson, President of the Metropolitan Museum, Ernest Hutcheson, President of the Juilliard School of Music, J. Fredrick Larson, whose architectural talent has recently been employed at Dartmouth and other colleges, at the International House in Paris, and at the School of Advanced Studies in Princeton, Randall Thompson, now head of the Curtis School of Music, Lorado Taft, the late Jonas Lie, Charles D. Coburn, Myron C. Taylor, John Erskine, and Herbert Putnam, the builder through the years of the Library of Congress.

The Association of American Colleges has conducted a continuous series of studies largely made possible through grants from the Carnegie Corporation. Many of these studies have eventuated in books and articles which help to mark the recent progress of artistic development in this country. The student of the subject is referred to the long list of these publications whose titles are included in the "References." Miss Lura Beam, who in 1927 made one of these studies, is now Associate in Arts in the staff of the American Association of University Women.

The Association has established a free advisory service in the field of architecture for members of the Association. It has arranged exhibits in New York, Washington, and elsewhere, and accumulated in the headquarters library much data of value to college executives and committees along architectural lines. Mr. Larson has been the consultant for this service for a number of years.

In addition to the moral and financial support which has been given to the Association's art program by the Carnegie Corporation, that Corporation has contributed generously to the College Art Association, has given valuable arts teaching equipment to many colleges, has provided fellowships for the preparation of teachers of art to meet the increased demand of the colleges, has distributed many sets of musical material, and in many other ways has become a leading exponent of American art education and appreciation.

In the year in which the Carnegie challenge was issued, only six of the 130 national academicians had the baccalaureate degree, and only six others had attended college at all. A few universities had schools of architecture, but their general relationship to university administration had been ironically expressed by a president of one of the larger institutions, "It has been the aspiration of our university to allow each graduate of our school of architecture to place one building on our campus."

In the same year the National Bureau for the Advancement of Music estimated that 250 colleges and independent schools of music were operating in this field. Of this number not more than seventy-five were demanding a quality of work that warranted such recognition as the degree of Bachelor of Music. Some institutions were virtually selling their degrees, and this statement applied to "conservatories" as well as to departments of music in not a few colleges. They were profit-making institutions. There were notable exceptions, but as late as 1927 the National Association of Schools of Music, which had been organized to set up standard minimum courses, consisted of only about twenty-five institutions,—10 per cent of the 250. Many state boards of education later appealed to that Association to protect the degree in courses in which public school music was a major, and this was done. It may be pointed out that, in general, music and the arts of a commendable quality appeared earlier in elementary and secondary schools than in colleges.

For the January meeting of the Association of American Colleges in 1931, it was arranged that Lorado Taft should speak on "Art and the College," and John Erskine on "Music in the Curriculum." This meeting, as it was intended to

be, became a landmark in the programs of college education
in the arts. Taft said, "After pleading with the citizens of
Chicago and much talking, we saved the old Field Museum,
the old art palace of the Columbian Exposition. We saved
it seven times. When we finally got it saved, our good
friend, Mr. Rosenwald, offered them his millions to supplement the millions set aside by the City of Chicago."

Erskine declared that while the colleges were teaching the
history, appreciation, and theory of music to a selected few,
they were doing nothing to aid the students who had come
from the secondary schools in larger groups and were dropping their music as soon as they came near a college. He
asked the college to consider music as a "practical study"—
as practical as mathematics or history or English. "We don't
pretend that the boys who take mathematics will turn out
to be great mathematicians, but we do hope modestly that
they won't know less mathematics when they leave college
than when they came in. This is all I hope for music."

The Association launched plans at once for a comprehensive study of the place of music in the colleges. A sponsoring committee was appointed and the next year Randall
Thompson began his work as Director of the Music Study.
After two years, Thompson found that three primary aims
were being sought in the music departments of the colleges—
more general appreciation, more general knowledge, more
general ability in practice; and that musical scholarship and
musical composition were secondary aims. He reported also
that the demand of the elementary schools for some technical
training in music had been met in some of the colleges by
developing types of music pedagogy.

Thompson put the cultural aim first and asserted that it
would be attained primarily as an intellectual performance
through the knowledge of the literature leading on to musical scholarship. He said that practicum should be taken
for granted. The real issue he stated concisely. "To advocate the inclusion of music as an essential subject of education is, at the present day, to beat at an open door. That

music shall be taught is now no question. How it shall be taught is a problem that music departments and college officers are honestly and modestly eager to solve." At last, the colleges have an open door to most forms of art!

His statement that practicum should be taken for granted, was accepted by about half of the members of the sponsoring committee. There was vigorous dissent by the others, and the book resulting from this study contains the arguments for and against practicum as a basis of credit, as set forth by Thompson and by a sub-committee of the dissenters. The critics protested that college music must not "go highbrow." In Thompson's view, applied music should be confined to the conservatories. On the whole, *College Music* is the classic work on music in the colleges. It was unfortunate that the main issue was not met, but that the committee became entangled in a problem of administration of means rather than ends. Already it has come to pass that music is an integral part of the curriculum and campus life of practically every college of liberal arts.

There came meanwhile a genuine awakening of the colleges along architectural lines. In 1924 only three institutions had a consistent architectural ensemble—the University of Virginia, Stanford University, and the University of Chicago. Since that time numerous colleges and universities have been built in entirety or in part along consistent and pleasing lines. Many first class architects are now emphasizing the various phases of college architecture.

Distinct progress was being made also in the quality of art teaching in the colleges. Eastern institutions, for the most part, were placing emphasis on the development of the individual student and the perpetuation of the history and tradition of art. Some colleges were coupling performance with appreciation and were recognizing responsibility for the artistic development of the country. In the early '30's an analysis of the content, nature and distribution of art courses offered in more than 400 institutions showed that over 73 per cent offered studio courses, over 66 per cent offered

courses in the history of art, over 37 per cent offered courses
in methods. Vassar was enrolling one-fifth of her students in
art courses; at both Vassar and Mills the Department of Art
was the third largest in enrollment. At Antioch every student was required to take an introductory course in the arts.
Various aspects of American art are now being offered in
more than sixty institutions. Among these, Lawrence College, the University of Chicago, and Rhode Island State
College are the pioneers.

   The American Art Annual for 1932 listed more than 200
Departments of Art in American colleges as well as 175
specialized art schools, and called attention to the fact that
instruction in art is included as an integral part of the curriculum in such recently organized colleges as Bennington,
Brooklyn, Brothers, Sarah Lawrence, and Scripps. Today
there are few colleges claiming to be liberal in objective that
have not recognized the irony of liberal arts colleges minus
the arts. Peyton Boswell, Jr. has expressed the belief of
many critics that "no longer is it necessary for American
youth to go to Paris, Rome or Munich for art training as
in the days of Whistler, Sargent, Chase, Duveneck and Ea-
kins. . . . It has long been voiced by critics that only when
Americans quit sitting at the feet of Europe and are willing
to obtain inspiration at home will the long desired 'American
Renaissance' be possible." Many facts of recent occurrence
give warrant to the conclusion that some phases of American
art, even if somewhat belatedly, have passed through their
adolescent period, are coming of age, and manifest an increased degree of self-determination. The Americanization
of the Metropolitan Opera is a case in point. Or consider
the recent development of so-called "regional painting" and
the veritable army of designers of industrial products—house-
hold equipment, automobiles, pottery and textiles.

   The Graphic Sketch Club of the University of Pennsylvania has stimulated the development of the "Cultural Olym-
pics" which, with tens of thousands of participants, is linking up history, literature, philosophy, religion, sociology,

ethnology, politics, and to some extent economics, through the means of the dance, music, public speech, dramatics, foreign language festivals. In all of this progress in making America conscious of the significance of beauty, our foreign-born population has made a great contribution.

A number of the land-grant colleges—Michigan, Kansas. Massachusetts—have taken the lead in developing music and the fine arts in connection with the curriculum of agriculture and home economics programs. This has been done by the integration and coordination of existing courses, the encouragement of new art interests, and the study of possible extensions. At Massachusetts State College a Fine Arts Council provides a continuing focus of art interests on the campus.

The movement in art education is still too young as yet to have produced many striking results among students in the display of creative ability, although several institutions have listed such results as among their objectives. This slow realization of creative objectives is due in part to the paucity of great teachers. One of the latest grants of the Carnegie Corporation affords Princeton University the means for conducting a five-year experiment in the various creative arts, including music and the art of writing. It is a part of Princeton's program in the humanities. The William Seymour Collection at Princeton offers opportunities for the scientific study of stage history and provides possible fields for research.

The latest barrier in the American tradition which has been broken down, that the arts might enter the colleges, is the theatre. With the exception of a very few institutions, the dance is still *non grata*. As late as the last quarter of the nineteenth century, the drama was not only an academic outcast, but the stage was by many considered essentially wicked. This conception was replaced by another that, although the theatre might be respectable, it was scarcely worthy of serious academic attention.

Today, theatre-goers' "Platitude No. 1" is the wail, "There's enough tragedy going on about us without having to see it on the stage too." But the obligation to carry on, no matter what the untoward circumstances may be, must be impressed upon men if they are to maintain their courage. The drama in literature, and on the stage, contributes mightily to the strengthening of the individual and social morale.

There has been something the matter with the theatre as well as with public sentiment toward it. It has been pointed out by a reliable authority that three-fourths of the plays written for Broadway production belong to the evasive category of a "tragi-comedy of the real." The friends of the theatre wish it to return to enduring and universal experience, clothed with beauty.

Time would fail to speak adequately of the pioneer work of Frederick H. Koch, early in the century, at the University of North Dakota and later at the University of North Carolina in laying the foundations for an American folk theatre; of the Carnegie Institute of Technology, which organized a department of drama and a course in theatre arts leading to the A.B. degree in 1914; of George Pierce Baker's "English 47" workshop at Harvard, and the theatre for the Yale School of Drama; of the National Theatre Conference, in stimulating interest and affording guidance in the development of the community theatre in its various forms; of Mr. and Mrs. Charles D. Coburn and President Dixon Ryan Fox, in demonstrating through the medium of the Mohawk Drama Festival the necessity of professional leadership and participation, if higher standards of achievement than those to be secured through amateur performance alone are to be preserved; and of the generosity of the Carnegie Corporation and the Rockefeller Foundation in contributions toward those and other artistic ends. In relinquishing some of its interest in established humanistic disciplines, the General Education Board in 1933 began to encourage the theatre, the museum, the community center, as well as the film and the radio, to become working mediums in a larger humanistic program. The National Theatre Conference reported in

June 1939 that through its royalty project it was in touch with 221 community theatres, 336 colleges, and 1,221 high schools.

The development in the theatre arts has been so rapid that Richard Ceough was able to report in 1936 that of the more than 400 colleges and universities offering some work in dramatic art, 33 have an expressed or implied cultural purpose. Seven institutions—Cornell University, Western Reserve, Wisconsin, Iowa, Michigan, Teachers College of Columbia University, and Louisiana State offer graduate concentration in dramatic art leading to the Doctor's degree. On the campuses of many institutions there are theatres; on that of the University of Washington there are three. Indiana University, Stanford University, the University of Wisconsin, Dartmouth College and Williams College are among those which, in 1939, were planning or constructing theatre buildings as a part of their campus expansion.

During the year 1939 the Julius Rosenwald Fund was spending $100,000 for art fellowships, the majority of the awards going to Negroes of demonstrated ability along artistic lines. The Negro schools and colleges have an Association of Music Teachers in Negro Schools and the Southern Association of Dramatic and Speech Arts. The capacity of gifted Negroes for artistic appreciation and performance is receiving general recognition and admiration.

The conviction is growing that the arts, properly understood and appreciated, form an important, often a determinative, function in the daily existence of every normal person. Art is inherent and discoverable in the common objects and experiences of the daily life of the people. Its conscious enjoyment is becoming more general in the United States, as it has been elsewhere for centuries. Without such appreciation and enjoyment, the realization of a full personality and of a rich community life cannot be achieved. Its influence is essentially unifying. Without it neither the nature of the world in which we live nor the constructive achievements of men can be understood. Critics agree that the arts are the symbol of the successive stages of civilization. As Charles Eliot Norton used art to give life to Greek histories and tragedies, so present-day teachers recognize that art values are to be found in all subject matter—not only music and the so-called fine arts, but in language and literature, home economics, physical education, the mathematical disciplines. Perhaps with deeper knowledge we will say "chiefly with mathematics," for now we are becoming familiar with the similarity of the lines of the spectrum, the lines of the musical scale, the lines of the Parthenon. Not only so, the California Institute of Technology now shows photographs of similar lines in microscopic manifestations of the life process. How many mathematicians have also been musicians!

The place of the history of art has been firmly established. The acceptance of the historical method of teaching follows. Appreciation is not a "field" of study but the outgrowth of a method of study, perhaps universally applicable. If art illustrates human history, it becomes enrolled with the other humanities.

While there is disagreement as to the wisdom of admitting practicum to the status of academic credit, the tide has been flowing for some time in that direction. Studies of art teaching show that the existence of a music department or an art department in a college has at present no necessary relation to the general appreciation of art by the members of the college. Singing, playing, landscape design, buildings, pictures, sculpture, students' rooms, house furnishings, restaurants, the ordinary routine of life, may be entirely unaffected by such departments because of their narrowness and exclusiveness. But the studio and the academy are finding their way into the college picture, and chiefly without the benefit of credit on the books of the registrar. The demonstration of the power of group singing given by the World War is being put into operation on many campuses. Only by actual contact with many college communities can the extent of this movement be realized. Practicing artists of many types are being brought to the college community to live and work. The scientific applications of drawing, of color, of design, now employed in business, are teaching their lessons. Picture rental collections and browsing rooms become vital instruments of instruction.

The fact that the arts do not have full academic status affords them an opportunity in considerable measure to transform and vitalize college work and life, just as the sideshows which Woodrow Wilson condemned have always done. They—the sideshows and the arts—are characterized by vitality rather than crystallization. They operate if and as they are not fettered.

Bennington College has taken advanced ground. Its program goes beyond the art department; it requires a faculty which lives art. The faculty preach what they call the "musical life." As Eric T. Clarke has observed, the difference between the function of the college and that of the conservatory is one of emphasis—not scholarship or dexterity, but scholarship and dexterity. Manifestly the degree of the one or the other will vary with the individual student as well as with the type of institution.

An Advance Step

At the annual meeting of the Association of American Colleges, in January 1936, an advance step was taken in the field of the arts. This step was a formal entry into the realm of extra-curriculum activities. It envisioned not merely additional opportunity for advancement on the part of the highly gifted student of the arts, but the establishment of means for the more general diffusion of artistic appreciation and performance within the colleges. The step was made possible by a number of grants from the Carnegie Corporation, announced simultaneously, for the development of designated arts projects. Eric T. Clarke was shortly transferred from the staff of the Carnegie Corporation to that of the Association, at the latter's request. Starting as Director of the Concert Project, his field has been expanded into an advisory service in the Association's entire Arts Program. In this work he has the counsel of a multitude of interested artists and administrative officers, as well as that of the Executive Board composed of college executives. Approval was given to the conception that the well-rounded artist recognizes and participates in the three phases of art—activity, study, enjoyment, and that the creative artist is a student as well as a composer, performer, or painter. This is Clarke's "Tripod."

The Director and his consultants were convinced that no art can flourish where it is merely inspected and talked about. The scholarly approach must be enriched by the simultaneous approach of the other aspects. Appreciation is only one leg of the tripod.

Upon the basis of such principles of procedure the Association formulated several projects. Underlying the entire series was the effort to place emphasis upon the imponderables inherent in the various forms of art as contrasted with, and in addition to, the curriculum program. The Association committed itself to a higher synthesis than that which had heretofore prevailed generally among the colleges.

A thoroughgoing study of the college library with a view to its recognition not only as a teaching agency but as a center of creative work was projected. It was hoped that as both the college and the library administration became more appreciative of the teaching function, the library might become a greater stimulus than at present to creative writing of both prose and poetry—that dynamically as well as potentially it might contribute more effectively to the recognition of the true nature of literature as an art. In addition, college libraries might become centers to some extent of the vast literature in the field of music and of the other arts. Out of such considerations grew the Library Project which has eventuated in Harvie Branscomb's *Teaching With Books*.

The Association emphasized the necessity of grants in aid

to teacher-artists of demonstrated quality in order that on leaves of absence they might devote themselves to available means in this and other countries of further preparation as college teachers.

It also sought the best means by which general participation in musical expression on the part of members of the colleges might be encouraged. As a preliminary step it provided for a Circulating Library of Choral Music consisting of a considerable number of vocal scores of leading works of J. S. Bach, Beethoven, Brahms, Franc, Handel, Haydn, Mendelssohn, Mozart, Verdi, Debussy, Pergolesi. This library is the property of the Association of American Colleges. The scores are available to singing groups in member colleges which are willing to pay nominal rentals based on handling costs and estimated depreciation, plus transportation charges from and to the central depository in Chicago. Subsequently, the University of Pennsylvania Choral Series was presented to the Association by Henry S. Drinker of Philadelphia, together with supplementary notations by the donor. The distribution is through the office of the Association in New York.

The most adventurous step of all was the Concert Project. It was grounded in the belief not only that the arts are a part of higher general education but that if the colleges were not merely giving lip service to this belief as a pious utterance, there was need for an agency which the colleges might feel to be their own which would stimulate creative work in contact with living artists. Since the profoundest significance of this project, which has now developed into the "Arts Program," is in the area of college teaching, fuller consideration is given to it in Chapter XX—"The Improvement of College Teaching."

CHAPTER XX

THE IMPROVEMENT OF COLLEGE TEACHING

THE miracle of furnishing the colleges with an adequate supply of good teachers has not yet been wrought. Great teachers have always come to the schools and colleges as manna from heaven. There is scarcely a college but that boasts of one or more great teachers during its history. These teachers have never been able to explain the secret of their power. They have usually been unconscious of it. Lists of the necessary qualifications of a good teacher have been made time out of mind. Experiments to produce good teachers synthetically have failed. Special units of education, both on the secondary and higher level, have been set up to put the parts together and turn out an ideal product. The sum of the parts does not equal the whole. What has been torn to pieces cannot be put together. This is a way most pedagogical axioms have. Apparently good teachers cannot be compounded of the known elements.

Or are the elements known? Has "knowledge" been confused with persistent presuppositions? A generally accepted presupposition is that if a college teacher knows his subject, he can teach it. The basic qualification then is scholarship. But an analysis of what passes for scholarship, or even knowledge, creates some surprises.

The accepted conception of knowledge has usually centered about that stock of curious and unrelated bits of information that is accumulated by taking courses in the several air tight departments of the college. You can pin your faith, it is confidently assumed, to these contributions of miscellaneous subject matter. By this measure, any college graduate can teach.

To make doubly sure, more recently the "fifth year" has been added. For a beginning teacher, this program of preparation now has general acceptance. The purpose of the fifth year is to turn the mind of the student to some of the problems of teaching. For the most part, it concerns itself with methods of conveying the information accumulated in the school and college. At its best, its purpose is to impress the prospective teacher, usually a candidate for a position in a secondary school, that his teaching ability in the long run will be measured by his attitudes, his sense of proportion, his relation to background. Einstein is quoted elsewhere in this book: "Education is joy and artistry." If the fifth year fails to put emphasis upon the inherent artistry of the teaching process, the magnetizing influence of the teacher, what the University of Pennsylvania has called the great teacher's "underground enlightenment available for sharing with others," it does not set the mark high enough.

But, of course, a Master's degree does not carry such guarantees. In the mind of the discriminating committee on teacher selection, the question continually arises as an applicant for membership in the staff is being considered: Art thou a master in Israel and knowest not—that to be a teacher in any school one must be born again?

Then there is the conception of knowledge held by the departments or schools or colleges of education, many of which are offsprings from and carry over into their programs the methods of the normal schools. Being professional schools they emphasize methodology. Since most of their students become teachers in secondary schools, their relation to college teaching is not so direct or extensive.

A third conception of scholarship is furnished by the graduate schools. Here is the field par excellence for the training of college teachers. This conception is equally misleading as an adequate preparation for teaching. The graduate schools persist in placing emphasis upon research. The usual test of the student's skill as a researcher is the ability to produce a thesis worthy of publication, which may be accepted as a contribution to the advancement of knowledge. The Doctor of Philosophy is a specialist who has written a book. Now, many more Doctors of Philosophy go into teaching than into research. Their tested ability to pursue an investigation to its sources and to do creative work is an invaluable qualification of a good college teacher. A teacher cannot teach for long unless he also is learning.

But the ability of teachers to adjust their knowledge to less mature minds, to extend their interests to fields beyond their specialties, to become comrades of students in creative pursuits is not necessarily inherent in the technique of research. These several types of the communication of knowledge and of inspiration, the graduate school usually, though fortunately not always, ignores. The college takes its newly coined Doctor into the faculty at its own risk. For the first few years, if he turns out to be a good teacher, he not only learns more than any of his students, but in point of fact he belatedly serves an apprenticeship.

The subject-matter approach is not sufficient. The conquest of subject matter may lead on to intellectual achievement. It does not make the full contribution to that broad and sympathetic intelligence which is necessary to account for the teacher.

There is a fourth conception of knowledge or scholarship. This conception lay at the basis of the Pennsylvania study carried on by the Carnegie Foundation for the Advancement of Teaching.* When the announcement was made in the public press that in the course of this study upper-class men had failed to make as good a showing as the same students while they were lower-class men, and with the same lists of questions, the conclusion seemed by many to be that the longer students were in college, the less they knew.

Many critics were disposed to discount the whole college enterprise. Others pointed out the possible insufficiency

* See References, p. 363.

and inadequacy of the selected questions to test student progress.   When the Carnegie Foundation elaborated its conception of knowledge, it appeared that neither the undergraduate type of knowledge, the pedagogical type, nor the graduate type of scholarship furnished a sufficient criterion. It was pointed out that the procedure of the study is based upon certain fundamental premises: that "education consists in thinking, in the perception of meanings and relationships among ideas that are true and important, and in the marshaling of an individual's natural emotions behind ideas in proportion to their truth and importance"; that, therefore, knowledge lies not with but "between those who consider it to be 'so very mere,' and those who consider it to be the ripe and finished product—the supreme goal of an effective education."   "Knowledge is the *product* of thought and not only or chiefly its raw material."

The first assumption was, therefore, that "knowledge must be a relatively permanent and available equipment of the student."   The second assumption was that knowledge, when used as adequate evidence of education, "should represent as nearly as possible the complete individual—that it furnish a coherent intellectual physiognomy."   This means that something very important has happened to "mere" knowledge.

This is a much abbreviated exposition of the theory of the study as given by Learned and Wood.   The practical justification is summed up in one sentence,—"To be valid, the scores made by the same students after the two-year period must show a gain, and they do so, except in the cases of certain individuals and occasional small groups."   That is to say, most students had learned to do some thinking, had gained in maturity.   The newspaper stories had been misleading.

As a further indication of the advance, or at least the extension, of a sounder theory of the teacher's knowledge, reference may be made to the discussion of "Scholarship and Teaching," in the report on some problems of personnel in

the Harvard Faculty of Arts and Sciences. This report was
made in response to expressions of discontent among younger
members of the Harvard staff, shared by the undergraduates, because, as was alleged, good teaching was not a serious
factor in promotion. The Committee which studied the
matter reached the conclusion:

> Scholarship and teaching present a sharp antithesis only
> when scholarship is identified with published research, and
> teaching with eliciting the interest and informing the minds
> of relatively immature students. . . . It is this antithesis
> which inspires the belief that the scholar-teacher, or teacher-
> scholar, is only a pious hope. . . . The first step in clarifying
> the issue is to redefine scholarship and teaching in terms of
> that intermediate zone in which they coincide; or in which
> teaching is a normal and appropriate expression of scholar-
> ship, and scholarship a condition of teaching. When this
> is done, the issue is largely resolved. . . .
> There is . . . a kind of good teaching which instead of
> being antithetical to scholarship is conditioned by it and
> constitutes one of its surest evidences. This is the teaching
> in which the creative processes of knowledge are shared with
> the student.

More than a decade before such rationalizations were made
public, indeed almost a quarter of a century before in some
cases, individual colleges had been proceeding in the same
direction not only in their thinking but in their planning
and in their practice. Today a large number of colleges are
moving in these directions. A few of the early pioneers may
be mentioned by name. They illustrate most of the principles of "coherent intellectual physiognomy" now in use.

Whitman College, Washington, had blazed the way in
introducing comprehensive examinations, and a year later
Reed College had made a careful selection of students, had
established a community life, had organized its program
without the complications and distractions occasioned by
fraternities and intercollegiate athletics. The faculty was
divided into four main divisions and began to develop techniques of teaching cooperatively, individually, unobtrusively,

informally. The desk and the raised platform had been eliminated from the classroom. Reed's greatest concern for a quarter of a century has been to preserve and develop unity of aim and spirit, though as might have been expected this has been a unity with expanding boundaries.

Harvard, largely under the leadership of President Lowell, had set forth its fourfold objective: to devote more attention to the undergraduate as an individual; to treat him as a whole being; to make him more largely educate himself; and to provoke in him an interest in doing so. This objective involved reorganization of the curriculum material, a redefinition of the elective system, the supplementing of the student's efforts with tutorial stimulation and guidance, the cooperative discovery of special student interest, the introduction and proper use of reading periods, and a definite improvement in methods of examination.

Princeton had found it necessary to depart from the almost universal method of conducting courses by means of lectures, and had introduced the preceptorial system. More recently, she had laid stress upon the examination, had required each student at the beginning of his junior year to choose a field of concentration and had developed many of the devices which, with modifications, are now the common possession of colleges in which honors courses are conducted. Princeton had laid special stress upon the plan of independent reading and had made progress toward the synthesis of courses in the several closely related departments. The college had announced that its ultimate purpose is to teach the undergraduate student how to help himself. In the graduate school definite steps had been taken to establish an awareness of the more general relations of knowledge, and in this the graduate school was depending almost wholly upon the natural effects of the intimate daily life of the students in a residential society.

The Graduate School of Princeton was a leader in graduate education in emphasizing the educational value of a small, compact, social unit. It has recently been achieved in the Houses and Colleges of Harvard and Yale. This conception has ever been the ideal of most of the detached colleges. Thus leading universities joined many of the smaller colleges in placing emphasis upon disciplined freedom worked out cooperatively by faculty and students, and preserving the ideals and aspirations of the institution as a whole, rather than of conflicting and competing groups within the institution.

Swarthmore had adopted a plan of teaching honors students, and had announced that the heart of it lies not in how these undergraduates are being taught, but in how they are learning. The ways in which honors undergraduates were learning were as varied as the personalities of the young men and women themselves. Much work was done individually in the library and elsewhere, and small honors groups including one or more faculty members frequently met for extended and informal reports and discussions. Students who were admitted to honors courses had previously demonstrated an active rather than a passive attitude toward their work. Plato's doctrine had become a motto: "A free spirit should learn no piece of learning with slavery." The comprehensive examination was being conducted by professors of other colleges and universities and served as the final test of attainment.

Antioch had rediscovered a number of the radical innovations which had been introduced by Horace Mann in the attempt to break free from the traditional concepts of college education. A cooperative effort on the part of the faculty was launched here to achieve internal integration and organization. A plan was announced as enabling the student in five or six years to obtain an exceptionally rich education centered in substantial preparation for a major life interest. This was accomplished by the integration with study of practical experience in living and working. The college had introduced a system of sectioning classes, had organized weekly discussion groups, and had thrown upon students the responsibility of distributing their own time and taking the initiative in their own education. Emphasis was laid upon community of thought and community of service.

Rollins had been operating on its "workshop method" by way of seminars of two hours' duration, which has become known as the Two-Hour Conference Plan of teaching. This plan is characterized by spontaneity of method in terms of student needs, but under constant faculty guidance.

Stanford had been developing its Independent Study Plan in the interest of a greater degree of self-determination on the part of a very limited number of exceptional students. This called for greater initiative, more self-direction, a higher type of thinking, not, however, without special faculty advisers. The plan did not then involve group study or any form of competition even in examination. Each student had individual instruction and opportunities had not been made for crossing department and subject lines. Improvements in the teaching technique were destined to come later.

Minnesota, before America entered the World War, had introduced an experimental study of the problems of educational guidance. Since the autumn of 1917, the army group intelligence examination "A" had been given, and other intelligence tests have been given since in different colleges in the University. Among the purposes with which these tests were and still are used have been the initiation of experiments in the technique of college instruction, the control of conditions in experimental studies of teaching, and the evaluation of numerous factors contributing to student success. Experimental studies had been made to determine the efficiency of instruction in large classes, to study current methods of instruction in the field of the laboratory sciences, to determine methods of reorganizing the curriculum. Minnesota's General College was to become later one of the distinguished outgrowths of these preliminary studies.

Among the colleges for women, Vassar, and later Oklahoma College for Women, introduced a division of Euthenics for the study of parenthood and the family; Sweet Briar, interdepartmental majors; Wells, independent study; Milwaukee-Downer, a course in occupational therapy—all requiring specialized teaching in relatively new fields.

A multitude of other colleges which must be unnamed have been devoting serious study to in-service improvement. The problems of teaching are often brought before the faculty by one of its own committees, which set up programs of discussion by the entire faculty. More serious study is being given to the matter than is generally understood. All agree that the teacher must be a Person.

Numerous colleges were becoming keenly aware of the possibilities of their libraries as the future intellectual centers, particularly of the social sciences and the humanities. Library administration was beginning to center upon the problems of teaching and many faculty members were beginning to appreciate the value of the library in reinforcing or even in partially replacing lectures and classroom instruction. This interest led, *inter alia,* to Harvie Branscomb's study of the library, under the aegis of the Association of American Colleges.

Another line of attack upon the problem of college teaching was inaugurated at Teachers College, Columbia University. There groups of college officials and teachers, usually on leaves of absence, began to come together to review such developments as have just been mentioned, to orient themselves in the midst of this crusade, and to project improvements. The University of Chicago soon established its Institute for Administrative Officers of Higher Institutions, which for a brief period during the summer quarter continues to draw to the University many administrators and teachers in service, for the consideration of special phases of the life and work of the college. New York University, Ohio State University, and the University of Minnesota became conspicuous in the same field. Hundreds of members of these groups of earnest and mature students are employed throughout the country as teachers and administrative officers. They serve as a backlog for all the fires that others are kindling.

In 1928, the Association of American Colleges, in collaboration with the Council of Church Boards of Education, formally agreed upon the study of college teaching as one of its primary policies. The annual meeting of the two organizations held in Chattanooga, in January 1929, took this topic as its theme. Following this meeting, the Commission on the Improvement of College Teaching of the Association addressed a letter to the deans of the graduate schools holding membership in the Association of American Universities, in which their cordial support was sought in the effort to develop a supply of college teachers with a keener appreciation of the values of good teaching. All of the deans made cordial acknowledgments, some of them showed genuine interest, and a few of them promised hearty cooperation.

About the same time, the North Central Association of Colleges and Secondary Schools became thoroughly dissatisfied with its effort to vitalize the schools and colleges through the means of minimum objective standards. This Association inaugurated a series of studies on the basis of the results of which it addressed itself to a complete reorganization of its methods of admission to membership. This process eventually led to its present plan of individual evaluation by an adaptation of the method by which physicians make diagnoses. That Association recognizes that the spirit, ideals, and methods of administration, including those of the president, the deans, and other officers, greatly affect the teaching processes and exercise significant influence in the development of the student in scholarship, personality, character, and all the other qualities of an educated man.

Later, the American Association of University Professors produced a significant study on college teaching as its special contribution.

Of the 10,792 teachers in Catholic colleges reported by the National Catholic Welfare Conference for 1938, 5,733 are lay instructors, men and women, and 5,059 are priests, Brothers and Sisters. The priests receive most or all of their education, extending over many years, in Catholic institutions in this country and Europe. Many of the Sisters enroll for special work in leading American universities, as do the lay instructors. Through a voluntary, country-wide organization, the National Catholic Educational Association, with its Department of Universities and Colleges, opportunity is given for the exchange of experiences and the pooling of ideas looking toward a steady growth in efficiency without the loss of local or individual initiative.

Experience has taught that the most effective cooperative procedure in securing good college teachers from the graduate schools has not been through an S.O.S. call from the colleges "to come over and help us." The more vital emphasis has been on the demand rather than the supply. College representatives are earnestly seeking teachers in the graduate schools who can meet needs inherent within special institutional objectives for which their curricula have been set up— objectives well defined and well known. A common basis of interest and sympathy between the college and the graduate school is being discovered. The colleges have become more discriminating in "shopping around" for additions to their faculties. They have more definite ideas of what they need. This is the most convincing argument for a better quality of "product."

There are many factors determining the types of teachers the colleges need. Knowledge of the background of students is recognized as so important that many colleges are changing their methods of recruiting in order to achieve a greater degree of homogeneity of student personnel. They prefer as recruiting agents understanding scouts rather than high-pressure salesmen. They establish close relationship with the secondary schools and accept as of high value the recommendation of secondary school officers and teachers. Many colleges throughout the country are cooperating in the Eight Year Plan of the Progressive Education Association in the effort to stimulate attitudes and formulate programs which will insure intellectual continuity as students proceed from the schools to the colleges. Here is a laboratory.

To this end such questions as these are considered: How may the students fit into the coherent program of the college? What intellectual power does the student have? Can he contribute to emotional harmony? What has he done besides making grades and passing exams? Does he give promise of broadening personality and creative achievement? Can he make some contribution to the social life of the college? Does he have wholesome ideas of what good conduct is? Has he shown evidence of power of self-propulsion?

The stated objectives of the colleges and their special types of experimentation are factors of significance in the selection of teachers. If the college has organized the curriculum into an upper and lower division, it has been done largely because different kinds of teaching are required in the two divisions. If the college holds that the curriculum should have justifiable relationships to the resources of the immediate community, it will seek teachers of a different type from that required in a college with a wider outlook.

If the college believes that intellectual achievement not permeated with ethical motives is a menace, it will choose its teachers accordingly. If the college is organized on the assumption that the religious spirit should permeate its entire program, it will seek teachers who are able to contribute to that end. If the college holds to the threefold objective of discipline of mind, ennobling tasks which endure, and intellectual curiosity which will not be sated, it will search for teachers who "gladly teach," as Chaucer expressed it. If a college is committed to the dictum, "Learn to do by doing," and would reproduce the history of the race in the experience of the student, it will establish workshop courses and seek teachers gifted in this form of artistry. Another college will choose its teachers on the assumption that the experience of the race has largely been deposited in compact, systematically developed subjects, and it will seek teachers who believe that the fibre of American education will be maintained and strengthened by the mastery of these subjects. If a college looks upon teaching as a science-in-the-making, it will move in the direction of objective tests, integrated by various short-form examinations, and will seek teachers who can manipulate such a testing program.

Such considerations as these are of greater weight in building a faculty than mere questions of methodology. Any method with constant use becomes sterile. The alert teacher will adapt his method to the situation at hand. He will not be the slave of any method, even though he be especially equipped for work in the classroom as a tutor, a lecturer, an interdepartmental teacher, a leader or participator in group thinking, or a roving professor. His value will be greatly enhanced if he is able in any situation to teach in the spirit of research.

There are certain characteristics, however, which are constants in this developing demand for good teaching in the colleges. Teachers are being sought, as has already been suggested, who have some dramatic element in their composition, who exhibit some magnetizing power, who seek the far distant as well as the near result, who are disposed to share what they have with their colleagues as well as with students, and who thereby contribute to institutional morale, who place a higher estimate upon values than upon facts, but who seek a union of knowledge and values that actually function in conduct, who consider what happens to the student as the most important outcome of their task.

In the light of such teaching procedure the ominous warning found in one of the important studies of college and university teaching against "inspectorial visitations," seems passé. The whole trend of the improvements in college teaching is in the direction not of widening chasms but of integrating subject matter, personnel, professional interest.

Thus far, all leaders of all types of schools frankly admit that the problems of good teaching and good teacher preparation have not yet been solved. No leaders are more critical of present methods than those who engage in the work of teacher preparation. They are baffled not only by the inadequacy of their own work, the rapid and conflicting changes in pedagogical conceptions, but also by many unforeseen complications. To be counted among these are the entrance of the motion picture and the radio into the teaching field; the continuous transfer to the school of responsibilities formerly assumed by the family and the church; the extension of their responsibility to the nursery school at one extreme, and to adult education at the other; the limitless multiplication of subjects of study. In the face of all these challenges, the fact remains that financial provision for teacher education in the universities falls far below that for other learned professions.

Two very significant developments are now in process which have within them great promise. One of these is the comprehensive study of teacher preparation which is now being made under the auspices of the American Council on Education; the other is the Arts Program of the Association of American Colleges. Each of these is progressing on the principle that the best way to learn to do a thing is by doing it.

The American Council's study envisions the total problem of teacher preparation. Representatives of thirty-four institutions, including twelve liberal colleges, are banded together to see the problem whole and to see it continuously for a period of five years. By the conference method they are isolating and evaluating the major problems of teacher education; as a second step they agree to make an experimental application of the methods and objectives agreed upon, in their respective institutions. First of all, they are demonstrating the values of group thinking, and they report that no irreconcilable differences have arisen. The vitality of the conclusions of the group, however, is to be tested in the crucible of experience before definite solutions of the problem of teacher preparation are proposed.

In the spring of 1936 the Concert Project of the Association of American Colleges was launched. Although the experiment might have started in any one of many fields, it was decided to begin in the field of music. It was felt that the use of philanthropic funds to compete with those who aim to extract a livelihood from the business of purveying artists would be unjustifiable. Features were introduced, therefore, which could not be secured through other channels.

Clearly, the first aim was to single out those concert artists who in their own lives typify liberal culture. This of itself was no easy task. For in a world of exhibitionists and one-sided specialists, such people are rare.

The next move was obvious—to arrange for them to be on the campus long enough to communicate their interest in general culture. Two-day visits as a minimum, therefore, were arranged.

Several well-known artists responded to the call, at special low fees, because they caught the educational significance of their visits and were assured that the public sale of admissions would be prohibited. Even on these terms it developed that the Project could not reach more than one-quarter of the Association's membership, for only 132 colleges admitted that they had spent $200 or more for any visiting artist within the past four years. Accordingly, in the first year of the experiment the head of a college music department who was a good performer was pried loose and offered for a half week to each of four colleges at such distance that the prophet should not be without honor.

This device opened up an entirely new field which has since become by far the most important feature of the Project. It blesses alike the colleges that give and them that take. To the musician there is a definite opportunity for an enlarged horizon.

The Project was further developed through the appointment and circulation on extended tours of teachers on sabbatical leave. Indeed, the demand for such visits soon far exceeded the supply of suitable visitors. For such purpose no college president as yet has refused to grant a reasonable leave of absence on full salary, but suitable faculty artists who maintain a high standard of performance and at the same time exemplify the higher general education to which the colleges are dedicated are very rare. The Director of the Arts Program has been appalled also at the number of college teachers in the arts who have allowed their fingers to grow literally and metaphorically stiff.

The extension of the plan has been undertaken as rapidly as possible. Representatives of the graphic arts, of the drama, and of history and the classics who are concerned with the arts have become participants. Indeed, the Concert Project, finding itself concerned with the effort of member colleges to make the degree granted at the end of four years' study the mark of a liberally educated person, has outgrown its skin. Under the second Carnegie Corporation grant for another three years, it has, for want of a better name, become known as the "Arts Program."

Under this new name further experiments include the circulation of workers connected not with colleges but with allied institutions. The Toledo Art Museum is glad to grant its Curator of Oriental Art a leave of absence to visit colleges, feeling that it is to such an extent thereby preventing the man from falling into a rut, as so many museum workers do.

The chief of the institutions which have caught this vision is the Library of Congress. Now, thanks to the insight and energy of the man who built it up through the years, Herbert Putnam, it has undertaken to grant leave of absence on full salary to as many of its Division Chiefs and Consultants as may wish to accept the unique proposal that they visit colleges. The Consultant in Comparative Literature of the Congressional Library, granted a leave for a year on full salary, and offered by the Arts Program on a regional tour, has been accepted by forty-six colleges. By this arrangement the riches of the potential fountainhead of national culture, "the peer in all respects of its great prototypes, the British Museum and the Bibliothèque Nationale"—to use the words of the American Council of Learned Societies—are brought by the Arts Program of the Association, through the human touch, to the member colleges.

Experiments are being made with artists' visits of longer duration—some for entire weeks. With one visitor the plan is for visits of three weeks on each campus. Thus the Program is heading directly towards a system of peripatetic professorships.

Such is the preoccupation with the arts as subjects of scholarship, that the Program has also experimented with the planting of artists in residence for a year at a time, a plan not new in a few alert institutions. These men, undertaking a mural decoration with the doors open and inviting student collaboration, are freed from official teaching duties, yet are actually teaching by the oldest of all methods—apprenticeship.

Whatever the lengths of their stay, be it from a half-week to three weeks, the Program is gradually gathering a list of suitable visitors. Few indeed have failed—almost all wish to repeat. By their influence the Program hopes in time to produce others.

There are now found on college campuses creative artists who are spreading the contagion of performance in vocal ensemble, instrumental music, and composition, in visual art work, graphic and plastic, in portrait, landscape, and mural painting, in etching, aquatinting, and photography. Artistic appreciation, performance, enjoyment, and creation are becoming more and more a part of the everyday life of college students.

This statement of the activities of what has become the Arts Program is offered as an illustration of the processes of cross fertilization which are superseding the old style encyclopedic lecturer from his elevated platform. The method is subject to great expansion and persistent experimentation. It is not easy. It requires humility on the part of the teacher. It demands a knowledge of the student as well as of the subject, and the art of bringing the two together. Its watchwords are cooperation, integration, socialization, understanding. It involves the newly discovered and the yet discover-able phases of concerted activity which are bound to appear in community of thinking and acting. It has been referred to in a previous chapter as a "method of orchestration."

Such things come not forth except with fasting and prayer. Perhaps this is what was meant by Robert S. Hillyer, newly chosen Boylston Professor of Rhetoric and Oratory at Harvard, following in the footsteps of John Quincy Adams, Adams Sherman Hill, LeBaron Russell Briggs, Charles Townsend Copeland, when he wrote in his "Letter to a Teacher of English, James B. Munn,"—

> That Chinese emperor who burned the books
> Succumbed to madness shrewder than it looks.
>
> . . . .
>
> The gift of Tongues without the Holy Ghost
> Becomes a Babel, not a Pentecost.

CHAPTER XXI

RELATIONSHIPS BETWEEN THE
COLLEGES AND THE CHURCHES

A QUARTER of a century ago a college senior, now the president of a nationally known university, was invited to attend a faculty meeting and interpret the student point of view on vital problems under consideration. After listening to some faculty speeches, he was impelled to observe: "Your thoughts are not my thoughts, neither are your ways my ways." The Founder of the Christian religion re-echoed this fundamental truth. He welcomed little children; he told a distinguished churchman and scholar, "Ye must be born again."

Recently many church communions sought to collaborate in the effort to discover their inherent principles of unity. Evidently they knew that between two persistent conceptions of religion a great gulf is fixed. Therefore they convened in two groups removed from each other not only in space but in time, one devoted to "Faith and Order," the other to "Life and Work." Thus were held the Ecumenical Conferences of Oxford and Edinburgh in 1937.

Two years later over 1700 picked young men and women from seventy-two nations gathered at Amsterdam for a ten-day conference. Two hundred and twenty separately organized religious groups and national churches were represented to consider "The Christian Community in the Modern World." They did not think that two separate conferences were necessary. They were willing, if they were able, to see religion whole. Of the seven sub-topics, the one entitled, "The Church: Its Nature and Function" drew a group triple the size of any other. The entire conference pledged allegiance to the church, even though disruptive forces among the churches were clearly recognized. These forces within the churches were dramatically exhibited when for the communion service the conference separated into four groups: Lutheran, Anglican, Orthodox, Dutch Reformed. Each group in succession participated in its service. "Others, or all, might observe; only selected ones might partake."

Some delegates recognized this merely as a series of educational exhibitions of a function of separate churches. Some were interested in the dramatic effect. Some recalled the persistent question, "If the church was founded by Christ, has it been confounded by men?" Many earnest people, young and old, are still seeking the basis of spiritual unity. How can two old institutions such as the church and the college, developed by men and women during the years, mediate in terms of children who are beginning to put away childish things?

There is probably not a liberal college in the United States which now considers its major objective to be the recruiting and training of clergymen. All colleges have a more comprehensive program. They recognize their obligation to serve the church, the state, and society in general, in innumerable ways. Liberal education cannot be held within a single channel of human experience. Colleges are devoted to the general welfare.

Generalizations do not usually apply with equal force to Catholic and Protestant colleges. The problem is considered first from the Protestant standpoint. The Catholic position and practice, often quite different, are then presented. The Jews have but one liberal college in the United States.

While most colleges related to the Protestant churches now have Departments of Religion or of Biblical Literature and extensive programs for assisting their own youth, very few undertake to offer even elective courses which interpret the peculiar doctrines of the denominations to which the colleges are related. They do not teach the creeds. The sectarian spirit has largely been eliminated. "Church-related colleges," a term which is applied for the present to those related to Protestant churches, attempt to teach religion as do also many not church-related. If they recognize that religion is to be taught both by precept and example, the members of the faculty must set the example. Many presidents of such colleges consider that faculty members must be chosen from among those who have a genuinely reverent attitude toward the things of the spirit. There are others who, in selecting suitable teachers, are not mindful of this consideration. Certainly specialized scholarship alone does not always tend toward the development of Christian graces.

There must be some members of the faculty who are able to lead in a scholarly interpretation of Biblical literature and other literature carrying a spiritual message. These interpretations, if scholarly and at the same time fruitful in the lives of students, will place emphasis upon what are generally considered the essentials of religion. There may be comparisons between the interpretations of one religious group and another, but these are chiefly set forth for purposes of illustration. The teacher is encouraged to express his own views in matters of doctrine, but is scarcely justified in exercising methods of propaganda for those views. In their religious views and decisions, students should be treated as in other areas of character building.

The colleges related to the Protestant churches make worthy contributions to the life of the churches. Many of them accept college graduates without extensive professional training as their pastors. While theological training is now segregated largely in seminaries—Catholic, Jewish, and Protestant—the majority of the Protestant candidates for church orders enrolled in the graduate seminaries, denominational and interdenominational, are drawn from the small, or at least the detached, church-related colleges. Some of the smaller denominations have never established seminaries. Their candidates for the ministry, if they seek further training, enroll in those under other denominational control or in non-denominational institutions.

These small colleges, therefore, are invaluable allies of the churches. They furnish them much of their human leadership. They not only contribute directly and indirectly a preaching ministry, but a ministry of teaching and of social service. Among these members of the ministry as thus broadly conceived are women as well as men. By no means all of them are ordained. Indeed, most of them serve as lay members of the churches.

There has been a remarkable transformation in most of the colleges in the personnel of administration. As has been pointed out in a previous chapter, most of the colleges were founded by home missionaries. The boards of trustees of these colleges and their faculties were identified with and chosen by the churches. Many of them were clergymen, as were nearly all of the presidents, including those of state-controlled institutions. While such organizational relationships have been changing for years, they have been accentuated within the present century. Dean Charles A. Baugher has recently furnished statistical evidence of these trends.* He shows that among Protestant institutions there has been a reduction in the number of trustees who are members of the related churches; in the number of clergymen on the boards of trustees, and in the number of faculty members who are affiliated with the churches to which the colleges are related; and that denominational characteristics in the religious activities of the colleges have decreased.

The leaders of these early colleges were not, for the most part, men of eminent scholarship. This was before the exodus of American students to Germany or the rise of excellent graduate schools on this side of the Atlantic. However, these early teachers had been educated in the schools of their day, and were quite at home in subjects taught in the colleges. They also had certain priceless possessions. They had the spirit of self-sacrifice, strength of character, loyalty to convictions, faith in ideals, devotion to a holy crusade. As President Donald J. Cowling has said, "The early teacher con-

* See References, p. 364.

tinues and always will continue to challenge the respect and admiration of all to whom character and ideals are a concern." It is easy to understand that with this type of personnel the early colleges were saturated with a spirit which in many colleges is lacking today. The old days with their daily chapel exercises, to indicate but one means of unified teaching, are not likely to return. Practically all of the students, whether voluntarily or through requirement, attended these exercises, which were attended regularly and led in turn by members of the faculty. Until the World War there were many such colleges in this country. Now, there are liberal colleges related to the churches in which the faculty is indistinguishable from the faculty of a state institution. Indeed, several of the state colleges are noted for the participation of faculty and students in all forms of religious activity.

The problem under consideration is complicated by the fact that an entirely new day has dawned in the matter of college enrollments. Within five years a change that is almost unbelievable has taken place. Of the million and a quarter students now attending our institutions of higher learning, more than half are enrolled in those which are publicly controlled. The scales were tipped in this direction about 1936 or 1937. Within the total enrollment of students in the colleges of nearly all of the denominations, a majority claim church membership in other denominations. This is not true of the students in Catholic or Southern Baptist colleges. The enrollment of students of all other denominations in most church-related colleges is larger than the enrollment from the homes of the sponsoring denomination. There are many cases in which the number of students affiliated with the sponsoring church is smaller than the number from other single denominations. The total number of students of a given denomination attending institutions of higher learning is often smaller in the institutions of the denomination than in other institutions. One major denomination reports that for every one of their own students in their own institutions there are four in other institutions. Speaking in general terms, neither the faculties nor the students have strong denominational consciousness. Very often there is not much religious consciousness. Interdenominational association among colleges has ceased to be a novelty. Such association has progressed much more rapidly than among the churches. The two types of institutions, again speaking generally, have become somewhat out of focus.

Perhaps the most marked change in the relationships between the colleges and the Protestant churches to which they are related has been in the sources of financial support. This change has been in the direction of sources other than the churches. Baugher's study shows that during the present century the percentage of annual operating income derived from contributions from individual congregations of the related churches has decreased as has also the income from denominational sources in comparison with non-denominational sources. At the same time, the percentage of annual operating income from alumni and from the local college community has increased. During the years from 1932 to 1937, while there was an increase of 79 per cent in our annual income as a nation, the contributions of twenty-five major communions and denominations decreased 21 per cent. The latter figure is not necessarily an accurate measure of the decrease in church appropriations to colleges, since the figure includes all church benevolences. Furthermore, contributions from alumni and the community include contributions from church members who are alumni or members of the community. In any event, many contributions have been made directly to the colleges instead of through the churches.

Many of the church-related colleges, however, have always depended upon contributions from individuals rather than upon apportionments made and collected by the churches. Such colleges have developed the practice not only of self-propulsion but of self-control. They have wished to be free from ecclesiastical as well as state interference. This has been particularly true of colleges having self-perpetuating boards of trustees.

When the colleges accustomed to financial aid directly from the churches found that such aid was becoming increasingly inadequate as an assurance of permanency to their work, they looked for financial support from other sources. Declining denominational apportionments, whatever the causes may be, tend to result in the surrender of such control as the denominations exercised. Not only are the boards of trustees becoming less insistent upon methods of maintaining denominational flavor in all the work of the colleges, but ecclesiastical agencies are less disposed to attempt to guide the policies of the institution into denominational channels. In the charters of many church-related institutions the provision is still to be found for the appointment by the church of a board of visitors in which is lodged the power to determine appointments to the faculties and the subject matter of the courses of study. These boards today have generally ceased to exercise their constitutional rights.

The full significance of such changes as these does not emerge from their mere enumeration. For a fuller understanding, the problem must be viewed genetically. A background must be held in mind of changes which have taken place within the churches, within the colleges, and within our national life and the life of the world.

For the first 250 years the task was relatively simple in most of the colleges. All of them were small, homogeneous in membership, denominational. Some of them were so sectarian in spirit that the tendency has been to attach the sectarian label to practically all of them. The decision of the Carnegie Foundation for the Advancement of Teaching, which was made soon after the beginning of the present century, that teachers in colleges under denominational control would not be eligible to become beneficiaries of its retirement pensions, had a profound influence on many colleges. Certain tests of denominationalism were announced by the Foundation in terms of which eligibility would be determined.

In the first list of fifty-two institutions whose teachers received allowances are found the names of fifteen institutions which had been founded through the influence of members of Congregational churches. These colleges were selected by the Foundation because of their historical and consistent lack of the sectarian spirit. From the beginning, they had adopted the policy of self-perpetuating boards of trustees. More than forty foundations have been laid by the Congregationalists upon which outstanding superstructures have been reared. In aggregate endowments, in personal and material equipment, in sound educational programs, and in academic prestige, this group is unsurpassed. Some of these colleges have made and are making distinctive contributions to minority groups—racial and social. Among the graduates of these colleges, as well as among the leaders of the churches to which they have been loosely related, have arisen many prophets and apostles of the interdenominational spirit.

There were a few colleges admitted to the Carnegie list which had historical or other affiliations with the Presbyterians, Methodists, Episcopalians, Baptists, Friends, and Unitarians. Some colleges immediately set about changing their charter requirements so that their teachers would be eligible to pension awards. One group in particular whose church had always officially opposed self-perpetuating boards of trustees, at that time with the approval of the highest judicatory body of the church, became aggressive in making the necessary methods of adjustment.

The original pension plan of the Foundation was later abandoned for reasons not pertinent to this discussion, and members of all colleges in good standing are now admitted on a contributory basis to the benefits of the insurance and annuity funds transferred by the Carnegie Corporation to an independent agency—The Teachers Insurance and Annuity Association of America.

It was not until after the organization of the Council of Church Boards of Education, several years later, that the United States Bureau of Education, upon the Council's representations, discarded the custom of listing in its annual reports all denominational colleges as "sectarian" institutions. It is now generally recognized by Protestant leaders of Christian education that there is no necessary relationship between the religious nurture of students and the official— that is, the legal—relationship of the college and the church. For a college to manifest the religious spirit, it is not required that it be church-controlled. The currents of spiritual life run deeper than this. However, the stimulus of church concern and motive power is likely to be of great assistance to officers perplexed with many phases of administration. The church-related colleges need have no inhibition in teaching religion. This is not true of some publicly controlled institutions.

In all due fairness, it must be pointed out that from the beginning of our educational history there have been times and places when the religious life on the campus was at a very low status. It is true also that even as far back as the colonial colleges, some institutions were measurably free from sectarian influences. Brown University is a notable example of this tolerant spirit. The old charter of that institution, still operative, provides that the board of control shall be made up of representatives of different denominations, and that students may be drawn from the four groups— "Protestants, Catholics, Jews, and Quakers"!

As the years went on, something happened in many colleges here and elsewhere. The students began to take matters into their own hands. The Christian student societies have operated within the colleges for 200 years. Methodism was an outgrowth of "an association of godly young men at Oxford in 1729." A strong impulse toward the religious life sprang up in American colleges among the students themselves. They did not look for guidance either to the colleges or the churches. Some of them started out along new paths.

The famous "haystack prayer-meeting" at Williams College, with five students present, launched what has become the foreign mission movement of the American Protestant churches. Under the active and persuasive influence of Dwight L. Moody and others, the interdenominational lay movement spread across the continent. This new force in the religious life of the people was accentuated by the founding of the Christian Endeavor Society and other youth centered organizations. Millions of young people espoused the Christian life and became identified with these movements.

The Young Men's and the Young Women's Christian Associations, to a large degree, assumed the leadership in this work in the colleges and the universities. The first Young Men's Christian Associations were founded at the University of Michigan and the University of Virginia in 1858-59. These Associations became very efficient instruments of the religious life of students of both sexes. They had extensive programs, carried out through local and intercollegiate organizations, far-flung missionary and international connections, all supervised by highly trained traveling secretaries. Church officials and college officers in all types of institutions generally received these workers gladly. It may be that because of the effectiveness of the Association workers, the sense of responsibility of the church and college officials in these fields was somewhat weakened. In any event, many students were disposed to look for leadership in their religious life to workers without official relationship either to the colleges or the churches. Under this leadership the religious life of the colleges became very largely student-centered rather than church-centered or college-centered. The religious nurture of college students was getting out of the hands of the churches. Clarence P. Shedd, who, under the title, *The Church Follows the Student,* has written in detail the thrilling story of all these developments, quotes a no less distinguished churchman than Joseph Wilson Cochran, a Presbyterian Church Board Secretary, as having said, "The World's Student Union (World's Student Christian Federation) is the most powerful organization of college men in existence."

At this time the churches were not prepared to follow their youth as each nation now attempts to follow its citizens into foreign lands. Historically, the Catholics as a group first realized the significance of the new issue. One of the earliest Catholic clubs to minister to Catholic students was formed at Wisconsin in 1880. Within the next decade similar clubs were organized at Yale, Harvard, and Michigan. The first Newman Club was formed at Pennsylvania in 1893, and later Pope Pius X issued an Encyclical which gave impetus to the teaching of religion at secular institutions. This was a document fraught with great possibilities and responsibilities not only in Catholic but in all other church circles. Today there are 262 such Catholic clubs in the United States.

Each church preferred to educate its own children in its own schools. Every church found that this was a dream which could not come true. Among the Protestant denominations the students and local church leaders began to organize student guilds and provide special equipment for church work with students. Under their influence various types of centers for Episcopalian, Presbyterian, and Methodist students were organized at Michigan, Illinois, Texas, and Colorado before the end of the century. Many forms of experimentation followed during the first decade of the twentieth century. Before the decade had elapsed the Presbyterian Church in the United States of America had formally accepted the challenge to follow its students into the universities. Other Protestant churches adopted the same policy.

For the detailed story of the belated effort of the churches to occupy what was being called the "most important home mission field"—the universities and the colleges—the reader is referred to Shedd's book. Most of the larger denominations began to develop and to employ specialized workers in the universities. The Episcopal, and to some extent the Lutheran, Church adopted the general policy of working through the local clergymen; the Disciples established chairs of religion on the ground that this gave to the workers academic standing; the Methodists developed the Wesley Foundations, and at the University of North Dakota, Wesley College. Other churches—the Catholics, the Jews, the Congregationalists, the Presbyterians, the Baptists, and the Disciples—also adopted the foundation plan and established foundation centers at the universities. Most of the churches relied chiefly upon university pastors. No denomination, however, adhered strictly to one type of leader. The university pastors multiplied rapidly in nearly all of the denominations. University Pastors' Associations were formed and the denominational workers and Christian Association secretaries soon entered upon cooperative work in the fellowship of a great cause. The Association of Church Workers in State Universities became the Conference of Church Workers in Universities and Colleges of the United States which functions today.

In 1912 the men devoting themselves exclusively to the religious interests of state universities totaled twenty-six, the Presbyterians having ten, the others representing the Disciples, Methodists, Episcopalians, Baptists and Congregationalists. Within three years thereafter the total had reached 128. The churches were professionalizing their student leadership. In 1911 the Council of Church Boards of Education was organized and began its work along the two lines of developing all forms of cooperation among the church-related colleges and in the area of the religious development of the students and faculties in tax-supported and independent universities. Two types of workers, therefore, were occupying the field which previously had been occupied exclusively by the local secretaries and the national and regional traveling secretaries of the student Young Men's Christian Association, Young Women's Christian Association, and the World's Student Federation. The peak of appropriations by the denominations for this rapidly enlarging work was reached between 1925 and 1930. After a few years of recession until 1935, a steady upswing has been apparent. Dur-

ing the years, the Jews, the Mormons, the Christian Scientists
and the Unitarians have come into the picture. At several
universities, notably Pennsylvania, Cornell, Illinois, Iowa,
the University of California at Los Angeles, some form of
inter-faith cooperation has been established.

At several colleges and universities a movement for the
centralizing of responsibility through official leadership provided by the institution has developed. Illustrations of this
trend are the deans of chapel at Princeton, Chicago, and
Syracuse; chaplains at Yale, Pennsylvania, and Smith; and
directors of religious life and activities at Columbia, Miami,
Northwestern, the Woman's College of the University of
North Carolina; counselors in religious education at Michigan.

Cooperative pastorates—one man serving the students of
two or more denominations—have developed at Massachusetts State College, New Hampshire, Vermont, Maine, and
Alfred Universities. In 1938 more than 200 men and women
were devoting from three-fourths to full time as denominational and university pastors.

Thus it appears that college students were given the opportunity to follow various types of leadership. There were
successively the clergymen connected with the colleges, the
leaders produced through the awakening of the laymen, the
specialized representatives of the Christian Associations, the
pastors of local churches in the independent and publicly
controlled university centers, the university pastors in the
universities, and church board secretaries who, in the larger
denominations, devoted their efforts chiefly to the students
in the church-related institutions. There was undoubtedly
some rivalry among these groups. The center of gravity of
leadership shifted from time to time to and from the campuses, to and from the local college churches, the laymen's
organizations, the Christian Associations, the church board
secretaries, student-pastors, deans of chapels, and other types
of workers. During all this time, within the institutions
themselves certain faculty members, without regard to de-

nominational affiliations or to the subjects they taught, were exercising profound influence among appreciative students. In a word, many other agencies besides the churches were contributing to the religious life and growth of American college students. The last few years since the student departments of the Christian Associations have ceased to function so effectively, the various denominations have developed Youth Programs adapted to what are believed to be the needs of all the youth of the church regardless of academic considerations.

In the midst of these various fluctuations of leadership, many of them frankly experimental, two definite trends may be noted: the trend toward student-centered religious activity, and the trend toward that which is church-centered. The Episcopalians, United Lutherans, Southern Baptists, and Presbyterians in the United States (South) magnify the importance of the local parish church; they attempt to develop church-centered student work. Another group, which has the largest total enrollment and employs three-fourths of the university pastors, is developing student-centered church work. This policy is illustrated by the Congregationalists, Northern Baptists, Methodists, Presbyterians in the United States of America, and Disciples. No church adheres exclusively to one point of view, however. It is the old conflict between institutionalism with its cramping tendencies and individualism with the possible loss of social insights. Enlightened leaders in all churches would hold the balance between the two.

The Catholic college situation offers a number of contrasts to the foregoing statement. It has already been pointed out that the Catholics were first to follow their students into universities not under their control, and that a majority of students in Catholic colleges are Catholics. Some Catholic bishops and many members of the teaching orders are participating in cooperative educational efforts. A few Catholic colleges are choosing teachers and even members of their boards who are not members of the Church. There is a dis-

position on the part of some of these colleges to make superficial modifications in their programs that they may conform
to the requirements of accrediting agencies.

The Catholic colleges, with the exception of eleven Dioc-
esan colleges, have never been under ecclesiastical control to
any great extent, as is popularly supposed. For the most part
they are administered by the teaching Orders of the Church,
not by the Hierarchy. The control, therefore, is internal
rather than external. Needless to say, the members of the
teaching Orders who comprise, as it were autonomous and
independent units within the Church at large, who obtain
their living from their Order to whose resources they directly
contribute by their labors, are loyal to Catholic faith and
practice. The responsibility for developing educational programs lies chiefly on their shoulders. This situation has not
changed from the beginning of Catholic higher education in
this country. In the case of the colleges of the Religious
Orders, there is no direct financial support from the Church
as such.

There is a basic philosophy which underlies all Catholic
education, consequently, Catholic higher education. This
basic philosophy may be summed up in the words of the
Encyclical on the Christian Education of Youth, by Pope
Pius XI:

> Since education consists essentially in preparing man for
> what he must be and what he must do here below in order
> to attain the sublime end for which he was created, it is
> clear that there can be no true education which is not
> wholly directed to man's last end, and that in the present
> order of Providence, since God has revealed Himself to us
> in the person of His only begotten Son, Who alone is "The
> Way, the Truth, and the Life," there can be no ideally
> perfect education which is not Christian education.

This statement expresses the motivating influence of Catholic higher education in this country. There has been no
change in this underlying philosophy down through the
years. Although Catholic colleges make no distinction of

creed in admittance, because of this basic philosophy, naturally the enrollment will be predominantly made up of adherents to the Catholic Church. The faculty, likewise, will be predominantly Catholic, and the whole environment and atmosphere will be Catholic. A distinctive practice follows a distinctive philosophy.

It is apparent that there has been no Protestant group which has seen the problem of the Christian education of college students steadily or seen it whole. Evidently the churches from which eventually leadership must come are not yet prepared either on the basis of knowledge or of mutual sympathy for such a comprehensive synthesis. The task itself is certainly sufficiently colossal to justify community of effort.

The first steps in this direction are now being taken in many denominations and by certain interfaith groups. There has never been a time when the churches were so keenly aware of the spiritual potentialities of their young people. By many of the churches efforts are being made on a national scale through the restudy of their own resources and obligations, by means of surveys and conferences, to envisage their potential as well as their actual contribution to their own membership, young and old, and to the unified ideal.

Space forbids even the mention of the specific efforts of the several denominations to discover the basis of a philosophy of higher education. Methodists or Presbyterians or Baptists would not proclaim a Methodist or a Presbyterian or a Baptist "philosophy of education." Such a philosophy must be more inclusive than denominational considerations. It would certainly include the elements that were manifested in the life and teaching of the Founder of the Christian religion. Christ broke down the wall which had been built around the Jews. He has a message for humanity. If progress toward a unity which comprehends religion and education, the individual and society, and their several organs of expression—the family, the church, the school, the state— seems slow, some ground for hope may be discovered by comparing present practice with the practice of the past. The reader is referred to the chapter on "Propagating the Species."

In view of the recent coming together of various branches of the Methodist Church, it is well to note a specific unifying influence which has been long operating within that group.

For many years at Boston University Borden P. Bowne taught large classes of students, drawn chiefly from the School of Theology. These young men became in considerable numbers the bishops, the presidents of the theological seminaries, the presidents of the colleges of the Methodist Episcopal Church, and the teachers of philosophy in Methodist and other institutions. Many of them were distinguished leaders in the Congregational and other churches. There is evidence to show that directly and indirectly his theistic philosophy was one of the influences which made possible the transition to a more liberal faith among the Protestant churches. Bowne made a remarkable contribution to the solidarity and cohesiveness of Methodism. Largely through his influence Methodism has steered clear of extreme leftist and extreme rightist thought and practice.

According to the late Chancellor E. N. MacCracken, Bowne taught that—

Theism is the fundamental postulate of our total life.

It is as legitimate to speak of an eternal intelligence as of an eternal energy.

The Power at work in the world is an intelligent Power.

This is a universe in which there is not only power, intelligence, life—but we are able to recognize that there is also feeling.

Power is known by its manifestations. Power manifested in the whole universe cannot be described as unknowable.

Men constitute a unit of independent, self-guided, rational beings held together by an inward motive and bound by bonds which are moral and spiritual.

Our interest at the moment is not so much in the ultimate validity of the details of Bowne's metaphysics, as in the fact that the leaders of Methodism for some generations have been profoundly influenced by a great teacher. They have been impelled by unifying aims. The lesson is worthy of imitation.

Now, the leaders of many of the churches are seeking unity as never before. They are less disposed to veer either to the left or the right in their theological interpretations, and in their conceptions of the essentials of religion. They preach a living God, here and now; the radiance of the Christian life; the destructive nature of sin; the power of individual and social redemption; the Fatherhood of God and the brotherhood of man. They are less inclined to try to climb into the Kingdom by some other way. They seek to retain or to regain the religion of youth.

What is most heartening of all, students in the schools and colleges in larger numbers than in the recent past are seeking the meaning of the ultimate issues of life. According to Gould Wickey, more than 88 per cent of college students now express a definite religious preference. In the church-related colleges 94 per cent claim church affiliation. At the state and municipal colleges, 85 per cent express church preference. Here is an unprecedented challenge to the colleges and to the churches. The time is ripe for wise, courageous, and tolerant leadership, a leadership which to be most effective must be buttressed by active interest and moral support on the part of the teachers in the colleges and the communicants in the churches. The outcome of this issue will determine very largely the character of our social order as the new generation assumes its place and responsibilities.

Is it possible that church and chapel attendance, and large mass meetings; that creeds and sermons setting forth man-made theologies; that particular ecclesiastical forms and orders have been relatively over-weighted? May these things be done and weightier matters be left undone? May the gnat be strained out and the camel be swallowed?

Jesus Christ placed the highest value on the human individual. He offered to remove fetters and set humanity
free, without regard to sex or color, or possessions, or rank,
or race. He extolled the value of peace on earth and good
will among men. He commanded his disciples when they
prayed to enter into their chambers and pray to the Father
who is in secret. He led them into the fields and taught
them to consider the lilies, how they grow. He set before
them marriage as a way of life. He promised them that they
should know the mysteries of a larger human brotherhood—
the Kingdom of Heaven.

Now these vital processes are being recognized as applicable not only in religion and education but in science and
democracy. If these are the weightier matters of the law,
then the colleges and the churches are not so far apart as
might appear when measured in terms of traditional standards. The leaven is at work in all four of the areas just
named.

CHAPTER XXII

RELATIONSHIPS BETWEEN THE COLLEGES AND THE STATE

THE principle of the separation of church and state is now quite clearly defined for all practical purposes. It is true that the state is taking over some of the functions formerly exercised by the church. The church, on the other hand, strives to serve the cause of good government, at times by supporting the policies of the state, and again by criticizing its policies, when those policies are not in its judgment well conceived from the standpoint of religious and ethical standards. The political organization in this country does not provide for a formal "opposition," as is the case in the parliamentary system of England. The church, the college, and other agencies of our culture, sometimes corporately, more often through the influence of individuals, serve this very worthy purpose.

The principle of separation of school and state is not so clearly defined. It is usually conceded that the public welfare is best served by a dual system of schools, one politically controlled, the other controlled through private organization. A very recent development recognizes the fact that both these types of schools are public schools, in that they are all supported by the public and all strive to serve the public. All these schools are finally a charge upon the financial resources of the people. The government, as well as the people, is now frequently though not consistently recognizing this distinction.

By common consent the state is assigned one fundamental responsibility with reference to all the schools and colleges.

It has the power to grant charters to the institutions. In practice it has exercised this power with greater generosity than wisdom. It has usually failed to take steps to assure to the people a superior quality of higher education, not to make a wider generalization, as the number of inadequately supported institutions bear witness. The state may be buttressed by the unthinking generosity of a people who possess a noble though sometimes blind devotion to anything called "education." The state may proceed on the prospect of power and patronage. It may be encouraged by the persuasive influence of great and good men who are achieving distinguished success in other situations. It may neglect to descend to such particulars as a proper distribution of institutions or of their adjustment to the actual needs of the people. Often publicly controlled colleges have been located through political log-rolling, and those under private control have been chartered without due consideration to field, constituency, or actual or potential resources.

Today there are some fifty privately controlled colleges in Pennsylvania, many of them on firm foundations, which produce thousands of candidates for teaching positions. In addition, the state supports thirteen teachers colleges. This is a new name for what historically have been normal schools—a type of institution rapidly vanishing from the picture. The Federal Government is now expending some fifteen million dollars for additional buildings in these thirteen teachers colleges and the state college. This gives to these institutions a new birth. It is in effect a new charter. The Federal Government is in this way accentuating a vast overproduction of prospective teachers. The young people who fail to secure positions because of this overproduction are the innocent victims. All teachers in the state are poorly paid. In the meantime the whole theory of teacher preparation is being challenged, and stubborn efforts are being made by highly competent and patriotic educators to develop adequate plans for meeting the needs of the profession.

The state is not entirely responsible for such situations.

It is in part due to the inadequate preparation of public officials for the high-grade service that such situations require.
In part it is an outgrowth of the dual system. In any event,
there has not been an intelligent and unified plan of procedure. The observation of Socrates has been forgotten:
"The unexamined life is no life at all." Quite recently steps
are being taken in some of the states to secure data in terms
of which at least some waste may be avoided and upon which
a reasonably unified system of higher education may be established, without interfering with the dual system of organization. Techniques are being developed for the attainment of
such a desirable end. Nine states, including Hawaii, are
now engaged in educational policy making—Florida, Idaho,
Kansas, Michigan, Minnesota, Nebraska, New Mexico, New
York. The successful issue requires the spirit of cooperation
among citizens primarily devoted to the public welfare. The
Regents' Inquiry into the Character and Cost of Public Education in New York recommends that the state "rely on the
. . . scholarship system, not on the Western state university
system, make grants to existing institutions, appropriate
no state funds for the establishment of any statewide system
of junior colleges or of a state university, and authorize no
city, county, or other area to set up any liberal arts college."
The Regents are attempting to set limits to the state's power
to grant charters. In other words, without endorsing all of
the particular steps recommended, it is at present noted that
the Regents are wrestling with their problem realistically and
in behalf of existing institutions. These are believed, with
proper adaptations and under proper guidance, to be competent to meet the needs of the state. In other states legislatures are frequently guided by their state boards of education
in formulating policies. Such policies, however, usually involve only state controlled institutions. What is required is
that a regularly constituted agency, or one created for the
specific purpose, view the problems involved comprehensively, with all important interests properly represented.

The power and interest of the state in the universities and

colleges are manifested in other ways than the mere granting of charters. All non-profit institutions of learning are classified by the state under the general head of charitable agencies. The nation—the people—subscribe to this classification. As with churches and hospitals, their property, in so far as it is used for benevolent purposes and not for profit, has been exempt from the ordinary forms of taxation. Contributions to these institutions up to 15 per cent of net income are deductible in computing federal income taxes. The government, whether federal, state, or local, relieves them of unnecessary burdens that their altruistic work may prosper. Governments and people approve the purposes of education, elementary and higher, to discover, develop, and integrate various forms of native excellencies. The colleges and universities are recognized in this larger sense as essentially service institutions. As such, the people have made education our biggest business. Thus would the state help to preserve our most valuable natural resources.

When recently the Federal Government, through the National Youth Administration, adopted the plan of making grants to college students to assist them in continuing their educational preparation, no discrimination was made between politically controlled and privately controlled institutions. In practice, more grants went to students attending privately controlled colleges. In 1937-38, for example, grants went to students in 618 publicly controlled institutions and to students in 1038 institutions under private control. This may be contrasted with the grants by the Works Progress Administration to 662 colleges and universities all under public control, for the expansion of their plants.

Again, when the Social Security bill was passed by Congress, all charitable institutions were placed on the exempted list. This was done not because the workers in these institutions were ignored, but to relieve such institutions from embarrassment as they develop their own systems of security. Indeed, the rejection later by the Congress of the proposal to extend the application of the bill to charitable institutions was an important factor in preserving the cherished tradition of freedom and independence of such institutions. This rejection was all the more praiseworthy, since many colleges joined in the hue and cry for federal funds even though it involved present expenditure on their part.

During the years in which the colleges have been particularly vigilant to improve their service to American youth and to discover and eliminate evil trends, the endowed universities have possessed themselves in a pleasant complacency. They have centered their efforts usually upon their graduate schools and have set them up as the test of university excellence. Upon the basis of the graduate schools, membership in the Association of American Universities has been determined. The graduate schools have extolled scholarship, particularly as manifested in the process and the product of research. Their proudest achievement has been in their lengthening processions of Doctors of Philosophy. While most of these Doctors have looked forward to teaching positions, their education has been as researchers. The graduate schools, with rare and notable exceptions, have resisted the call for any form of teacher preparation. They have looked patronizingly upon the struggles of the schools of education to gain status, but they have ignored their objectives. Although a thousand colleges of many standards of excellence were conferring the baccalaureate degree, the holder of that degree from any college was admitted to membership in the graduate school. Although the requirement that candidates for the doctorate be able to read German and French was made before the United States offered graduate work, and long before German universities were impoverished by regimentation and by the elimination of vast numbers of distinguished scholars, the requirement remains and its enforcement is often a notorious farce. Many such examinations mean little or nothing. Certain undergraduate colleges secure better facility in reading German and French from their honors students than do most graduate schools, because they require it as a prerequisite of admission to honors standing.

The examinations themselves as ordinarily conducted are tests of memory or in other particulars fail of their purpose. Relatively few Doctors of Philosophy are competent to carry on research of a high order. Germany, France and England continue to lead in the number of Nobel awards. Fewer still are able to write theses which demonstrate capacity for clear and precise expression, much less mastery of form and style, as in the French university.

In the meantime the state universities have forged forward. Their power to attract students has been greater than that of the endowed universities, their salaries have been increased, millions of money have been expended through federal aid lavishly given for campus and building improvements; the sense of possession on the part of the people has been vitalized. In many cases connections have been made throughout the state between the university and the daily life of the citizens. A pervasive expectancy of favors yet to come has been aroused.

The full extent of federal activities in education has been outlined in a book of 151 pages by the Educational Policies Commission of the National Education Association of the United States and the American Association of School Administrators.*

While the depression has been stopping the material expansion of the endowed universities, it has been giving to the state universities, with the help of the Federal Government, the means of rebuilding their physical superstructures. At the same time certain new criteria to guide educational procedure have been handed down by the United States Supreme Court. In the case of Allen *vs.* Regents of the State University of Georgia, concerned with the tax on tickets to athletic contests, the Court declared: "When a state embarks in a business which would normally be taxable, the fact that in doing so it is exercising a governmental power does not render it immune from federal taxation."

"Three major conceptions," Alexander Brody points out.

* See References, p. 365.

"emerge from this decision: first, the United States Supreme Court will continue to apply the governmental-proprietary test to educational activities undertaken by a state university, at least for purposes of taxation; second, educational functions undertaken by a state do not *ipso facto* become tax immune; third, the federal tax will not be held invalid although it may directly burden the state or its university."

In a case involving the refusal of the University of Missouri to admit a Negro to its law school, the Court held that this was "a denial of equal protection of the laws." This decision was made in spite of a legislative declaration of purpose to establish a separate law school for Negroes, not yet fulfilled and in spite of a statute which provides for the payment by the state of tuition for attendance at a law school in another state. "The basic consideration . . . is as to what opportunity Missouri itself provides for white students or denies to Negroes."

Such grandeur of achievement as the state institutions have experienced has its abuses as well as uses. Fanatical devotion and lavish expenditure invite political intrigue. The picture of the state universities is not all rosy. The inevitable desire to control follows the gifts of the government.

There has been much criticism of the loose manner in which work projects have been assigned both to college students on National Youth Administration appointments and to the young men enrolled in the Civilian Conservation Corps camps. It is generally agreed that there have been many abuses and much waste. "Research work," to select one from many types of projects carried on under the auspices of the student aid program, for the Public Works Administration, the Civil Works Administration, and the Works Progress Administration, has often resulted in the degeneration of research in the public opinion. May we give the floor to some state university presidents? The late Lotus D. Coffman, President of the University of Minnesota, in 1936, raised his voice in alarm:

I have observed with no little anxiety the continued and increasing pressure of the Federal Government to dictate the educational program of the country. . . . Every school superintendent knows that during the last three years there have been at times as many as three, and sometimes more, federal officers seeking jurisdiction over some of the youth of his community. In setting up the National Youth Administration the educational officers, federal, state, and local, were ignored; authority was centralized in the hands of persons inexperienced for the most part in educational work; there was a duplication of agencies, federal and state, with attendant expense and machinery. . . . It would be an easy step from this to a situation where the materials of instruction were suggested and then required from Washington.

A year later Alexander G. Ruthven, President of the University of Michigan, sounded the same warning:

The present position of most tax-supported colleges and universities is a striking illustration of the recent tendency of faculties and administrators to barter freedom for financial considerations. . . . For many years it has been the aim of those desirous of improving the educational opportunities of their citizens to protect these schools from their most imminent danger—partisan political influences. But while it has been the dream of educators to see state-supported colleges and universities safe from party and faction, and faculties and administrators of state schools continue to give lip service to this ideal, according to a recent report, in only six of these schools do the governing boards now occupy a position of independence in regard to the powers of state executive officials and agencies.

Furthermore, most of the state colleges now receive their support by direct legislative appropriation. With increasing frequency also they are accepting bills carrying riders which dictate details of operation. In a number of states the governor appoints the trustees and in some he is ex officio member of the governing body.

The evil results of these and other administrative procedures which make the institutions subservient to political influences are all too apparent and need not be illustrated by examples. Suffice it to say, more than ever before faculty members are compelled to live in apprehension of dismissal,

administrators are handicapped in directing the growth of
their schools, and selfish interests and non-educational
agencies are modifying the curriculum and directing staff
appointments and activities. To make matters worse, in
order to escape in some measure from state control and to
secure additional cash, some administrators, educational
politicians, and professors themselves are now apparently
ready further to strangle state-supported education by seeking, and, indeed, by engaging in unseemly struggles for,
federal subsidies.

The practice of creating federal subsidies for state schools
is increasing. . . . It scarcely seems possible that educators
can be so heedless or myopic as to be unable to discern the
evil consequences of these subsidies. Federal grants, unless
carefully made, mean competition between institutions, continuing struggles for ever greater support of the same kind,
the gradual assumption of the power to dictate operations
by small bureaucrats, and ultimately political domination.

The basis of such fears has been set forth statistically by
John H. McNeely of the United States Office of Education.
McNeely shows that almost every phase of the internal management and administration of state institutions is included
among the powers conferred in one state or another on the
officials and agencies of the state. Specifically these are:

Budgetary and financial affairs, 47 states; prescription of
accounting system, 42; acquisition, disposal, or inventory of
property, 40; printing and binding, 38; investigation of management, administration, and operation, 31; purchase of supplies, materials, and equipment, 30; publication of bulletins,
pamphlets, and reports, 21; construction and alteration of
buildings, 20; investment of permanent funds, 17; staff and
faculty personnel matters, 13; travel of staff members, 13;
insurance on buildings, 7; educational and academic program, 1.

In one state, Virginia, the Governor possesses power over
the educational and academic program itself, being given
the authority of prior approval before the governing boards
are permitted to introduce any new or additional courses
of study at the institutions. This power applies to all the
state institutions of higher education in Virginia.

Such data seem to justify the question, "For what purpose is the endless stream of questionnaires from federal and state authorities for information concerning higher institutions?"

The endowed universities recognize that they face a new and difficult situation. Relatively speaking, they have lost prestige. Some of them have been forced to draw upon financial reserves, although quite recently Harvard, Northwestern, and Chicago have had many millions added to their endowments. On the other hand, there is much to be said in their behalf. They are virtually free both from state and ecclesiastical control. They are, in this respect, preserving the American tradition. They develop their own policies and programs. Their trustees are becoming better equipped for their responsibilities. These trustees are less disposed to interfere with educational programs. These universities are more experienced in the processes and attitudes of research. They are free to limit enrollment that they may conform to self-imposed educational standards, as well as to material and personal equipment. They are free to indulge in experimentation. They aspire to be better if not larger. They count it a privilege to minister to a more limited group. They depend less than formerly upon their prestige. Following the example of the colleges, they are beginning the process of perpetual self-examination. Their obligation to their students and to society is being clarified. Their policies for the future are not so complex as are those of the state institutions, since they do not so fully face the question whether apparent gains made during the depression may eventuate in less desirable ends. President Dodds has summed up the situation thus:

> It is my honest conviction that we have in this sense of ownership (by donors to private institutions) a foundation on which to build, stronger and more conducive to the purposes we profess than any system of national tax support could provide; and so delicate as to be easily destroyed if we permit a Washington overlord to be set up over us, as we probably shall if we turn for financial help to Uncle Sam, who after all is not as rich as many seem to think.

The American plan requires that education be controlled as well as supported by the people through their understanding and sympathetic representatives. The fundamental principle for given situations is local control. In the light of this principle the method of choosing these representatives is of secondary importance. Such representatives are found on multitudes of managerial boards in both publicly and privately controlled institutions and systems. This is the theory behind the organization of America's thousands of boards of education, often composed for the most part of laymen. It is democratic and on the whole it is amazingly satisfactory. The principle of local control in many areas of American education is being supplanted by the principle of centralization. This is particularly true among tax-supported institutions. Theoretically these forms of centralization have great value. Under such pressure the little red schoolhouses have given way to fewer and better equipped consolidated schools. To some extent forms of centralization of control have been applied in the development of state systems of higher education, as in Montana, Georgia, Oregon. Such forms of control afford opportunities for economies and also offer greater temptations to self-seeking politicians. The temptations may or may not be resisted. These forms should result in a higher type of administration.

With the mounting debts of the Federal Government and the states, many encroachments are being made upon what the colleges have rightly or wrongly held to be their reserved areas of freedom. Government authorities are less generous than formerly in the matter of taxation. In their search for new sources of revenue they are exploring the twilight zone between education and government. Numerous cities in which colleges or universities are located are seeking out college property not used for educational purposes. In the judgment of the institutions they are also encroaching on definitely educational values. Municipal governments complain that the presence of so much college property, which must be provided with the usual public improvements and upkeep, makes too heavy a drain upon civic administration. In some instances there has been heated controversy over this question. The antagonism between the town and the gown has been revived, as each has stoutly set forth its grievances. A university in one small city has voluntarily made monetary contributions to civic government. Colleges and universities today cannot, as in medieval times, readily pull up stakes and move to another location.

In several instances the demand for revenue from the colleges has become state wide. Bills have been introduced in the legislatures which if enacted would not only impose heavy burdens on the institutions of higher learning but would in some instances imperil their existence. There has been a purpose to tax intangible values.

The most serious interference with the work and the freedom, particularly of privately controlled institutions, comes by way of the paralyzing taxes on corporations, with which much of their permanent funds—estimated at something like $2,000,000,000 in value—is invested. Add to this the confiscatory taxes on private wealth and income and the long continued business depression, and it is easily understood that such institutions have some basis for the fear that their surplus wealth may also be appropriated by the state and the federal governments. The situation is all the more critical since funds from privately controlled colleges taken by confiscatory taxes are used in part to found and enlarge duplicating and competing institutions under political control. In view of such considerations most institutions under private control decline to sell for a mess of pottage the right to say how they shall be run. The publicly controlled institutions, through necessity as well as inclination, have their ears to the ground. They have a sensitive awareness to the complicated changes now operative in our social life. They are taking a comprehensive view of educational problems—elementary, secondary, and higher. They strive to adjust their programs to the changing needs in each of these areas. They are attempting to make education socially effective.

Since the beginning of this century there has been a slow-ing down of population growth. The restriction of immi-gration and a declining birth rate tend toward stabilization or decline in population. Family limitations are more com-mon among urban than rural groups. Within a hundred years the average age of population has risen from seventeen to twenty-seven. The number of children is decreasing, the number of adults is increasing. The rates of increase and decrease favor the rural communities. From certain sections there has been an exodus of adults with a corresponding in-crease of adults in other sections. Technological changes, soil erosion, drought, have reduced the numbers of our citi-zens who are engaged in extractive occupations in certain sections.

The automobile is helping to determine educational poli-cies. It has created 6,000,000 jobs. With the aid of rural electrification and the movement toward decentralization of industry, it is making rural life more attractive. All such widening differences are recorded in elementary and second-ary school attendance. There are signs that they are begin-ning to affect college attendance even though the colleges have more distant educational ends in view. The publicly controlled institutions have a keen awareness of all these changes and are preparing to provide for them.

It was the rural communities which originated and demon-strated the effectiveness of our democratic policies of educa-tion. Once more, if adequate financial administration can be assured, the rural communities are coming into their own.

These trends cannot be met successfully if the mistake is made of separating our work and our culture. Nor can they be met if our family life and our educational life are sepa-rated. These are dangers which face the colleges. Some of the colleges for women are alert in meeting these problems. They see clearly the necessity of social service programs which tend to unify the family, the home, and the school.

Nor can these trends be met if public control means politi-cal control. It is against this danger and practice that state university heads have protested so vigorously. It is against this that the Educational Policies Commission has declared that educational authorities need a wide range of freedom in determining and carrying out policies for the schools. The Commission declares, "Schools should be protected against sporadic raids by those who are not responsible."

The national correlation of the state planning agencies, to which reference has been made in this chapter, is being attempted by this Educational Policies Commission of the National Education Association and the American Association of School Administrators. The Commission is composed of selected representatives of all grades of educational work, including both publicly and privately controlled institutions of higher learning. It has 2,200 ex officio consultants, each the head of an educational organization. They constitute an effective liaison with the profession and the public. The Commission is dedicated to the task of drafting a pattern of progress for American education. It is engaged in long-time educational planning. A number of its publications are listed in the bibliography. Among the numerous principles of administrative procedure approved by this Commission is this: that legislation for federal support to education, if and when passed, should specifically forbid and prevent federal control and administration of education.

With reference to this principle, the traditional attitude of privately controlled institutions is that the way to play safe is not to accept appropriations. In the nature of the case, appropriations must be accompanied by stipulations as to the availability of funds and followed by reporting, counseling, and auditing. The colleges desire to be controlled professionally, not politically. Since the time that the people of Virginia, through their assemblies, tried to stop the slave trade and were baffled by interests powerful with the British Government, the American people have had repeated warnings against the practice of remote control.

By the elemental device of object lessons, the colleges are being persuaded anew that eternal vigilance is the price of liberty—vigilance against propaganda in favor of existing regimes, against prohibition of free investigation and free speech, against arbitrary selection of students and of subjects of study, against dictation and regimentation in any form.

CHAPTER XXIII

THE RESPONSIBILITY OF THE COLLEGES FOR THE GENERAL WELFARE

ASSOCIATE Justice Louis D. Brandeis has said:

> The peculiar characteristics of a profession as distinguished from other occupations, I take to be these:
>
> First, a profession is an occupation for which the necessary preliminary training is intellectual in character, involving knowledge and to some extent learning, as distinguished from mere skill;
>
> Second, it is an occupation which is pursued largely for others, and not merely for one's self;
>
> Third, it is an occupation in which the amount of financial returns is not the accepted measure of success.

In offering an "opinion" from a member of our highest court as a basis of this discussion, it is not assumed that all college men and women who render public service exert their influence through the medium of a profession. There is a sentence in the writings of the Father of Medicine, quoted with full approval of Sir William Osler,* which associates one's love of humanity with the love of his craft. In this sentence the magic words *philanthropia* and *philotechnia* are joined. It is now suggested that as philanthropy is joined with philosophy the colleges are justified of their children.

It is true that law, medicine, theology, and the newer professions developed as human relationships multiplied, have usually furnished the men and women of the greatest distinction. The large majority of college-bred men and women, however, who are impelled by the love of their fellow men, render public service of priceless though often of unrecog-

* See References, p. 368.

nized value. The term public service then has a wide content. It cannot be applied only to great men or only to men
in public life. The colleges contribute to the general welfare.

In the preface to this book the thesis is set forth that the
social function of the colleges is two-fold. If the *corpus
politicum* shows symptoms of *rigor mortis* the function of the
colleges is to administer stimulants. If on the other hand a
paroxysm of delirium is observed, the colleges must suggest
a very different treatment. The work of the colleges is justified then, if it offers helpful interpretations of the social concepts of the epoch, or of the higher genius of the people, or
of the still more comprehensive nature of man and his world.

It would not be too much to say that the chief architects
and builders of the American state were college men. To
insure a foundation that would last during the centuries they
dug down to rock bottom. They succeeded through trial
and error in erecting a superstructure which integrates the
individual life with a group life directed toward ethical purposes. Such a government hath foundations. The United
States Government is now the oldest government in the
world. It is the invariably cited model for new structures of
permanence achieved, projected or prophesied.

It was while a student at Harvard that Samuel Adams became a disciple of the English philosopher, John Locke, and
the other Natural Rights philosophers. Adams had the insight to see that previous decades and centuries were not dead
but contained the germs of life. He started the American
Revolution in his Master's thesis. He became the political
leader of Massachusetts. His beneficent influence percolated
into every nook and corner of the colonies. He was the
Father of the American Revolution. His political children
sprang up like magic.

Among them was Elbridge Gerry who succeeded him in
Massachusetts in the succession of major political prophets.
Gerry's task was different, but his spirit was the same. He
became a member of the Continental Congress, a signer of

the Declaration of Independence, a signer of the Articles of
Confederation, and a member of the Congress of the Confederation. He and Rufus King, also a member of the same
Congress, emerged from this laboratory in democratic government with a strong conviction. The government had
failed because it was decentralized, therefore weak. These
statesmen were impelled by the high resolve that strong men
should be sent as delegates to the Constitutional Convention
of 1787. John Hanson of Oxon Hill, Prince George's
County, Maryland, was the first president of the United
States—in Congress assembled under the Articles of Confederation. The ashes of the sovereign nation of which he was
chief fertilized the nation about to germinate.

Seventeen hundred and eighty-seven was an epoch-making
year in the formation of the American state. It was signalized by the framing of the Constitution and by the proclama-
tion of the Ordinance of 1787, both products very largely of
college men. Of the fifty-five delegates to the Constitutional
Convention who were present at some of the sessions, thirty-
two were college trained and most of the others had minds
enriched by reading, thought, and experience. Among the
latter were the two geniuses, Washington and Franklin, who
became founders of colleges and honorary alumni of Harvard. The determination, just attributed to Gerry and
King, to send men of scholarship and wisdom to the Convention was certainly shared by most of the colonial leaders.
This Convention reached the high water mark during all
history in political theory and purpose. The flexible form
of the Constitution and its capacity to keep intact constantly
quickening content are the marvel of students of political
science. The various state constitutions followed with the
same type of organization and under the leadership, for the
most part, of college men.

It was a college man, a graduate of Yale, Manasseh Cutler,
who inspired if he did not write the Ordinance of 1787. It
became the educational as well as the political Magna Charta
of the trans-Allegheny region and eventually of all the terri-

tory to the Pacific. In this instance, the framers of it far out-
ran in idealism the possibility of immediate realization, but
the states of Ohio, Indiana, Illinois, Michigan, Wisconsin,
and others later, eventually were vitalized to a high degree
when it became measurably operative.

Each of these states has developed a superior system of free
public schools extending from the lower grades to graduate
education. Each has an adequate supply of good colleges
and universities on private foundations. Michigan led in
organizing the first great state university and has also a great
state college. Illinois has within its borders the second center of population of the country and three universities holding membership in the Association of American Universities.
The University of Wisconsin set the example to other state
universities in widely extended service to the citizens of the
state. Ohio, the "Mother of Presidents," has a multiple system of state universities, and Indiana, a special locale for the
flowering of letters, has a great school of engineering in Pur-
due University and Indiana University which has led in furnishing superintendents of town and city schools for the
nation. No other section of equal area in the United States
has so great a population of happy and contented people.
The latest statistics of President Raymond Walters show that
nearly one-fifth of the full-time enrollment now in American
colleges and universities is found in the 119 institutions of
these five states.

The United States Government, during its early days, was
very largely guided in its several departments by men of
scholarship and culture. The founding fathers were concerned that public service should be of the highest order.
This was illustrated in the constitutional provision for presidential electors, which is now inoperative, although it remains in the Constitution. They established the basic conditions for a merit system in the national government.

The exponents of the Jacksonian principle of public service broke completely with these ideals, and educational institutions became concerned with the preparation of their stu-

dents for business and other private professions. Until the
War between the States there was undoubtedly a recession in
some of the departments of the government. During this
period, however, some of the most brilliant defenders of the
Constitution appeared, led by Dartmouth's Webster.

Certainly the series of compromises that characterized the
great game of politics for some decades before the fateful fir-
ing on Fort Sumter demonstrated the capacity of American
statesmen to preserve the balance between opposing forces.
To do that was to preserve a cardinal principle of the Constitution.

Other distinguished college men of this period besides
Webster were Sumner, Phillips and Seward. Opposing their
views were men of great native ability put to persistent use,
such as Hayne, Clay, Calhoun, Douglas, Davis, Stephens. Of
these, Davis was a graduate of the United States Military
Academy, and Calhoun and Douglas had attended colleges
in New England. Union College furnished William H.
Seward, the Secretary of State of the United States Government, and also Robert Toombs, the first Secretary of State of
the Confederacy. The two generals who in the field bore the
heaviest responsibilities of war and eventually of peace,
Grant and Lee, were graduates of the United States Military
Academy, then as now essentially a liberal arts college. The
servant of all the people, North and South, who came forth
from the wilderness and whose message straight from heaven
sounded out above the noise of battle, was untaught both in
the forms of the college and of the church, although he was
the embodiment of the spirit of both.

It is well to recall that just as the college men of the
formative days established a high order of Civil Service in
the Federal Government, so the excesses which reached their
climax after the War between the States drove other college
men into revolt. Carl Schurz, Charles Francis and Henry
Adams, Whitelaw Reid, John Hay, Charles W. Eliot, George
William Curtis, among many others, fought valiantly for
Civil Service reform. President Hayes committed the gov-

ernment to a study of the British Civil Service and took other notable first steps at Washington toward healing the gaping wound between the two sections. In all this work good and conscientious men and great newspapers wielded their influence regardless of the accidents of education or party or creed. The regenerative forces of American life were again at work.

The social ferment of the 1890's which followed the business depression, agricultural distress, currency troubles, the closing of the geographical frontier, and other conditions gave government on all levels more and more complicated functions to perform. John R. Commons, at the University of Wisconsin, began at that time to send young men trained in political science and economics into the service of the state. Many universities eventually followed Wisconsin's example. Much of the history which has been written during the last few decades in the effort to democratize American politics and at the same time to improve the Civil Service has been inspired by highminded men of education and culture. It was to center and guide the efforts of such men that in 1912 the American Political Science Association appointed a committee on Practical Training for Public Service.

During the past few decades the great surge toward orderly and progressive economic reform has made more progress perhaps than that toward political reform. This economic reform was given legal sanction in 1890 by the Sherman Antitrust Act, was dramatized repeatedly by William J. Bryan, was put on the stage in somewhat different form and with more success by Theodore Roosevelt. It has come through the fires of controversy somewhat purified, and now has the approval in principle, though not in every detail and emphasis, of the factions of both political parties. Certainly Raymond Moley could not be counted among the conservatives. He has recently pointed out that the economic reform covering this period of political history is comparable to the movements for political reform in England and the sweep of republicanism on the continent after the Napoleonic wars.

While it has at no time fully obtained its objective, it is proving itself more persistent and stable than the decisive trend toward democratic government after the World War. In spite of the acknowledged flaws in the political and economic procedure of the United States, the plans for a United States of Europe or of the world now being set forth as the only possible means of preserving civilization, are based upon political principles enunciated in the Constitution of the United States, and upon economic principles which have been taught for years in American institutions of higher learning. Some of these principles have entered into administrative processes.

There are no comprehensive statistical data which show the extent to which college men and women have contributed to the various phases of public and social service. Much of their contribution has been of the intangible kind, not subject to objective measurement.

The contribution of the educated ministry to American life, a contribution which cannot be characterized in a few words, has been made possible in large measure by the opportunities and the inspirations which have been offered by the colleges and seminaries as well as by the homes and the churches. The work of the minister is not confined to his parish. Experience over long periods of time shows that the sons of ministers attain distinction for service rendered to the community quite out of proportion to their number. The stimulative and formative influence of the manse has been well established. There is a sort of royal succession of mind and spirit. Intellectual and spiritual awakenings often, though not always, go hand in hand. The most striking evidence of its far-reaching power furnished by the statisticians is in the hundreds of descendants of Jonathan Edwards, generally considered America's greatest intellectual personage, in spite of the "irresistible implications" of his theology. One may scarcely venture to mention other names. The list is too long. America has been and still is fortunate in her great families, the names of many of whom are almost invariably associated with the churches.

A few definite samples of the vocational distribution of college alumni are offered.

The *Harvard Alumni Directory* for 1937 classifies the more common occupations under sixty-five heads. Of course there are innumerable refinements. A sampling of these statistics discloses the fact that representatives of the law stand first in number, followed by those of education, finance, medicine, mercantile work, manufacturing, the ministry, and other pursuits with definite social content. From another source it is learned that of the 690 members of the Foreign Service of the United States in 1939, 77 were graduates of Harvard. This indicates a present day alertness to public affairs in marked contrast to that of 1860 when Robert Todd Lincoln entered Harvard. He came, according to Edward Everett Hale, with letters of introduction from his father and Stephen A. Douglas, but it became necessary for Professor James Russell Lowell to explain to the other members of the faculty who Abraham Lincoln was.

The distribution of the former students of a very different type of school is indicated in the statistical report issued by Cumberland University, a small institution with an endowment of $105,000, located in a small community among the hills of Tennessee. This list, covering the history of the institution, counts the present Secretary of State Cordell Hull, 2 Justices of the United States Supreme Court, 12 Federal District Judges, 6 Federal Circuit Judges, 4 Generals of the United States Army, 12 United States Senators, 68 members of the House of Representatives, 42 State Supreme Court Judges, 13 Judges of the Court of Appeals, 4 United States Ambassadors.

Among the alumni of the school there have been counted 1205 ministers, and a vast number of missionaries and church workers of the lay as well as of the professional order.

This little university's contribution to education is

measured in terms of 47 college presidents and long lists of other officers and teachers of all types of schools.

While this is a notable record, no claim is made that it surpasses that of some other small institutions. A special study has been made of the graduates of institutions of higher learning in Tennessee who are rendering public service, from which it appears that 39 per cent of those now living in that state were educated in Tennessee colleges, chiefly those under private control. These persons in order of the frequency of their occupations are: educators, clergymen, lawyers, physicians, judges, congressmen, authors.

Another sampling may be submitted from the list of American Rhodes Scholars. In 1938, of 870 Scholars, about 40 per cent were engaged in educational work, chiefly as presidents, deans, and teachers in colleges and universities. Other vocations represented in order were law, business, government service, and nine others. There is now reported by President Frank Aydelotte a very decided trend toward forms of political activity among these Scholars. The indication is strong that Cecil Rhodes's hope that American Oxford students might participate in public life is likely to be realized.

A study based upon the 250 most recently starred scientists* in the 1938 edition of *American Men of Science* showed that they studied at more than 120 different colleges. No college or group of colleges has a monopoly in good science teaching. Of the 11 institutions which conferred the Bachelor's degree on 4 or more of these scientists, all but 2 are privately controlled. These figures indicate a widened interest in science among the smaller institutions. The study notes a decline in the East, considerable gain in the Midwest, a sharp rise in the West. In proportion to college population, the South produced fewer subsequently starred scientists than any other section. The wider distribution of stimulating teachers, the advances being made in numerous

* Two hundred and fifty men and women designated periodically by their colleagues for the exceptional quality of their work.

state universities and in the South promise an increase of the
total output of eminent scientists.   State universities conferred the Bachelor's degree on only 86 of 1000 scientists
starred in 1903.   Of this group only 25 had their doctorate
from state universities.   Of the 750 younger scientists starred
in 1932 and 1937, state universities graduated 176 and 9 received their doctorates.

The editors of *Who's Who in America* for a number of
years have been setting forth the educational preparation of
the persons listed, who now number in the neighborhood of
30,000.   The proportion of college graduates runs all the
way from 70 per cent to 85 per cent.   Many of the others
have had some college education.   In the most recent study
of the representation of the colleges in this publication by
Kunkel and Prentice a constant increase in the percentage
of college and university alumni is noted.   The endowed
liberal arts colleges—both of the university and of the detached college types—are making the greatest gains in this
respect.   Among the 20 institutions which in 1928-29 stood
first in their representation, there were only 4 which are
publicly controlled.   In later editions, several such are shown
to be making large numerical gains.   This indicates a trend
of considerable significance in the matter of the production
of distinguished professional leaders.   For many years the
presidents of tax-supported universities and colleges have
been very largely graduates of privately controlled institutions—in numerous cases graduates of the small colleges.   Today the numbers break about even as between the two types
of institutions.

Perhaps the greatest contribution of the colleges to the
social order has been in furnishing educational leadership.
This leadership has affected every phase of formal education.
The responsibility for this leadership centered on the colleges in the nature of the case, for from those who have received much, much is expected.   The turn of events also con-
spired to place it there.   American education began to grow
at the top.   After the colleges, came the secondary and the

elementary schools.   The problem of the colonial colleges was to preserve and perpetuate racial inheritances.   This required a form of isolation from the physical task of conquering the continent.   If the colleges did not offer courses on blazing trails through the forests, on waging warfare on the Indians, on finding means of subsistence in the deserts, on approved methods of discovering gold, on the conservation of natural resources, they did preserve some of the wisdom and culture of the past and found in it life-giving springs with marvelous fructifying potency.   They were captivated by the "baffling task," as André Siegfried has phrased it, for modern men and women "of studying the depths of the currents that are still only uncertainly seen on the surface." They preserved some of the elements of a former epoch, now all but lost in some other countries, which contribute much to our present conception of life.

The Ordinance of 1787, largely inspired if not actually written by a graduate of Yale, carried over to the Mississippi Valley some of the elements of this life and set them forth in its famous Preamble.   "Religion, morality and knowledge," the forerunner of the "whole man" conception now so generally accepted, belongs in the same category of excellence as the aspiration "to promote the general welfare" of the Constitution's Preamble, and the inspiring shibboleth of Daniel Webster—"Liberty and union."

It was a college man, a graduate of Brown, Horace Mann, whose persistence in pleading the cause of the children in Massachusetts laid the foundation for the comprehensive system of free elementary education in the United States.   It was an undergraduate of Yale, William T. Harris, who eventually gave philosophic interpretation to this document and made education a national issue, with federal implementation but without federal control.

It was chiefly through the influence of Jonathan B. Turner, of Illinois College, that the ideals of vocational and cultural education were combined in what became the Morrill Act. Eventually, through the persistence of Senator Justin S. Morrill, the Act was passed and Abraham Lincoln made it effective by his signature.

Through these land-grant colleges and the state universities in which they are found or with which they cooperate the boys and girls of the farms and the shops have been led into paths of usefulness and happiness in the rural regions as well as the urban centers.

A multitude of college men and women such as Henry Barnard, Mary Lyon, Emma Willard, Booker T. Washington, and many others unnamed through the demands of time and space, have been promoters of education as a necessary phase of the democratic ideal. In all this work such leaders had the approval of the American people through their universal passion for education.

Scholars have been accused of wishing to preserve the *status quo* as if that of itself were a capital crime. The history of American education only partially confirms this charge. The colleges and universities have not despised the *status quo* if no better status seemed possible as a substitute. They think twice before throwing out the baby with the bath. They have been chary of changes for the sake of change. But among them have been those who have led all other agencies in setting experimentation and research free from the shackles that bound them. They have developed a generous and cooperative spirit so that today the neglect or persecution of an adventurous experimenter or researcher does not come chiefly, as it once did, from the scholars. They have developed a type of scholarship which is permeated with the grace of humility. Joseph T. Mackey strikingly illustrates this transformation of attitude. He has taken the pains to discover that, when the prediction was made by a scientific authority about 1880—" 'Physics and chemistry have reached a stationary condition,' Thomas Edison was 39 years old, Albert Michelson 34, Henry Ford 23, Charles Steinmetz 21, Thomas Morgan 20, Robert Millikan 18, Madam Curie 19, Orville Wright 15, Marconi 12, Einstein 7, and that the Compton brothers had not yet been born."

There has been no more doubtful discrimination between the possible functions of the colleges than that prompted by the belief that they should be composed of reflective groups but not of pioneering groups. It would be easy to err on the side of optimism by asserting that in all colleges reflective groups are to be found. But in any event the colleges cannot be assigned entirely to the roll of monasteries. Many of them are pioneers on the campus, and more of their former students are pioneers off the campus. They are the primary seats of research and the training grounds for it, along the far-flung horizons of knowledge. Most of the research work under the auspices of the universities is being done in the graduate schools. In some universities one-fourth or more of the budget is expended upon the work of research. In undergraduate colleges where honors work is carried on under favorable conditions there are the beginnings of research by students as well as teachers on both an individual and a cooperative basis. Some undergraduate colleges fit up private laboratories for special or continuous research activity. For three decades federal and state authorities have stimulated the development of specialists in forestry and agriculture in publicly controlled institutions.

There are many laboratories, some of them on the campuses, in which the nature of and remedy for the diseases which affect the human system are being discovered. In these, practicing physicians find ready-made many of their prescriptions. Since the World War a score of institutions have experimented in the field of preparation of students for consular and diplomatic posts.

The services of college graduates who have distinguished themselves in the various fields of research are sought by the foundations, the special research institutes and institutions, industrial and commercial concerns, social and welfare agencies. Tens of thousands of these alumni are occupied in this way. The colleges mark out the straight and narrow path which leads to the fields of research.

Industries devoted to the production of steel, oil, automo-

biles, to the radio and motion picture, to the telegraph and
the telephone, expend larger sums in their research divisions
than the entire budgets of leading universities. Research in
industrial laboratories alone involves an annual expenditure
estimated at $100,000,000. In 1936-37 the Federal Govern-
ment expended $120,000,000 in research. College men di-
rect these investigations.

These expositions have been made, with some exceptions,
from the standpoint of quantity rather than quality. It is
one thing for college men to participate in public service;
it is another thing for them to participate in the interests
of public welfare. It must be admitted that college men in
public life have not always been guided by the north pole
of morality. They have not always been shining Galahads,
Parsifals and Siegfrieds. On the other hand, men like Wilson
and Hoover, interestingly enough sons of ministers, who have
been so guided, have been subjected to ridicule because they
were not "good politicians," a fact which makes it possible
to evaluate their service. In the field of economics many
college men with political responsibilities have failed to
follow the teachings of Perry, Walker, Sumner, Dunbar,
Taussig, Hadley, Howison, and John Bates Clarke. Some
"good politicians," either college graduates or under the
special tutelage of college graduates, have developed into
infamous and others into famous bosses.

Certainly it is evident that intelligence, education, even
culture, do not furnish the full equipment for public service. The Ordinance of 1787 mentioned also morality and
religion. The authors of the Ordinance held to the eternal
sanctions of oughtness without which there can be no social
science.

College men have undoubtedly become notorious for their
manipulations in the fields of public utilities, banking, real
estate, the stock exchange. In an address a few years ago at
an annual meeting of the Association of American Colleges
Paul H. Douglas, of the University of Chicago, now incidentally a member of the City Council of Chicago, after

naming numerous bosses with unsavory reputations, declared, "if we were to take a census . . . of college men in politics it is probable that we should find more of them in the thick of machine manipulations, than among the forces of reform." This opinion at least calls attention to the dark side of the picture. The actual "census" referred to has not been taken. When and if the complete census is taken, on the good side will appear the names of most of the presidents and secretaries of state for the past fifty years, outstanding among whom in national and international service are John Hay, Theodore Roosevelt, Elihu Root, Charles Evans Hughes, Woodrow Wilson, William Howard Taft, Frank B. Kellogg, Herbert Hoover. It will contain the names of multitudes of others who have served mankind with devotion to the interests of humanity. Among them will be the names of great educators, clergymen and social workers, who have served as ambassadors with and without portfolios,— Henry Ward Beecher, James B. Angell, Andrew D. White, Jacob G. Schurman, Nicholas Murray Butler, William E. Dodge, Owen D. Young, Jane Addams, Mary Emma Woolley, S. Parkes Cadman.

There are colleges by the score, and foundations and councils made up of college men, which are addressing themselves to the task of prevention and correction of abuses. This is true even in the field of research, which carries with it the implication of disinterestedness. It is becoming clear that the maintenance of the true spirit of research, when conducted under the auspices of the national, state, or municipal government, requires cooperation between such agencies and agencies independent of government control. Politicians may have mixed motives. Here the foundations and research institutes, all directed by college men, may supply highly qualified advisers. The true worth of these institutes has not yet been fully recognized. Cooperative forms of research between universities and even between international agencies are setting a worthy example. At least in the field of research evidence is being offered that Benjamin Frank-

lin's saying that it is hard for an empty sack to stand upright
may have some refinements of interpretation.   The school
of experience teaches the lesson that public servants, regardless of college experience, if they are to have the permanent
confidence of the people, do not need to have the sacks filled
in the sense implied by Franklin.   There has been no better
illustration of this fact than Franklin himself.   As long as
colleges teach morality they will furnish men whose sacks
can be filled with values other than loot.

When and if the Civil and Diplomatic Services adopt more
intelligent measures of recruiting, placement and in-service
training, high-mindedness as well as keen-mindedness will be
at a premium.   The plan of assignment of men in some forms
of government service to interneship training in the universities will undoubtedly be greatly extended.   The United
States Government is greatly in need of career personnel in
the Civil, Diplomatic and Research Services.   Some progress
is being made but the government has far to go before the
dream of President Hayes is translated into practical experience.

When it is recalled that one out of every forty citizens of
the United States works for some branch of local, state or
national government, as an engineer, financier, auditor, doctor, teacher, lawyer, criminologist, buyer of merchandise, or-
ganizer, etc., the magnitude of the task of educating men and
women for this type of public service becomes apparent.

The *Municipal Year Book* in 1939 listed 150 colleges which
now offer courses in public administration.

The Georgetown University School of Foreign Service is
celebrating in 1940 its twenty-first anniversary.   Its graduates
are scattered in fifty-seven consulates and legations throughout the world.   It is thus using education as the primal factor toward the great end of world friendship.   It provides
training also for domestic service.   Its course spans five years
and includes instruction in French, German, Spanish, Portu-
guese, Chinese, Japanese, Italian and Russian.   Its 575 students are accepted on the basis of high scholastic averages.

Its class work is supplemented by lectures by Ministers and Ambassadors resident in Washington. Authorities in various fields of service offer counsel and advice in informal seminars. Visits are made to legations, government bureaus, and Atlantic seaports. Annual trips are made to foreign nations.

The University of Southern California's School of Citizenship and Public Administration was started ten years ago as a one week's intensive professional course of study. In 1932 its name was changed to the School of Government. Two years of college work are required for admission. Undergraduate and graduate courses are offered leading to the Bachelor's and Master's degrees in public administration. The School now enrolls some 2,000 students. It is designed to serve four groups: (1) men and women engaged in public service who desire a plan of study which will bring together the resources of the University and the political knowledge of persons in public service; (2) selected men and women who are preparing for careers in public administration, in research, and the performance of official functions in public agencies, national, state and local; (3) college students as well as adults in active life interested in a broad training and preparation for the duties and the practice of citizenship; (4) individuals charged with specific governmental responsibilities.

Princeton's School of Public Affairs has also been operating for ten years and has become an integral part of the University. The students are grounded thoroughly in the social sciences—history, politics, economics. They are faced with the realities of current public and business problems as men in public life are brought to the campus. They visit centers of political activity. They are instructed in methods of independent investigation, drilled in the organization and presentation of facts and arguments, trained to speak effectively in conference. The men are the "top tenth in academic standing." An early project was participation in a survey of the state government of New Jersey by the University made at the request of the governor of the state. Princeton was fertile ground for such a development as this. The influence of Princeton graduates and faculty members in the area of international relationships is more conspicuous perhaps and for a longer time than that of any other American college or university. In 1844, under the leadership of Edward M. Dodd this development began in the Near East, and it has continued without interruption for almost a century. During the nineteenth century numerous Princeton graduates went to the Near East as missionaries. Others have held responsible positions in the diplomatic service or as advisers on economic questions. The work of Edwin Walter Kemmerer and his associates as economic counsellors in many countries of the earth has probably not been surpassed. More students have been chosen for Rhodes Scholarships at Oxford from Princeton than from any other American institution.

The National Institute of Public Affairs is a non-partisan, non-political, privately financed and self-governing organization which enjoys the cooperation of the Federal Government and brings winners of scholarships to Washington for a period of two months. These scholars with a substantial grounding in political science and related subjects become internes in a government agency of particular interest to the individual students.

When the gift from Lucius N. Littauer was announced in 1935 for the establishment at Harvard of a graduate school of public administration, a commission appointed by the University set about the task of devising a plan for realizing the best results from such an effort. They drew upon the experience of some thirty-five colleges which were experimenting in this field. They found that all special efforts on the part of the colleges to train men in the affairs of government had their beginnings during this century.

After some years of careful study of the issues involved, in which heavy drafts were made upon the experience of government officials as well as faculty groups representing economics, politics, law and business administration, the Harvard plan of procedure was announced. The plan provides that effort shall be focused upon quality rather than quantity. Provision is made for various types of personnel: Fellows drawn from college and university graduates who have had some experience in public administration; junior consultants detailed by their administrative superiors for a period of study; officials in responsible administrative positions in federal, state and local governments; selected members of the Harvard faculty. The students are to spend their first year in research and study, the second year in field work as apprentices in government departments, and the third year in the effort to integrate the theory and actual practice of public service. The school opened in 1938 with fifteen Fellows enrolled.

The Institute of Government of North Carolina, with headquarters at the state university, now has 2,000 public officials in its membership and is enrolling private citizens of all ages. It employs a staff of six full-time experts who work from town to town and county to county in community service.

Some most interesting phases of the development of a sense of civic and social responsibility are found in a number of the colleges for women. There is an increasing realization among women that the nation as well as the home is theirs. Without their aid democracy cannot work. Among the colleges pioneering in this field are Barnard, Hunter and Skidmore, New York; Connecticut College; Wheaton, Massachusetts; Pembroke, Rhode Island; Goucher, Maryland; Sweet Briar, Virginia; Agnes Scott, Georgia. An endowed chair to be devoted to public service has been presented to Sweet Briar by the friends of Senator Glass, a member of the board of trustees and a brother of President Meta Glass. This foundation emphasizes the sense of civic and social responsibility which was already recognized as a part of the college program. In all these colleges the most enduring service to the public welfare, entirely immeasurable, is in preparation for home making.

This persistent and quickened sense of social responsibility is inspiring all educational leaders to a restudy of the means of preserving human values. It has become an educational movement. The Educational Policies Commission of the National Education Association is outlining practical plans for developing this sensitiveness in the children of all grades and types of schools. Suited to the growing capacities of youth, the program involves teaching in social justice, social participation, social understanding, critical judgment, tolerance, conservatism, social applications of science, law observance, political citizenship, economic literacy, devotion to democracy, world citizenship.

Among the professional schools the medical colleges as a group have been leaders in recognizing and in emphasizing human values. Dr. Fred C. Zapffe, the Executive Secretary of the Association of American Medical Colleges, is aggressive in this leadership. He is showing that from year to year, as selective admission is put into operation, qualities of mind and spirit weigh more heavily than technical preparation. Concretely, more A.B. graduates than B.S. graduates are being accepted by the 77 colleges in the United States having membership in the Association. The greater per cent of freshmen are drawn from the upper brackets of school achievement. Medical colleges are advising against pre-medical courses, chiefly in science. Thus the most sacrificial of all the professions is pointing the way to the realization of higher social education.

The engineering schools are making notable advances in integrating social, economic, and humanitarian studies with those of science and technology. As more basic subjects are being introduced into the preparatory work, less attention is being given to the minutiae of technical application. The California, the Carnegie, and the Massachusetts Institutes of Technology were pathfinders in this area of development, but they in no sense stand alone now. There is much to indicate that a revolution in engineering education is taking place, and this is all the more significant since engineers, unlike ministers, physicians, and lawyers, deal only indirectly with social and human material.

The tragic events which have driven to this country from the totalitarian states vast numbers of intellectuals and artists have resulted in the enlargement and improvement of college faculties. President Hutchins, of the University of Chicago, recently testified that every department from arts to zoology at that institution has been stimulated by these refugees, and he observed that it may turn out that Hitler and Mussolini will be the University's greatest founders.

That the colleges themselves and their graduates as a group have been slow to make adjustments to the changing social order is often greatly to their credit. It has been a fault that a considerable part of the growth of higher education has been opportunistic in nature. On this principle, if it may be so called, the colleges are approved by those who adopt the American watchword, "Bigger and Better." On the ground that nearly half of the nation's adults have not finished the elementary school, that probably a fourth of them have not finished the fourth grade, and that 3,000,000 or more of them are illiterate in the ordinary interpretation of that term, colleges are urged to lower standards of achievement and make quick adjustments. Most of them have not been willing to sell their birthright for such a price. For this they have been called prophets of intellectual celibacy. They have been condemned for attempting to escape from social responsibility. They have been denounced for their unawareness of human needs. But they have taken to heart the lesson of the tortoise and the hare. They are disposed to hold fast to the conception that education is growth and it is the part of wisdom to recognize that normal growth is slow.

It is now clearly recognized that certain social trends are operative which come as peculiar challenges to the colleges.

Society realizes that the minds and hearts of men must be internationalized and the movement in behalf of peace and good will is incorporated into the school and college programs.

The prevalence of lawlessness and crime threatens to destroy the moral fiber of the people and men like J. Edgar

Hoover and his colleagues are demonstrating that society need not be supine in the presence of such evil doing.

The centralization of business in the hands of a few men is undemocratic and dangerous and already the process of decentralization is making progress. Great industrial and railroad corporations are transferring their headquarters from New York to Pittsburgh, Chicago, San Francisco. The directorates of others are being reorganized. Absentee managers are being eliminated. The new personnel contains many college men drawn from the "grass roots" section of the country. Other corporations are deliberately placing university men, who have no financial interests in the business, on their boards of trustees. Slowly the breach between the capitalistic system and democracy is being healed.

The forces of society are greatly extending the leisure time of the people, and the schools and colleges are responding to the call to make persistent re-examinations of the objectives of education and life.

Society is learning anew that morality and education are inseparable elements of life and the makers of educational programs are placing increasing emphasis upon the necessity of emotional adaptability as a fundamental guarantor of dependable character.

There is a persistent demand for educational opportunities for every individual. The higher and lower courts are requiring, as cases arise, that provision be made to meet this demand, and the educational leaders are more and more depended upon as guides in this extension of opportunities.

The danger of too early specialization is more clearly seen than heretofore, and this insight demands more productive correlations and syntheses of knowledge and life. It is being recognized that just as ideologies alone train for a world that does not exist so does specialization alone train for a world that tomorrow will become passé.

In a word, there is an enlarged sense of responsibility for men and women of scholarship and wisdom to contribute to the public welfare.

As constructive forces of society the colleges are called to assume their part of the responsibility for seeing that there is maintained a better balance between the privileges and the services of the few, the rights and duties of the many.

CHAPTER XXIV

THE GOLDEN THREAD THAT BINDS

IN ATTEMPTING to estimate imponderable values it is well to bear in mind what H. G. Wells once so well expressed, that to achieve a result and to claim to have achieved a result are not exactly the same thing. That there are degrees of achievement as well as of claims among the colleges need not inhibit the effort to clarify their aims.

The "oneness of the universities" whose loss in modern times is so frequently chronicled and deplored was a oneness of European not American institutions. It was, furthermore, in reality a tripartite oneness. It was a oneness of subject matter, a oneness of objective, and a oneness of relationship to the social order. These onenesses seem to have a familiar sound on this side of the Atlantic even during these dark days for the world of learning and of man.

During the years the discovery has been made by some that we live in an expanding universe and that that expansion has come about by the application of new methods of thought. The content oneness of the colleges could have been maintained in something like its original form and substance if the deductive method had been unchallenged and if all men had accepted the major premise arbitrarily defined, or even defined by "reason." The coming of the inductive method and the multiplication of restless and inquisitive souls upset the apple cart. Put the blame where it belongs —on the inevitable urge of the pioneer spirit, operating in the realm of the mind. This urge was compounded of initiative, resourcefulness, boldness, tenacity of purpose, and an increasing tolerance of opinion. As a matter of fact, there are more Americans studying Latin and Greek literature, mathematics, and philosophy today than during the palmiest days of the colonial colleges. Not so large a proportion of college students, to be sure, are studying Latin and Greek, but those who do seek this type of oneness do so more effectively, more comprehensively, with a higher degree of perspective. The first-class colleges have not abandoned learning; they have expanded it by extending its boundaries, and this has been done largely through cooperative effort. This is true in England as well as in America. Albert Mansbridge says that with the exception of subject matter of two technical schools, Oxford and Cambridge between them offer work along all lines that are now offered by London and Birmingham.

A similar expansion has come about in the matter of the college objective. The colleges still seek an "elite," but they give it a broader and more flexible definition. They even have a new name for it. They may call it the aristocracy of the mind, or capacity for leadership, or personality, or social effectiveness. Perhaps they are able to deliver to society as representatives of the higher life as large a proportion of their students (which means a very much larger number of them) as the old classical colleges did. It must be remembered that the rigors of the old classical course drove many students out. Most colleges now make the modest claim that 10 per cent or 20 per cent of their students develop into the higher reaches of intellectual achievement. In a few colleges undoubtedly the percentage is larger. In some it well-nigh reaches the vanishing point. We do not call these students "intellectuals"; neither do the colleges despise the other 90 per cent or 60 per cent. One college follows the Oxford terminology and frankly calls them "pass men." They recognize that it takes more than an elite arbitrarily defined to build a democracy. England thinks well of Cecil Rhodes—a rather distinguished pass man. In America those who fail to qualify as honors students are very often not without honor. They have their own qualities of excellence. The greatest of all values, a by-product of teaching—character—is an imponderable of college life and study. There is a serious as well as a comic meaning to Max McConn's delightful satire, *Studies Are Not Everything*. The colleges would develop qualities of mind and of spirit. It is fortunate, indeed, if the two are combined in one person.

Nor have the American colleges abandoned their interest in the social order. They have extended and intensified this interest. The current preponderant enrollment in the social sciences indicates the attitude of the present-day faculty and students. Here the argument can readily be turned against the traditional American college. For it, as for the colleges of today, Plato was an inexhaustible storehouse of thought. But many colleges of the earlier era failed even to seek the complete Platonic program of education, much less attain it. They picked and chose in accordance with the accepted opinions of their day. In developing his program Plato had drawn from the various manifestations of Athenian culture, as Thomas Jefferson drew from the Natural Rights metaphysics. The Puritans did not go all the way with Plato. Plato had interpreted Greek life at its best. He was a supreme artist as well as a master of thought, and a no mean wrestler. Today, the colleges go so far as to include music and dancing and intramural and intercollegiate games. They are developing a taste for the beautiful. They have found values in Plato called new, which were there all the time. The Puritans, to take liberties with Goldwyn's phrase, "included those subjects out."

The colleges have abandoned the oneness of pattern. They hold tenuously or tenaciously to the original elements of oneness. These elements governed the culture of Europe prior to the seventeenth century. They were preserved to mankind by the Roman Catholic Church. Their greatest exemplar has been Cardinal Newman.* In their adaptation, in which process the Catholic colleges quite recently are beginning to participate, they retain a tremendous and increas-

* See References, pp. 366, 368.

ingly meaningful vitality. President Hyde, of Bowdoin College, detected and proclaimed four of these elements in the Greek Academy: two primary, wisdom and justice; and two secondary, courage and temperance. These are now component elements of the American collegiate theory and practice, as they are of the institutions of higher learning in other democratic countries.

The motto of the American college as of the American state is *E Pluribus Unum*. The colleges are approaching a degree of inner and spontaneous unity, with all their diversities. This unity is achieved through the synthesis of inherent, permanent, and timeless values. President Lowell called it "the eternal thread that runs through all the changes that occur."

This fixity of purpose, with attendant flexibility of method, has been illustrated in each of the growing but distinctive sectional cultures of our broad land. When Wheelock established Moore's Indian Charity School, he entered upon the experiment of the direct teaching of wild Indians in order that they might be fitted more effectively to meet the competition of "civilized"—that is, white—men. Wheelock's experiment was admittedly unsuccessful.

Professor Richardson has shown that Dartmouth adopted the Wheelock experiment as its central purpose, but with an entirely new technique. Dartmouth would teach white men rather than Indians to become in turn the teachers of the Indians in their local habitat. The enterprise was still missionary in purpose and, within the boundaries first established, was again almost a failure. The college has never abandoned her primary purpose. Today, with appropriate expansions and modifications to meet the exigencies of the times, Dartmouth's objective is unchanged. Dartmouth, like all other self-respecting colleges, is committed to certain universals and constants. Dartmouth still holds up the torch of service to mankind.

The dynamic power of such central values has operated in the South as well as in New England. It knows neither time nor place. It is the essence of liberal education. The University of Georgia, as President Sanford has said, was first fitted to the political and social conditions of a land-owning aristocracy. In such an environment the word "gentleman" had a context of its own. Perhaps this accounts for the persistence through the years of "gentleman" and "gentlemanliness" as prominent words in the vocabularies of Southern educators. It is the basis of the honor system of the University of Virginia. To be sure, the idea is present elsewhere, though not so frequently and consciously expressing a meaning peculiar to that region. But as the years went on and the universities persisted in the fearless inquiry and the maintenance of truth, they broke the shackles which had confined intellectual liberty to narrower and predetermined bounds, and a broader democracy has emerged—a democracy which embraces twentieth century thought, considerably outgrown from that of the eighteenth century. The South is no longer characterized by blind partisanship. There is the same old value with broader dimensions and modern manifestations.

Now what are some of the strands of this golden thread that binds the colleges together? What are the enduring values? Even though they may be forgotten in some colleges, what are they?

For purposes of illustration reference will be made to *learning, thinking, service* (the *"ministry"*), *freedom,* in terms of the old formulas and their vastly richer content and wider applicability. It is not claimed that these are the only "elements." This is a problem of bio-chemistry, not chemistry. Since these elements tend to merge into each other, the total complex may be approached from other points of view. The differences are functional and this is the underlying thesis of this discussion. It is of relatively small importance that the old forms are not always maintained.

Learning. The colleges have been and are devoted to learning. Otherwise, why do they exist? They seek it partly for its own sake. To appreciative minds it is an investment upon which dividends constantly accrue. In a larger measure than that usually applied to investments, it is inherently profitable. Learning does not need to be "placed out to usury." This is not to say it should not become capital. Indeed, its chief value to society lies in its applications.

To be sure, in the present organization of American education, "scholarship" is seldom attained by the undergraduate. The more modest term "knowledge" should be used. But knowledge and scholarship differ chiefly in degree. Furthermore, either requires the same essential delimitation. It has to be pointed up and clarified. Learning, whether of the knowledge type or the scholarship type, furnishes the forms, the boundaries of education. "Whatsoever things are true, . . . think on these things." Even if perchance you think on other things, the thought must have its delimitations. These necessary limits have been extended during the centuries. Admitting that learning now spreads over much territory, it must not run indiscriminately over any lot. The streams of knowledge must have banks, however the volume may increase or the currents change. There must be precise discrimination, if there is to be clear and effective thinking. Let the dictionaries and encyclopedias grow thicker. They must keep their place in the total program of education. That place is to contribute raw material conveniently classified for the structure of thought. Architects do not ignore structure; least of all, architects of thought.

Research was once the entire prerogative of the universities. It is now carried on also through special foundations of their own, through other contributory bodies, and through marvelous research departments in commercial corporations. The budgets for research in these private corporations, under normal conditions, sometimes exceed in amount the total budgets of leading universities. The American Chemical Society has estimated the 1937 expenditures for research and training purposes of commercial and industrial organizations at $100,000,000. Other estimates are higher. Here, as at other points, education and industry join hands in a common effort to extend the bounds of knowledge.

At this moment the whole complicated and highly technical system of objective tests and measurements, one of the very latest manifestations of progressiveness in education, to use a single illustration, emphasizes the enduring value of the structural side of education. These tests and measurements assume the value of knowledge and, further, the value of possessing it. They stimulate the assembling and organization of facts. They by no means ignore the use of knowledge. It must not be despised. Reading still maketh a full man. Be it admitted to our chagrin, America has not yet produced her ratio of scholars. This is a challenge yet to be answered.

But knowledge cannot form the basis of a complete educational program. Whitehead observes that knowledge keeps no better than fish. Even in the field of mathematics, which has been considered an "absolute" science, the area par excellence of "pure intellect," solutions have been multiplied from Euclid to Einstein for no "practical" purpose, but because they were so beautiful. The mathematical basis of music has been often observed. Research in mathematics leads to music and vice versa.

Thinking. Knowledge discovers facts. It respects facts and holds on to them. It furnishes the form, the structure of the phenomenon called education. Thinking represents the process. It does something with facts—and opinions. It makes deductions, determines policies. It requires not so much the "wit of an intellect," as the penetration of a mind. Its highest achievements come through the conflict and the ultimate accord of penetrating minds. The philosophers have laid stress, almost without exception, not upon truth as a possession but upon the pursuit of truth. Hamilton pointed out a hundred years ago:

> Considered as ends and in relation to each other, the knowledge of truths is not supreme but subordinate to the cultivation of the knowing mind. The question, Is truth

or the mental exercise in the pursuit of truth the superior
end? is, perhaps, the most curious theoretical and certainly
the most important practical problem in philosophy.

In our changing world fluidity of thought, flexibility of
mind, capacity for quick uptake and adjustment, the application of tested principles to new situations, are the chief
desiderata of the liberal colleges. The resourceful mind has
facts and ideas and concepts at command, and the excellence
of its operation is dependent upon their usability, clearness,
and adequacy. The greatest shift that has ever occurred in
our colleges is from the emphasis upon the restricted body of
knowledge to emphasis upon the interests and capacities of
students. This does not ignore the body of knowledge. This
"ought ye to have done, and not to leave the other undone."

Knowledge and thinking are correlative terms. The con-
tainer is quite as necessary as the thing contained. Neither
knowledge nor thinking can serve its true function without
the other. Man has put spiritual substance into the body.
The most heated controversies at this moment about the
program of American higher education are concerned with
comparative excellencies of the one or the other. In the
nature of the case it will always be a drawn battle. There
can be no finality in the one apart from the other. Each has
a value realized only through synthesis of the two. The
teacher who does not stimulate the student to think, the
college that does not afford the student time to think, is engaged in malpractice.

Service. A nearer approach to the synthesis of knowledge
and thinking is possible through the inclusion of a third enduring value. Thought has an inherent power of propulsion. If it cannot progress without knowledge, it cannot
reach its goal without service. If knowledge implements
thought, service sets up an objective. Thought cannot survive in a vacuum.

Harvard's primary concern was that the priceless value of
scholarship might be perpetuated by those who were constrained to minister in the churches to their fellow men. For

the "ministry," Yale substituted the more inclusive term service—"service in the Church and Civil State." Princeton first laid stress upon personal culture, but her program was soon expanded to include this same growing conception of scholarship and a sense of social responsibility. At King's College (Columbia), "a serious, virtuous and industrious course of life" was to be provided, following which there was to be personal culture, and finally "knowledge of themselves and of the God of Nature and of their duty to Him and to themselves and one another." Thus was forecast the remarkable enrichment that was to occur in the content of the germinal idea of the minister. With the growing conception of the ministry, this value remains at the heart of every American college. The problem of the college today is to retain the vitality of this rapidly expanding value. The record of these four universities, named for purposes of illustration, in furnishing leadership during recent decades is more conclusive than the citation of their official declarations.

The churches themselves have eventually encouraged and aided this enlargement of the value of the term minister. This has come about through the emphasis they have latterly placed upon the significance of the social gospel within boundaries greatly exceeding those of the earlier personal gospel. Somewhat belatedly perhaps, but nevertheless certainly, they have contributed to the development of the various phases of the ministry of the layman—men, women, children, home and foreign missions, medicine, law, diplomacy, in a word to public service broadly conceived as contrasted with the work of the clergy more technically defined.

Never has there been within the colleges a more distinct concern that young men and women may develop a sense of responsibility and make some adequate preparation for fruitful social and public service. The social sciences lead the natural sciences in enrollment; both seek to serve. In order that this purpose may not be defeated, the more seasoned liberal colleges proceed on the faith that the best way to prepare students for the "new age" is to prepare them to stand on their feet in any age, or as another has phrased it, "that they may become not only more agreeable companions to themselves through life but more potent forces for good in any environment in which they may find themselves."

That the narrower definition of the ministry as conceived by the earlier colleges persisted to a remarkable degree in New England is evidenced by the fact that for the five decades preceding 1870 the percentages of ministers to graduates were —Amherst 46, Bowdoin 21, Dartmouth 24, Harvard 11, University of Vermont 24, Williams 33, Yale 24. Most of the clergymen still reach their parishes by way of the colleges and the professional schools.

It has already been pointed out that the churches were the primary agency in the multiplication of colleges in the South, the Middle West, and the Far West, and that during the period of their rapid multiplication the earlier conception of the ministry prevailed. As has just been said, it prevails today. To speak in general terms, the percentage of ministerial candidates in the earlier meaning has decreased as the conception of the ministry has enlarged. This is a natural outgrowth of the dynamic power of the teachings of Jesus Christ, who "draws all men to Himself," and is not to be urged as an indication that the colleges formerly called denominational but now more properly referred to as church-related are abandoning this elemental objective.

Freedom. The most liberal colleges hold tenaciously to the paradox recently expressed in the apt phrase of Thomas Mann concerning phases of our turbulent contemporary life, "To live in freedom is to compose (these) opposites."

It has been shown that the colleges have stood for stability in the midst of change and they still so stand. They also stand for self-determination in the midst of authoritarianism. When the world is disintegrating they emphasize integrating forces. When the world becomes sluggish and impotent they not only welcome but initiate experimentation. They prize their freedom to steer their course in terms of existing conditions, never losing sight of their ultimate goal. They do not accept "adjustment to environment" as their most worthy procedure. At times, it is true, they follow developments in society; at other times they lead. They do not accept the philosophy of opportunism.

Independence has always been the administrative watchword of the colleges. Being free, they chose at first to operate along traditional lines. This choice involved a degree of dependence upon both the church and the state, and raised problems that still linger in most institutions. That is to say, the colleges did not at once adopt the principle of freedom as an operating administrative formula. The principle was not extended either to faculties or students. The founders of the early colleges like the citizenry in general were under the spell of the Natural Rights metaphysics. They were winning freedom, not dispensing it. They frequently dispensed with it. They enforced external discipline. They conducted their work on the basis of authority. The curriculum and the rules of conduct were prescribed. Discipline by way of freedom was a paradox largely unresolved. Discipline through liberty, that is self discipline, was not set up as an end. It is an ideal which an increasing number of college students are achieving today.

The prevailing conception of freedom did not include tolerance of opinion, much less of faith and of life. The colleges' formula for freedom did not involve the Golden Rule. Perhaps they were too jealous of their own prerogatives. They brooked no arbitrary interference. In administrative matters, in curriculum building, and in methods of teaching they did not seek or welcome suggestions, as has been shown.

Since these early beginnings wider conceptions of freedom have arisen. New methods of implementation have been introduced. Colleges at times and places harbor bulls in the china shop. It has been well demonstrated that while the fate of the nation and its culture are tied up in the same bundle, for the purposes of democracy they must be tied rather loosely. It is not strange that the colleges are frequently accused of seeking isolation from society or of being in actual opposition to current trends. They are disposed to accept cheerfully such penalties of independence. They place liberty and freedom above security in the table of values.

The colleges are learning to compose the opposites inherent in disciplined freedom. They cannot be free unless they are moral. William T. Harris, destined to be the John Marshall of the United States Office of Education, a fearless champion of the public schools, insisted that every class recitation in every subject should be utilized for the teaching of morality. This would seem to be beclouding subject matter in the interest of an issue. While the forms and methods may have changed, the requirement of integrity still persists. Morality is inextricably bound up with the search for truth, the possession of truth, and the efforts to apply it to human experience. Morality does its best service when guided by religion. Individual morality has taken on the additional content of social responsibility. An enlarged sense of duty, of social and public service, is being recognized as a sense of morality and remains a growing aspiration of the colleges, an aspiration sometimes partially achieved.

Today the mental hygienists are pointing out the necessity of guiding the student's physiological, social, and ethical as well as his intellectual development. It is this type of "co-education" which L. P. Jacks so valiantly defends. The admission into the content of educational theory and in less gratifying fashion into practice, of these real dynamos of personality, sets further limitations upon freedom. Aristotle knew that man is a political animal, by which he meant that the release and control of his social, moral, and religious impulses can no more be neglected than his appetite for knowledge. The wellsprings of human life are deeper than the knowing or the thinking process. The high rates of divorce, crime, imbecility, and insanity cannot be ignored by school and college program makers, nor by the builders of national and international society.

The colleges demand the freedom to cultivate the suspended judgment. They are not easily stampeded, for they have caught the spirit of the scientific method. Research is uncongenial to coercion. Many leaders of industry extend this freedom to their research men. These men are increasingly free to pursue an investigation without thought of immediate profits. Nearly all of them are college-bred men.

The colleges listen to propagandists that a balance of truth may be discovered. They align themselves with the courts which hand down decisions in terms of the law and the evidence. Colleges and courts both make and follow law. The Constitution contains certain principles inviolate and at the same time makes provision for unseen developments in the social life. This is another road to the higher freedom. Just as on the intellectual side the colleges exercise their insight, their versatility and adaptability, so on the moral side they cultivate such qualities as "veracity, probity, equity, fairness, gentleness and amiableness," to quote from John Henry Newman, who also points out that the full development of the moral nature is possible only through the offices of religion. Thus the colleges seek to serve the body politic in various situations as dynamos, as balance wheels, safety valves, governors.

The colleges did not so early discover what Socrates well understood, that if the true and the good were to shine resplendent it would be because their inherent beauty had been discovered by eyes that could see. A fuller understanding and evaluation of the esthetic in nature and in life and conduct now constitutes one of the most significant emergent contributions to the higher freedom.

A large measure of the greatness of the world's great teachers—Confucius, Socrates, Jesus, St. Augustine—is disclosed in their comprehension of these paradoxes of freedom. They do not substitute blind authority for abandoned reason. They point the way to a real, not a fictitious, unity. The good life is the unified life, achieved too seldom, as the individual becomes a person and is fused into an encompassing unity. This is the academic spirit at its best. Most men accept it on Christmas. The true insight was expressed in the words—"And ye shall know the truth and the truth shall make you free."

Colleges are happy to be able to work so largely as they do under those compulsions which are inherent in their task. The freedom from external control, if and when realized, carries with it a number of complementary responsibilities. The friends of the colleges recognize these responsibilities and are trying to meet them. When they work in the spirit of freedom, they also may work in the spirit of cooperation. College administration thus finds within the process itself principles which are self-regulatory. These principles point the way to actual as well as potential harmony. They point the way to ultimate human unity through freedom.

The colleges have faith in enduring values and all the more so because values which endure are values which possess creative power. The ability to grow and to serve is measured in terms of the freedom of the college and of the individual to express himself with increasing understanding and power,—freedom of thought, freedom of worship, freedom of speech, freedom of the press, freedom of assembly, freedom of enterprize.

With the guarantee of such freedom, guided by a keen sense of responsibility, men and society reach their highest fruitage in scholarship, thought and service, in science, democracy, and religion.

However well or poorly equipped college alumni and alumnae may be, there are two million of them who are now called to serve as leaven in the lump of American society.

SOME MOTHERS OF COLLEGES

1. AMHERST

   Alumni founded 1 institution of higher education in the United States.

   Alumni founded 4 foreign educational institutions.*

   17 alumni are presidents or presidents emeriti of higher institutions in the United States.

   1 alumnus is president of a foreign educational institution.

2. BOSTON UNIVERSITY

   Alumni founded 15 institutions of higher learning in the United States.

   Alumni founded 6 foreign educational institutions.

   151 alumni are, or have been, presidents of higher institutions in the United States.

   39 alumni are or have been presidents of foreign educational institutions.

   Of the total of 190 presidents, 17 pursued the liberal arts course at Boston. It is significant that 125 were enrolled in the School of Theology. At least 89 are or have been presidents of Methodist higher institutions in the United States.

3. INDIANA UNIVERSITY

   Alumni founded 17 institutions of higher learning in the United States, of which 14 are teachers' colleges or normal schools.

   An alumnus founded 1 foreign educational institution.

   68 alumni are or have been presidents of higher institutions in the United States—27 of whom are or have been heads of teachers' colleges or normal schools.

   3 alumni are or have been heads of foreign educational institutions.

* Foreign educational institutions of all grades have been included, as no satisfactory classification at the several levels can be made.

4. JOHNS HOPKINS UNIVERSITY

Among the living alumni of Johns Hopkins are—
40 who are or have been presidents of higher institutions in the United States.
8 who are heads of foreign educational institutions.
Of the above, 3 received the A.B. degree from Johns Hopkins.

5. UNIVERSITY OF MICHIGAN

52 alumni are or have been presidents of higher institutions in the United States.
3 alumni are or have been heads of foreign educational institutions.
Of the 55, 39 did their undergraduate work at the University of Michigan.

6. MOUNT HOLYOKE COLLEGE

Alumnae founded 3 colleges in the United States.
Alumnae founded 10 foreign educational institutions
—or at least were strongly influential in their founding.
3 alumnae are or have been presidents of colleges in the United States.
26 alumnae are or have been heads of foreign educational institutions

7. NORTHWESTERN UNIVERSITY

14 alumni are or have been recently presidents of higher institutions in the United States.
Of these, 10 hold the Arts degree from Northwestern.

8. OBERLIN COLLEGE

Alumni founded 6 institutions of higher learning in the United States and one foreign educational institution.
130 alumni are or have been presidents of higher institutions in the United States.
13 alumni are or have been heads of foreign institutions.
Of the 143, 22 took their undergraduate degree at some other institution; 121 did undergraduate work at Oberlin.

9. PRINCETON UNIVERSITY

Alumni founded or were prominent in the founding of 21 institutions of higher education in the United States and 1 foreign educational institution.

102* alumni are or have been presidents of higher institutions of learning in the United States.

20 are or have been heads of foreign educational institutions.

10. STANFORD UNIVERSITY

29 alumni are or have been presidents of institutions of higher learning in the United States.

11. YALE UNIVERSITY

Yale still claims the title which has frequently been assigned her, "Mother of Colleges," but the detailed list of Yale men who founded colleges is not available. Tewksbury states that at least sixteen colleges were founded before the Civil War largely under the guiding hand of Yale College and its graduates.

In 1936 Yale University listed 50 Yale men who were then presidents of American colleges and universities. The claim was made that of the 184 colleges and universities which rank highest among American institutions of higher learning, more than one-third at one time or another have been presided over by men who had received Yale training.

* Princeton Theological Seminary has had several Princeton men as presidents. Number was not indicated. Counted only once above.

STATEMENT ON
ACADEMIC FREEDOM AND TENURE

Adopted by the Association of American Colleges, Philadelphia,
January 12, 1940.

The purpose of this statement is to promote public understanding and support of academic freedom and tenure and
agreement upon procedures to assure them in colleges and universities. Institutions of higher education are conducted for
the common good and not to further the interest of either the
individual teacher* or the institution as a whole. The common
good depends upon the free search for truth and its free exposition.

Academic freedom is essential to these purposes and applies
to both teaching and research. Freedom in research is fundamental to the advancement of truth. Academic freedom in its
teaching aspect is fundamental for the protection of the rights
of the teacher in teaching and of the student to freedom in
learning. It carries with it duties correlative with rights.

Tenure is a means to certain ends; specifically: (1) Freedom
of teaching and research and of extra-mural activities, and (2)
a sufficient degree of economic security to make the profession
attractive to men and women of ability. Freedom and economic
security, hence tenure, are indispensable to the success of an
institution in fulfilling its obligations to its students and to
society.

ACADEMIC FREEDOM

(a) The teacher is entitled to full freedom in research and
in the publication of the results, subject to the adequate performance of his other academic duties; but research for pecuniary
return should be based upon an understanding with the authorities of the institution.

(b) The teacher is entitled to freedom in the classroom in

---

*The word "teacher" as used in this document is understood to include
the investigator who is attached to an academic institution without teaching
duties.

discussing his subject, but he should be careful not to introduce into his teaching controversial matter which has no relation to his subject. Limitations of academic freedom because of religious or other aims of the institution should be clearly stated in writing at the time of the appointment.

(c) The college or university teacher is a citizen, a member of a learned profession, and an officer of an educational institution. When he speaks or writes as a citizen, he should be free from institutional censorship or discipline, but his special position in the community imposes special obligations. As a man of learning and an educational officer, he should remember that the public may judge his profession and his institution by his utterances. Hence he should at all times be accurate, should exercise appropriate restraint, should show respect for the opinions of others, and should make every effort to indicate that he is not an institutional spokesman.

ACADEMIC TENURE

(a) After the expiration of a probationary period teachers or investigators should have permanent or continuous tenure, and their services should be terminated only for adequate cause, except in the case of retirement for age, or under extraordinary circumstances because of financial exigencies.

In the interpretation of this principle it is understood that the following represents acceptable academic practice:

(1) The precise terms and conditions of every appointment should be stated in writing and be in the possession of both institution and teacher before the appointment is consummated.

(2) Each institution should define with great care the probationary period and notify every appointee of its precise length and its terms. Notice should be given at least one year prior to the expiration of the probationary period if the teacher is not to be continued in service after the expiration of that period.

(3) During the probationary period a teacher should have the academic freedom that all other members of the faculty have.

(4) Termination for cause of a continuous appointment, or the dismissal for cause of a teacher previous to the expiration of a term appointment, should, if possible, be considered by both a faculty committee and the governing board of the institution. In all cases where the facts are in dispute, the accused teacher should be informed before the hearing in writing of the

charges against him and should have the opportunity to be heard in his own defense by all bodies that pass judgment upon his case. He should be permitted to have with him an adviser of his own choosing who may act as counsel. There should be a full stenographic record of the hearing available to the parties concerned. In the hearing of charges of incompetence the testimony should include that of teachers and other scholars, either from his own or from other institutions. Teachers on continuous appointment who are dismissed for reasons not involving moral turpitude should receive their salaries for at least a year from the date of notification of dismissal whether or not they are continued in their duties at the institution.

(5) Termination of a continuous appointment because of financial exigency should be demonstrably bona fide.

DATA RELATIVE TO PROBLEMS OF ACADEMIC FREEDOM FOR THE FIVE YEAR PERIOD 1934 - 1938

	1934	1935	1936	1937	1938
Number of new cases	40	56	31	42	52
Number of cases held over from the previous year	8	11	13	10	35
Total number of cases dealt with during each year, including cases revived from former years after having lapsed	60	74	48	58	94
Number of the above cases withdrawn in successive years	5	18	7	4	11
Number of cases rejected as being trivial, or the facts were manifest and required no investigation or public notice	28	27	10	2	10

SAMPLES OF COLLEGE PUBLICITY

Under the title, "Jack Sprats in Education," an executive of a small college writes in a publicity leaflet:

At a recent inauguration of the president of a small college of liberal arts, I was embarrassed for the small colleges represented. . . . We listened to the parade of speakers announcing that the small college was the sole builder of character, the sole source of intellectual vigor, the sole breeding place of great leaders, the sole hope of democracy.

"A college must be good because it is small"; this is a popular fiction. There are small colleges which for their intellectual integrity, their strong, loyal faculties, their endeavor to add the spiritual note to education, are eminently worthy of hearty commendation and larger public support. And there are small colleges where smallness appears to be a lonely virtue.

One president, after looking through some of the "promotional literature" issued by sister colleges, comments in his own college "organ":

But the exercise has left me depressed. And a question lingers to plague my mind: How vital are some of these scenes to the process of education? A drowsy student shutting off an alarm clock, students with handsome luggage crowding into automobiles, hundreds dancing with the abandon of the less educated, a lovely girl adjusting a flower in her hair—are these so fundamental to the experience of education that when we come to tell in pictures the story of our college (presumably for those for whom the printed page makes small impression) we turn to them and say, "See, here is education on our campus"?

The following quotations appear in publicity material issued by: (a) A state university:

343

The high school graduate who decides to spend four years in intellectual endeavor; who wishes an opportunity to train his mind and spirit; who hopes by thought and study to equip himself more thoroughly not only for making a living but even more for living life itself; who believes that these four years in college will help to prepare him for the enjoyment of life's benefits and for the fulfillment of life's obligations, for the undertaking of a profession or business, and even for the perceiving of new needs to be met by him; such a boy or girl, having resolved that he will go to college, may well decide to enter the University of . . . . .

(b) An independent college:

The outstanding characteristics of . . . . are the strong health and physical education programs built around intramural and individual sports; the autonomous plan of study, which permits students above the rank of sophomore to work out courses "on their own", by the use of syllabi and through regular conferences with instructors; a group of courses covering all the major divisions of human knowledge, taken by all the students regardless of their subject of concentration; special training in the field of special interests; the general and field comprehensive examinations, given each year to seniors; and the cooperative system of alternating work and study.

(c) A church-related college:

The educational objective of a small college may well be the building of mature students possessed of integrated personalities. Such is the objective of . . . . The purpose is to provide a challenging environment which continuously encourages the development of students whose intellectual, emotional, spiritual, social, and physical characteristics are harmoniously unified. . . . Through this life it is hoped that the graduate may have achieved an insight into an understanding of our society, an understanding of the intellectual approach to the solution of our problems, be imbued with an altruistic outlook toward the needs of society, and have attained social poise and maturity of judgment.

(d) A church-related college in the South (from the president's annual report for 1938) :

The ideal of .... has been summarized in two words—genuineness and excellence. This ideal, so clearly and completely illustrated in its plant, is the very warp and woof of this institution. Under difficult conditions, ... is endeavouring to do in this section a piece of quality education, which unfortunately is being appreciated only by the discriminating minority.

... It is to the church colleges, particularly in the South, that we must look primarily as bulwarks of our hard won liberties, for there are in this section comparatively few independent institutions, which, like the church college, are untrammeled by political considerations. These church colleges are vital to the welfare of the Republic also for the reason that they are quietly combating that grave peril of the divorce of religion and education, bearing an unfaltering testimony to the fact that Christianity is not incompatible with enlightenment, endeavoring to develop their students into well-rounded personalities in whom the fear of God, which is the beginning of wisdom and the foundation of democracy, and a sense of social responsibility are emphasized.

(e) A college for women:

The story which accompanies these views will introduce to you what .... College can contribute to your preparation for life and to your future happiness.

Our first distinctive contribution is a beautiful location. . . .

The program of education at .... College is also distinctive. Here one dares to be one's self. We call it "individualized education." That means . . . that you are recognized as a personality different from all others and that you are encouraged to realize your own potentialities. . . .

Our objectives are simple: to teach our students to think regardless of what they learn; to acquaint them with the best thought and experience of man down through the ages; to teach them to live with people, to be refined, to be religious, and to have a genuine appreciation of the beautiful, to give them opportunity to develop strong bodies and to provide a program for keeping them strong; to prepare them to perform useful functions in American life; and to come to the realization that these functions are to be performed in terms of intelligent and useful citizenship.

(f) Another woman's college:

Four years of your youth in .... College! An academic home of simple beauty, rooms with book-lined walls and the leisure to linger in their midst; wide lawns trimmed with crataegus bushes and pleasant months to watch while blossoms grow to scarlet berry; broad gardens and shady pools for quiet study and friendly conversation. Pungent eucalyptus paths leading out and up to hilltop and to hall! Four years in exchange for self-knowledge humbly sought and self-mastery gradually acquired. Four years to open the doors of historic epochs, and behold oneself welcomed as a kinsman by all countries and peoples. Four years in which to learn that the arts may be for you an ever increasing joy, science a daily miracle, and your particular task a diurnal blessing. Four years to train the sinews of your mind and the wings of your spirit. Four years of your youth for concentrated study, for experiment in sharing responsibility and play, for practice in the crafts of life to the end that you may become a worthy heir of the treasures of the past and a happy and intelligent citizen of the challenging present. Four years of your youth in exchange for comradeship in ambition, in inspiration, and in goal. To master the riddle of the sphinx, to find the foot of the rainbow, to discover the philosopher's stone, to search for the River of Yarrow; here are fellows for the journeys, both travelers who have blazed the trail and those who take the road for the first time.

REFERENCES AND NOTES

A selected list of references is submitted, arranged alphabetically by authors when practicable. Manifestly, samples only of pertinent material could be included.

The Bulletin of the Association of American Colleges is basic source material. This Association holds to institutional membership and concentrates on college problems. All types of colleges of liberal arts and sciences are represented. Recent volumes of the Bulletin contain volume indexes, to which general reference is now made. Typical citations appear below. In connection with Chapter XIX they are assembled in a group at the head of the list.

Unless otherwise indicated, the statistical data found in the text are drawn from the reports of the United States Office of Education or its predecessor, the United States Bureau of Education. These reports are ordinarily available at cost from the United States Government Printing Office, Washington, D. C.

The following abbreviations are used in references pertaining to the publications of well-known educational organizations: AAC Bul. (Bulletin of the Association of American Colleges), AACR Jour. (Journal of the American Association of Collegiate Registrars), AAU Proc. (Proceedings of the Association of American Universities), AAUW Jour. (Journal of the American Association of University Women), IIE News Bul. (Institute of International Education News Bulletin), NASU Proc. (Proceedings of the National Association of State Universities), NSSE Yearbook (Yearbook of the National Society for the Study of Education). Shortened forms indicate the names of other journals and publishers frequently repeated, e.g., Ed. Rec. (Educational Record), Jour. Higher Ed. (Journal of Higher Education), P.S.P. Co. (Public School Publishing Company), Sch. and Soc. (School and Society), Teachers College (Bureau of Publications, Teachers College, Columbia University), etc.

Roman numerals in parentheses immediately following a reference indicate the chapter of the book to which it pertains.

CHAPTERS I–IV

I The Early American Tradition   III Why Colonial Colleges?
II The Genius of Citizenship   IV Propagating the Species

Adams, Ephraim D. *The Iowa Band.* Boston: Pilgrim Press, 1868. 240 pp. (IV)

Adams, Henry. *The Education of Henry Adams, An Autobiography.* Boston: Houghton, 1922. 519 pp. (I)

Adams, James Truslow. *The Epic of America.* Boston: Little, 1933. 446 pp. (I)

American College and Education Society. Annual Report, 1839; (American Education Society) Annual Report, 1874. Boston: Congregational Ed. Soc. (IV)

Boone, Richard G. *Education in the United States; Its History from the Earliest Settlements.* New York: Appleton, 1902. 410 pp. (IV)

Bryce, James Bryce, Viscount. *The American Commonwealth.* New York: Macmillan, 1927. 2 vols. (I, III)

Clemens, Samuel Langhorne and Charles Dudley Warner. *The Gilded Age.* New York: Harper, 1915. 336 pp. (I)

Dunning, Albert Elijah. *The Congregationalists in America.* Boston: Pilgrim Press, 1894. 552 pp. (IV)

Duvall, Sylvanus M. *The Methodist Episcopal Church and Education Up To 1869.* New York: Teachers College, 1928. 127 pp. (IV)

Eaton, Edward Dwight. *Historical Sketches of Beloit College.* New York: Barnes, 1935. 323 pp. (IV)

Edmonds, Walter D. *Drums Along the Mohawk.* Boston: Little, 1936. 592 pp. (I)

Erskine, John. *Democracy and Ideals.* New York: Doran, 1920. 152 pp. (III)

Godbold, Albea. *Some Factors in the Rise and Character of the Church Colleges in the Ante-Bellum Seaboard South.* A dissertation accepted in partial fulfillment of the requirements for the degree of Doctor of Philosophy in the Graduate School of Arts and Sciences, Duke University, 1939. Durham, N.C. Unpublished MS. 433 pp. (IV)

Kelly, Robert L. *The Influence of John Locke on American Political Ideals.* A thesis accepted in partial fulfillment of the requirements for the degree of Master of Philosophy at the University of Chicago, 1899. (The thesis was documented by works on political theory of Locke, Hobbes, Rousseau, Montesquieu, Paine, and the American statesmen mentioned in the text; the Journal of the House of Commons; American public documents, biographies, criticisms.) Chicago. Unpublished MS. 28 pp. (II)

Limbert, Paul M. *Denominational Policies in the Support and Supervision of Higher Education.* New York: Teachers College, 1929. 242 pp. (IV)

Maxey, Chester C. *Political Philosophies.* New York: Macmillan, 1938. 692 pp. (II)

Morison, Samuel Eliot. *The Founding of Harvard College.* Cambridge: Harvard Univ. Press, 1935. 472 pp. (III)

O'Connell, Geoffrey. *Naturalism in American Education.* New York: Benziger, 1938. 285 pp. (II)

Patton, Jacob Harris. *A Popular History of the Presbyterian Church in the United States of America.* New York: Mighill, 1900. 560 pp. (IV)

Rammelkamp, Charles Henry. *Illinois College; A Centennial History, 1829-1929.* New Haven: Yale Univ. Press, 1928. 605 pp. (IV)

Society for the Promotion of Collegiate and Theological Education at the West. Twenty-six Annual Reports (Theron Baldwin, 1843-64), (Absalom Peters, 1865-69). Boston: Congregational Ed. Soc. (IV)

Taylor, Graham. *Pioneering on Social Frontiers.* Chicago: Univ. of Chicago Press, 1930. 457 pp. (III)

Tewksbury, Donald G. *The Founding of American Colleges and Universities Before the Civil War.* New York: Teachers College, 1932. 254 pp. (IV)

Walsh, James J. *Education of the Founding Fathers of the Republic.* New York: Fordham Univ. Press, 1935. 377 pp. (III)

Wertenbaker, Thomas Jefferson. *The First Americans, 1607-1690.* History of American Life Series, Vol. 2. (Arthur M.

Schlesinger and Dixon R. Fox, eds.). New York: Macmillan, 1927. 358 pp. (III)

—————. *The Founding of American Civilization, The Middle Colonies.* New York: Scribner's, 1938. 367 pp. (III)

CHAPTERS V–VIII

V   The Rise and Fall of the "Intellectuals"
VI   The Scrambled Decades
VII   Collegiate Variants
VIII   A New Era Emerges

Adams, James Truslow.   (See reference, Chaps. I - IV)   (V)

Berle, Adolph A., Jr. and Gardiner C. Means. *The Modern Corporation and Private Property.* New York, Chicago, Washington: Commerce Clearing House. Loose Leaf Service Division of the Corporation Trust Co., 1932. 396 pp. (VI)

Brooks, Van Wyck. *The Flowering of New England, 1815-1865.* New York: Dutton, 1937. 550 pp. (V)

Christy, Arthur E. *The Orient in American Transcendentalism; A Study of Emerson, Thoreau, and Alcott.* New York: Columbia Univ. Press, 1932. 382 pp. (V)

The Congregational Quarterly, 1870. Boston: Pilgrim Press. (VI)

Cyclopedia of Education. Paul Monroe, ed. New York: Macmillan, 1926, 5 vols. (VII)

Emerson, Ralph Waldo. Quoted by John Erskine in *Democracy and Ideals* (see reference, Chaps. I-IV), p. 52. (V)

Foerster, Norman. *The American State University; Its Relation to Democracy.* Chapel Hill: Univ. of North Carolina Press, 1937. 287 pp. (VII)

Groves, Ernest R. *The American Woman; The Feminine Side of a Masculine Civilization.* New York: Greenberg, 1937. 438 pp. (VII)

Hare, Lloyd C. M. *The Greatest American Woman: Lucretia Mott.* New York: American Historical Society, Inc., 1937. 307 pp. (VII)

Harper, William R. *The Prospects of the Small College.* Chicago: Univ. of Chicago Press, 1900. 46 pp. (VIII)

James, Henry. *Charles W. Eliot.* Boston: Houghton, 1930. 2 vols. (V, VIII)

Josephson, Matthew. *The Politicos, 1865-1896.* New York: Harcourt, 1938. 750 pp. (VI)
————. *The Robber Barons; The Great American Capitalists, 1861-1901.* New York: Harcourt, 1934. 474 pp. (VI)

Kelly, Robert L. "The Future of the Liberal Arts College." NASU Proc., Vol. 28, 1930. (VII)
————. "The Prospects of the Liberal Arts College." *The Liberal Arts College Movement* (see Archie M. Palmer, ed.), Chap. 1. (VIII)

Kotschnig, Walter M. and Elined Prys, eds. *The University in a Changing World: A Symposium.* London: H. Milford, Oxford Univ. Press, 1932. 224 pp. (V)

Moore, Elsa Adrienne. *Rammohun Roy, His Possible Influence on American Thought, With Special Emphasis upon Periodicals.* A thesis submitted in partial fulfillment of the requirements for the degree of Master of Arts at Columbia University, 1935. New York. Unpublished MS. (V)

National Education Association. Annual Reports. Proceedings (National Teachers Association) 1857-70; 1871-1939. Washington, D. C. (VII)

Palmer, Archie MacInnes, ed. *The Liberal Arts College Movement.* Proceedings of a Conference held in Chicago, March 1930. New York: Little & Ives, 1930. 187 pp. (VIII)

Pendleton, Ellen F. "Changes and Experiments in Colleges for Women." AAUW Jour., Washington, D. C. Vol. 24, April 1931. (Available also as a reprint, 8 cents.) (VII)

Robinson, Charles Mulford. *Modern Civic Art, or The City Made Beautiful.* New York and London: Putnam, 1903. 381 pp. (VI)

Ryan, W. Carson. *Studies in Early Graduate Education.* Carnegie Foundation for the Advancement of Teaching, Bulletin No. 30. New York, 1939. 167 pp. (VIII)

Shepard, Odell. *Pedlar's Progress, The Life of Bronson Alcott.* Boston: Little, 1937. 546 pp. (V)

Tewksbury, Donald G. (See reference Chaps. I-IV) (VII)

United States Office (Bureau) of Education. Report of the Commissioner of Education, 1870. Washington, D. C. (VII)

Walters, Raymond. "Statistics of Registration in American Universities and Colleges." For 1938, Sch. and Soc., Vol. 48, Dec. 17, 1938. For 1939, Sch. and Soc., Vol. 50, Dec. 16, 1939. (VII)

Ward, Harold. "American Cities on the March." Travel, Vol. 71, July 1938. (VI)

Woody, Thomas. "Colleges for Women." *A History of Women's Education in the United States,* Chap. 4. New York: Science Press, 1929. 2 vols. (VII)

Works, George A. and Barton Morgan. *The Land-Grant Colleges.* Washington: U. S. Govt. Printing Office, 1939. 141 pp. (VII)

CHAPTERS IX–X

IX   The Colleges Learn to Cooperate
X   From Provincialism Toward An International Mind

American Friends Service Committee. Annual Reports: 1937, 1938, 1939. Philadelphia, Pa. (X)

Aydelotte, Frank. *The Vision of Cecil Rhodes.* The Marfleet Lectures at the Univ. of Toronto, 1939. Princeton Univ. Press. (X)

Butler, Nicholas Murray. Annual Report of the Director of the Division of Intercourse and Education, Carnegie Endowment for International Peace. Year-Books: 1937, 1938, 1939. Washington, D. C. (X)

Cherrington, Ben M. "The Division of Cultural Relations of the State Department." IIE News Bul., Vol. 14, May 1, 1939. (X)

Committee on Friendly Relations Among Foreign Students. *The Unofficial Ambassadors.* New York, 1938. 20 pp. (X)

Cyclopedia of Education. (See reference, Chaps. V-VIII) (IX)

Duvall, Sylvanus M. (See reference, Chaps. I-IV) (X)

Ford, Guy Stanton. "The American Scholar Today." . . . *On and Off the Campus.* Minneapolis: Univ. of Minnesota Press, 1938. (IX)

Institute of International Education. *Institute of International Education: Its Organization, Aims and Activities.* 17th Series. Bul. No. 2. New York. March 1936. 21 pp. (X)

Institute of Oriental Students for the Study of Human Relations. *An Experiment in Oriental-American Friendship.* Handbook. Chicago: Brent House, 1934. (X)

International House, University of California. Report of Activities, July 1, 1937—June 30, 1938. Berkeley, Calif., 1938. (X)

International Student Service. Annual Report, 1935-36. Geneva, Switzerland. (X)

"Junior Year in Switzerland." IIE News Bul., Vol. 13, Feb. 1, 1938. (X)

Kelly, Robert L. and Others. A Bird's-Eye View of the Entire Foreign Scholarship Situation as Related to the United States. AAC Bul., Vols. 4—6, 1918-20. (X)

Limbert, Paul M. (See reference, Chaps. I-IV) (IX)

MacCracken, John H. "These Twenty Years." Ed. Rec., Vol. 18, July 1937. (IX)

Maiden, Arthur L. Analysis of Educational Studies Made Under the Auspices of the Association of American Universities from 1900 to 1931. Unpublished MS. (IX)

"More Statistics on Rhodes Scholars." American Oxonian, Vol. 25, January 1938. (X)

Rockefeller, John D. "That Brotherhood May Prevail." International Quarterly, Vol. 2, Winter 1938. (X)

Shotwell, James T. Annual Report of the Director, 1938, 1939. Division of Economics and History, Carnegie Endowment for International Peace. New York. (X)

Spivac, Robert G. "International Student Service." IIE News Bul., Vol. 13, Dec. 1, 1937. (X)

Stoker, Spencer. *The Schools and International Understanding.* Chapel Hill: Univ. of North Carolina Press, 1933. 243 pp. (X)

Student Institute of Pacific Relations. Proceedings. Annual Conference, 1936 (Eleventh); 1937 (Twelfth). San Francisco. (X)

Tewksbury, Donald G. (See reference, Chaps. I-IV) (IX)

Ware, Edith E., ed. *Study of International Relations in the United States.* Survey for 1934, 503 pp. Survey for 1938, 540 pp. New York: Col. Univ. Press. (X)

Wellard, James H. "International House—An Experiment in Human Relations." Harvard Ed. Review, Vol. 7, May 1937. (X)

"World's Student Christian Federation and International Relations." Student World, Vol. 23, Second Quarter 1935. (X)

Zook, George F. and M. E. Haggerty. *Principles of Accrediting Higher Institutions.* Evaluation of Higher Institutions, Vol. 1. Chicago: Univ. of Chicago Press, 1936. 202 pp. (IX)

CHAPTERS XI–XII

XI Academic Freedom and Academic Tenure
XII Publicity and Propaganda

"Academic Freedom" (editorial). Harvard Al. Bul., Vol. 38, Feb. 17, 1936. (XI)

"Academic Freedom and Academic Tenure" (editorial). Harvard Al. Bul., Vol. 40, Oct. 22, 1937. (XI)

American Association of Collegiate Registrars. Proceedings, 1930-1939. E. C. Miller, Sec'y, Univ. of Chicago, Chicago, Ill. (XII)

American Association of University Professors. *College and University Teaching.* Washington, 1933. 122 pp. (See also AAUP Bul., Vol. 19, No. 5, Sec. 2, 1933.) (XI)

————. Committee A. "Academic Freedom and Tenure." Reports. AAUP Bul., Vols. 21 (February 1935), 24 (February 1938), 25 (January 1939). (XI)

————. Committee Y. *Depression, Recovery and Higher Education.* Prepared by Malcolm M. Willey. New York and London: McGraw-Hill, 1937. 543 pp. (XI)

Anderson, Ruth E. "The Colleges in Current Literature." AAC Bul., Vols. 13 (November 1927), 14 (December 1928), 15 (December 1929). (XII)

————. "The Colleges in the Popular Magazines." AAC Bul., Vols. 16 (December 1930), 17 (December 1931). (XII)

Boas, George. "The Complete Scandalmonger." Harper's, Vol. 175, August 1937. (XII)

Capen, S. P. "The Responsibility of Boards of Trustees for the Preservation of Academic Freedom." AAUP Bul., Vol. 21, October 1935. (XI)

Carlson, A. J. "Freedom of Thought, Speech, and Teaching." AAUP Bul., Vol. 23, January 1937. (XI)

"Chastity." Newsweek, Vol. 9, April 10, 1937. (XII)

Cowley, W. H. "President Coffman on Academic Freedom." Jour. Higher Ed., Vol. 8, February 1937. (XI)

Duggan, Stephen P. "International Propaganda." IIE News Bul., Vol. 13, Nov. 1, 1937. (XII)

Eells, Walter C. Surveys of Higher Education. The Carnegie Foundation for the Advancement of Teaching. New York, 1937. 538 pp. (XII)

————. "Criticisms of Higher Education." Jour. Higher Ed., Vol. 5, April 1934. (XII)

Flint, Charles W. "Academic Freedom." Ed. Rec., Vol. 16, October 1935. (XI)

"Football Flasks." Literary Digest, Vol. 122, Oct. 31, 1937. (XII)

Fraser, Mowat G. The College of the Future. New York: Col. Univ. Press, 1937. 529 pp. (XI)

Good, Carter V. "Freedom of Teaching in the Public Schools." AAUP Bul., Vol. 24, May 1938. (XI)

Haggerty, Melvin E. The Faculty. Evaluation of Higher Education, Vol. 2. Chicago: Univ. of Chicago Press, 1937. 218 pp. (XI)

Halle, (Kleeman) Rita. "Is My Daughter Safe at College?" Good Housekeeping, Vol. 87, September 1929. (XII)

Harlow, R. F. "The Stanford School-Press Relations Investigation." Excerpts from Daily Newspaper and Higher Education. Sch. and Soc., Vol. 48, Oct. 8, 1938. (XI)

Meiklejohn, Alexander. "Teachers and Controversial Questions." Harper's, Vol. 177, June 1938. (XI)

Miller, Clyde R. "What the New York Times Wants in the Way of College News." Publicity Problems. Report, Annual Convention, American College Publicity Association, 1937. Pittsburgh: Univ. of Pittsburgh. (XII)

Moore, Henry T. "Women's Colleges and Race Extinction." Scribner's, Vol. 87, March 1930. (XII)

National Catholic Educational Association. Statement on Academic Freedom. AAUP Bul., Vol. 22, October 1936. (XI)

Olmstead, John G. *Alumni Achievement.* Ithaca, N. Y. American Alumni Council, 1931. 150 pp.

Proface, Dom. "Collegiate Drinking." Commonweal, Vol. 25, Apr. 2, 1937. (XII)

Propaganda Analysis. Vol. 1. October and November 1937; February and June, 1938. New York: Institute for Propaganda Analysis. (XII)

Sheehy, Maurice S. "College and the Work Habit." Commonweal, Vol. 23, Mar. 27, 1936. (XII)

Tyler, Henry W. and Edward P. Cheney. "Academic Freedom." Annals of the Am. Acad. of Pol. and Soc. Science, Vol. 200, November 1938. (XI)

Van Duzer, C. H. "The Meaning of Propaganda." Social Frontier, Vol. 4, May 1938. (XII)

"Youth in College." Fortune, Vol. 13, June 1936. (XII)

CHAPTER XIII

The Financing of Colleges

American Alumni Council. "Statistics." Report, Twenty-fourth Annual Conference. Ithaca, N. Y. 1938.

American Association of University Professors. Committee Y. (See reference, Chaps. XI-XII)

American Universities and Colleges. 3d edition. Clarence S. Marsh, ed. Washington: American Council on Education, 1936. 1129 pp.

Anthony, Alfred Williams, Robert L. Kelly, and Others. *Safeguarding Funds.* Baltimore: Stohlmann, 1925. 130 pp.

"Appropriations of the Philanthropic Foundations." Sch. and Soc., Vol. 49, May 20, 1939.

Arnett, Trevor. *Observations on the Financial Condition of Colleges and Universities in the United States.* General Education Board. Occasional Papers, No. 9. New York, 1937. 25 pp.

————. *Trends in Tuition Fees in State and Endowed Colleges and Universities in the United States from 1928 through 1936-37.* General Education Board, Occasional Papers, No. 11. New York, 1939. 113 pp.

Baugher, Charles A. *A Determination of Trends in Organization, Finance, and Enrollment in Higher Education in Church-Related Arts Colleges Since 1900.* A dissertation accepted in partial fulfillment of the requirements for the degree of Doctor of Philosophy at New York University, 1937. New York. Unpublished MS. 192 pp.

Bowman, Isaiah. "Financial Outlook for Institutions of Higher Education." Proceedings, Southern University Conference, 1937. Nashville, Tenn.

General Education Board. Annual Reports, 1914-1939. New York.

Gerlinger, Irene H. *Money-Raising: How To Do It.* Los Angeles: Suttonhouse, 1938. 311 pp.

Gifts and Bequests to Colleges and Universities in Good Times and Bad Times. New York: John Price Jones Corp., 1938.

"Gifts and Bequests to Universities and Colleges." Sch. and Soc., Vol. 49, Apr. 8, 1939.

Hollis, Ernest V. *Philanthropic Foundations and Higher Education.* New York: Col. Univ. Press, 1938. 365 pp.

————. "Philanthropy's Future in Higher Education." Sch. and Soc., Vol. 49, Jan. 28, 1939.

"The Julius Rosenwald Fund." Sch. and Soc., Vol. 49, Mar. 25, 1939.

Kelly, Frederick J. and John H. McNeely. *The State and Higher Education; Phases of Their Relationship.* The Carnegie Foundation for the Advancement of Teaching in cooperation with the U. S. Office of Education. New York, 1933. 284 pp.

Kelly, Robert L., ed. *The Effective College.* By a group of American students of higher education. New York. Association of American Colleges, 1928. 302 pp.

Limbert, Paul M. (See reference, Chaps. I-IV)

McNeely, John H. *Authority of State Executive Agencies Over Higher Education.* U. S. Office of Education. Bulletin, 1936, No. 15. Washington, 1936. 67 pp.

Marts, A. C. "Advancement Voluntarily or by Statute?" Social Science, Vol. 11, October 1936.

Marts, A. C. "Do Taxes Kill the Golden Goose?" American Scholar, Vol. 7, Summer 1938.

————. "Philanthropy Under the New Deal." Christian Century, Vol. 5, Aug. 15, 1934.

Palmer, Archie MacInnes. "The Quest for Bequests." Sch. and Soc., Vol. 45, Mar. 27, 1937.

Reeves, Floyd B. "What Should Education Cost in an Effective College?" AAC Bul., Vol. 12, May 1926.

"Reunion's Top Feature—Alumni School—Attended by 9,700." Univ. of Chicago, The Alumni Bulletin, Vol. 5, July 1939.

Russell, John D. and Floyd W. Reeves. *Finance.* Evaluation of Higher Institutions, Vol. 7. Chicago: Univ. of Chicago Press, 1935. 133 pp.

Sears, Jesse B. *Philanthropy in the History of American Higher Education.* U. S. Bureau of Education. Bulletin, 1922, No. 26. Washington, D. C. 112 pp.

Stanford, Edward V., O.S.A. "The 'Living Endowment' of Catholic Colleges." Catholic Ed. Review, Vol. 35, April 1937.

CHAPTERS XIV–XVIII

Barr, Stringfellow. "St. John's Hails New Curriculum." New York Times, July 3, 1938. **(XVI)**

Dartmouth College. Report on Undergraduate Education by the Senior Committee, May 15, 1924. Hanover, N. H. 42 pp. **(XVI)**

Eliassen, R. H. "Survey of 'New' College Plans." Jour. Higher Ed., Vol. 10, May 1939. **(XIV, XV)**

Flexner, Abraham. *Universities, American, English, German.* New York: Oxford Univ. Press, 1930. 381 pp. **(XVI)**

Gideonse, Harry David. *The Higher Learning in a Democracy.* New York and Toronto: Farrar, 1937. 34 pp. **(XVII)**

Harper, William R. *The Trend in Higher Education.* Chicago: Univ. of Chicago Press, 1899. 390 pp. **(XIV)**

Hollinshead, Byron S. "The Relation between the Liberal Arts College and the Junior College." AAC Bul., Vol. 26, March 1940. (XVIII)

Hughes, J. M. "Curriculum Organization and Integration." Jour. Higher Ed., Vol. 10, May 1939. (XIV, XV)

Hutchins, Robert M. *The Higher Learning in America*. New Haven: Yale Univ. Press, 1936; London: H. Milford, Oxford Univ. Press, 1936. 119 pp. (XVI)

Institute for Administrative Officers of Higher Education. Proceedings (W. S. Gray, ed.)
Recent Trends in American College Education, Vol. 3 (1931);
Provision for the Individual in College Education, Vol. 4 (1932);
General Education, Vol. 6 (1934);
Current Issues in Higher Education, Vol. 9 (1937). Chicago: Univ. of Chicago Press. (XIV, XV)

Jefferson, Thomas. Letter of June 22, 1822, addressed to the Rev. Thomas Whittemore, Cambridgeport, Mass. Tufts College Library. Tufts College, Mass. MS. (XVII)

Johnson, B. Lamar. "The Junior College." *General Education in the American College*, Chap. 7. NSSE Thirty-eighth Yearbook, Part II (Guy M. Whipple, ed.). Bloomington, Ill.: P. S. P. Co., 1939. (XVIII)

Jones, Edward S. *Comprehensive Examinations in American Colleges*. New York: Macmillan, 1933. 437 pp. (XVI)

McGrath, Earl J. "Liberal Education under a Tutorial System." AACR Jour., Vol. 13, January 1938. (XV)

McHale, Kathryn and Frances V. Speek. *Newer Aspects of Collegiate Education*. A Study Guide. Washington, D. C.: American Association of University Women, 1936. 67 pp. (XIV)

Meiklejohn, Alexander. *The Experimental College*. New York: Harper, 1932. 421 pp. (XVI, XVII)

National Society for the Study of Education. *Changes and Experiments in Liberal Education*. Prepared by Kathryn McHale. Thirty-first Yearbook, Part II (Guy M. Whipple, ed.). Bloomington, Ill.: P.S.P. Co., 1932. 267 pp. (XIV, XV)

National Society for the Study of Education. *General Education in the American College.* Thirty-eighth Yearbook, Part II (Guy M. Whipple, ed.). Bloomington, Ill.: P. S. P. Co., 1939. 382 pp. (XV, XVI)

The New Program at St. John's College in Annapolis. Supplement to Bulletin. Annapolis, Md., July 1937. (XVI)

Park, Marion E. "The Long Future of the College." Bryn Mawr Al. Bul., Vol. 19, July 1939. (XVII)

Richardson, Leon B. *A Study of the Liberal College.* Dartmouth College, Hanover, N. H., 1924. 282 pp. (XVI, XVII)

Ross, Sir William David. "The Faculty Member as a Cultural Force in the Community." AAC Bul., Vol. 25, March 1939. (XVI)

Showerman, Grant. "A Most Lamentable Comedy." Sch. and Soc., Vol. 33, Apr. 11, 1931. (XVII)

Wriston, Henry M. "A Critical Appraisal of Experiments in General Education." *General Education in the American College,* Chap. 14. NSSE Thirty-eighth Yearbook, Part II (Guy M. Whipple, ed.). Bloomington, Ill.: P.S.P. Co., 1939. (XV)

Wunsch, W. R. "Plot Own Courses at Black Mountain." New York Times, Dec. 4, 1938. (XIV)

CHAPTER XIX

The Growing Influence of the Arts

Association of American Colleges Bulletin
    Association of American Colleges. Commission on the Arts. Annual Report. Vol. 26, March 1940.

    ——————. Commission on College Architecture and College Instruction in the Fine Arts. Annual Reports. Vols. 9 (May 1923), 10 (May 1924), 13 (Feb. 1927), 15 (March 1929).

    ——————. Executive Director (Secretary). Annual Reports. Vols. 2-26 (1916-40).

    Beam, Lura. "The Place of Art in the Liberal College." Vol. 13, May 1927.

    Ceough, Richard. "Facts and Figures Concerning the Theatre Arts in American Colleges and Universities." Excerpts from a Doctor's thesis entitled *The Universities, Colleges and the Theatre.* Vol. 22, November 1936.

Clarke, Eric T. "The College and the Fine Arts." Vol. 22, December 1936.

————. "The Union of the Arts in the Liberal Arts College." Vol. 23, December 1937.

Elliott, Huger. "The Study of Art in Our Colleges." Vol. 12, April 1926.

Erskine, John. "Music in the Curriculum." Vol. 17, March 1931.

Hubbard, Henry V. "The Teaching of Landscape Architecture in Liberal Colleges." Vol. 12, April 1926.

Kelly, Robert L. "Creative Education." AAC Bul., Vol. 17 No. 4, December 1931.

Kelly, Robert L. and C. C. Zantzinger. "Practical Problems in College Architecture." Vol. 11, December 1925; Vol. 12, April 1926.

Keppel, Frederick P. "The Place of the Arts in American Education." Vol. 11, April 1925.

Larson, J. Fredrick. "Individual Character in College Architecture." Vol. 15, December 1929.

Moore, Charles. "The Place of the Fine Arts in Education." Vol. 16, March 1930.

Nimmons, George F. "A College Course in Art Appreciation." Vol. 11, April 1925.

Noble, Eugene A. "The Study of Music in the Liberal College." Vol. 12, April 1926.

Boswell, Peyton, Jr. "Schools and Progress." Art Digest, Vol. 7, May 15, 1933.

Carnegie Corporation of New York. Annual Reports. 1922-39. New York. 18 vols.

————. *The Place of the Arts in American Life.* Memorandum by a special committee, 1924. Unpublished MS. 90 pp.

Clarke, Eric T. *The Artistic Tripod.* Address at Fisk University, Nashville, Tenn., 1938. 10 pp.

Kelly, Robert L., ed. (See reference, Chap. XIII)

Keppel, Frederick P. and R. L. Duffus. *The Arts in American Life.* New York and London: McGraw-Hill, 1933. 227 pp.

Klauder, Charles Z. and Herbert C. Wise. *College Architecture in America and Its Part in the Development of the Campus.* New York and London: Scribner's, 1929. 301 pp.

Koch, Frederick H. *Carolina Folk-Plays.* Introd. to Third Series. Cited by Frank Durham, "Dramatic Art at the University of North Carolina." AAC Bul., Vol. 22, November 1936.

Larson, J. Fredrick and Archie MacInnes Palmer. *Architectural Planning of the American College.* New York and London: McGraw-Hill, 1933. 181 pp.

National Theatre Conference. Quarterly Bulletin, April and June 1939. Western Reserve University, Cleveland, O.

Palmer, Archie MacInnes and Grace Holton. *College Instruction in Art.* New York: Association of American Colleges, 1934. 62 pp.

Paris, W. Francklyn. "France-America," and "The Statue of Liberty in 1883." Legion D'Honneur Magazine, Vol. 10, July 1939.

The Significance of the Fine Arts. Association of American Colleges and the Committee on Education of the American Institute of Architects. Boston: Marshall Jones, 1926. 483 pp.

Swift, Emerson H. "A Rebirth of the Arts in America. AAUW Jour., Vol. 22, April 1929.

Swales, Francis S. "The Beaux-Arts Influence in American Art." Legion D'Honneur Magazine, Vol. 10, July 1939.

Thompson, Randall. *College Music.* New York: Macmillan, 1935. 279 pp.

Watson, Forbes. "The Roots of Art." AAUW Jour., Vol. 22, April 1929.

CHAPTER XX

The Improvement of College Teaching

American Association of University Professors. *College and University Teaching.* (See also AAUP Bul., Vol. 19, No. 5, Sec. 2, May 1933.) Washington, D. C. 122 pp.

American Council on Education. *Cooperation in the Improvement of Teacher Education.* Washington, D. C., 1939. 19 pp.

————. Proceedings. Twenty-first Annual Meeting (1938); Twenty-second Annual Meeting (1939). Ed. Rec., Vols. 19 (July 1938), 20 (July 1939).

Bowman, Isaiah. *The Graduate School in American Democracy.* U. S. Office of Education. Bulletin, 1939, No. 10. Washington, D. C. 70 pp.

Branscomb, Harvie. *Teaching with Books.* Chicago: Association of American Colleges and American Library Association, 1940. 258 pp.

Brown, Elmer Ellsworth. "The Obligations of a University to the Social Order." A Summary. AAC Bul., Vol. 18, December 1932.

Burstall, S. A. *Retrospect and Prospect: Sixty Years of Woman's Education.* New York: Longmans, 1933. 301 pp.

Carnegie Foundation for the Advancement of Teaching. Annual Reports, 1907-39. New York. 32 vols.

Chen, Theodore H. E. *Developing Patterns of the College Curriculum in the United States.* A thesis accepted in partial fulfillment of the requirements for the degree of Doctor of Philosophy at the University of Southern California, 1939. Los Angeles, Calif. 154 pp.

The College Teacher. Proceedings of the Fifteenth Annual Meeting, Association of American Colleges. AAC Bul., Vol. 15, March 1929.

Glass, Meta. "The College Curriculum for Women." AAC Bul., Vol. 14, March 1928.

Harvard University. Special Committee appointed by the President. *Some Problems of Personnel in the Faculty of Arts and Sciences.* Cambridge: Harvard Univ. Press, 1939. 165 pp.

Hillyer, Robert S. "Letter to a Teacher of English—James B. Munn." Atlantic, Vol. 161, November 1936.

John, Walton C. *Graduate Study in Universities and Colleges in the United States.* U. S. Office of Education. Bulletin, 1934, No. 20. Washington, D. C., 1935. 234 pp.

Johnson, Palmer O. *Aspects of Land-Grant College Education.* Minneapolis: Univ. of Minnesota Press, 1934. 271 pp.

Learned, William S. and Ben D. Wood. *The Student and His Knowledge.* A report on the results of the high school and college examinations of 1928, 1930, and 1932. New York: Carnegie Foundation for the Advancement of Teaching, 1938. 406 pp.

National Survey of the Education of Teachers. U. S. Office of Education. William John Cooper, Director; E. S. Evenden, Associate Director. Washington: U. S. Government Printing Office, 1932-36. 6 vols.

Payne, Fernandus and Evelyn W. Spieth. *An Open Letter to College Teachers.* Bloomington, Ind.: The Principia Press, 1935. 380 pp.

Perry, Bliss. *And Gladly Teach.* Boston: Houghton, 1935. 315 pp.

Reed, Anna Y. *The Effective and the Ineffective College Teacher.* New York: American Book, 1935. 344 pp.

CHAPTERS XXI–XXII

XXI   Relationships Between the Colleges and the Churches
XXII Relationships Between the Colleges and the State

Baugher, Charles A.   (See reference, Chap. XIII)   (XXI)

Board of Christian Education of the Presbyterian Church in the United States of America. Annual Report, 1938. Philadelphia, Pa.   (XXI)

Board of Education of the Methodist Episcopal Church. *The Record of the Years.* Report. Chicago: February 1939. (XXI)

Board of Education of the Northern Baptist Convention. Annual Report, 1939. New York, 1939.   (XXI)

Board of Education of the United Lutheran Church. *Lutheran Higher Education.* Biennial Survey, 1936-38. Washington, D. C., 1938.   (XXI)

Brody, Alexander. "Federal Relations to Higher Education." Sch. and Soc., Vol. 49, March 4, 1939.   (XXII)

Burns, James Aloysius and B. J. Kohlbrenner. *A History of Catholic Education in the United States.* New York: Benziger, 1937. 295 pp.   (XXI)

Christian Education Handbook. Robert L. Kelly and Ruth E. Anderson, eds. Edition of 1928, Christian Education, Vol. 11, May 1928. 201 pp. Edition of 1931, Christian Education, Vol. 14, January 1931. 360 pp. Edition of 1934, Christian Education, Vol. 17, April-June 1934. 353 pp. Washington: Council of Church Boards of Education. (XXI)

Christian Higher Education: 1940. A Handbook. Gould Wickey and Ruth E. Anderson, eds. Washington: Council of Church Boards of Education, 1940. 342 pp. (XXI)

Coffman, Lotus D. "Federal Support and Local Responsibility for Education," Proceedings, National Ed. Assn., 1936, pp. 413-21. Washington, D. C., 1936. (XXII)

Dodds, Harold W. "Problems Arising from the Relationships of Educational Institutions to the Government." AAU Proc., Thirty-ninth Annual Conference, 1937. Chicago: Univ. of Chicago Press. (XXII)

Dunning, Albert Elijah. (See reference, Chaps. I-IV) (XXI)

Duvall, Sylvanus M. (See reference, Chaps. I-IV) (XXI)

Executive Committee of Christian Education and Ministerial Relief of the Presbyterian Church in the United States. Annual Report, 1939. Louisville, Ky., 1939. (XXI)

Frazier, William F. *Rethinking Congregationalism.* Committee of the International Council of the Congregational Churches. New York. 1938. (XXI)

General Board of Christian Education of the Methodist Episcopal Church, South. Annual Report, 1939. Nashville, Tenn. 1939. (XXI)

Hutchison, Ralph. "Fascism and Higher Education." Atlantic, Vol. 163, June 1939. (XXII)

Judd, Charles H. "Federal Aid to Education." Sch. and Soc., Vol. 49, May 6, 1939. (XXII)

Kelly, Frederick J. and John H. McNeely. *The State and Higher Education; Phases of Their Relationships.* (See reference, Chap. XIII) (XXII)

Moore, John M. "Is the Church Achieving a Policy for Its Colleges?" Christian Education Magazine (M.E.So.), Vol. 28, March-April 1938. (XXI)

National Education Association. Educational Policies Commission. Deliberative Committee Reports. Washington, D. C., 1938. (XXII)

——————. Educational Policies Commission. *The Purposes of Education in American Democracy.* Washington, D. C., 1938. 157 pp. (XXII)

——————. Educational Policies Commission and the Department of Superintendence. *The Unique Function of Education in American Democracy.* Washington, D. C., 1937. 129 pp. (XXII)

——————. Educational Policies Commission and the American Association of School Administrators. *The Structure and Administration of Education in American Democracy.* Washington, D. C., 1938. 128 pp. (XXII)

Newman, John Henry. *The Idea of a University Defined and Illustrated.* London: Basil Montagu Pickering, 1907. 527 pp. (XXI)

O'Malley, Austin. "Catholic Collegiate Education in the United States." Catholic World, Vol. 47, June 1898. (XXI)

Patton, Jacob Harris. (See reference, Chaps. I-IV) (XXI)

Ruthven, Alexander G. "Leadership or Regimentation in Higher Education?" Ed. Rec., July 1937. (XXII)

Ryan, John K. "The Goal of a Catholic Education." Catholic Ed. Review, Vol. 32, January 1934. (XXI)

Shedd, Clarence P. *The Church Follows Its Students.* New Haven: Yale Univ. Press, 1938. 327 pp. (XXI)

Stanford, Edward V., O.S.A. "Are We Headed for Governmental Control of Higher Education?" Catholic Ed. Review, Vol. 36, March 1938. (XXII)

Tewksbury, Donald G. (See reference, Chaps. I-IV) (XXI)

Zook, George F. "Who Should Control Our Institutions of Higher Education?" Ed. Rec., Vol. 20, January 1939. (XXII)

CHAPTERS XXIII–XXIV

Bryant, E. R. "The Fate of the Scholar." Muskingum College Faculty News Bul., Vol. 10, October 1939. (XXIII)

Carlson, A. J. "The Colleges and Public Service." AAC Bul., Vol. 24, March 1938. (XXIII)

Castle, William B. "Harvard Men in the Foreign Service of the United States." Harvard Al. Bul., Vol. 27, Sept. 25, 1929. (XXIII)

Cattell, J. McKeen. "The Distribution of American Men of Science in 1932." Science, Vol. 77, Mar. 10, 1933. (XXIII)

Clark, Austin H. "Harvard Participants in the Constitutional Convention of 1787." Harvard Al. Bul., Vol. 41, Oct. 21, 1938. (XXIII)

Douglas, Paul H. "Has Higher Education Failed?" AAC Bul., Vol. 19, March 1933. (XXIII)

Eaton, Edward Dwight. (See reference, Chaps. I-IV) (XXIV)

Fetter, Frank A. Democracy and Monopoly. Stafford Little Lecture, Princeton University, 1939. Princeton, N. J. 22 pp. (XXIII)

Hamilton, Sir William. "Metaphysics." Lectures on Metaphysics and Logic, Vol. 1, H. L. Monsel and John Veitch, eds. Boston: Gould and Lincoln, 1860. (XXIV)

Harvard Alumni Bulletin (editorial). Dedication of the Littauer Center. Vol. 41, May 12, 1939. (XXIII)

————— (editorial and report, J. B. Conant). Purpose of the Littauer School of Public Administration. Vol. 39, July 2, 1937. (XXIII)

Harvard University. Commission on University Education for Public Service. Report. Harvard Al. Bul., Feb. 5, 1937. (Also available as reprint.) (XXIII)

Industrial Price Policies and Economic Progress. Brookings Institute Monograph. Prepared by Edwin G. Nourse and Horace B. Drury. Washington, D. C., 1938. 328 pp. (XXIV)

Johnston, J. B. "How Shall the College Discharge Its Obligation to Society?" AAC Bul., Vol. 11, April 1925. (XXIII)

Keppel, Frederick P. Philosophy and Learning With Other Papers. New York: Col. Univ. Press, 1936. 175 pp. (XXIV)

Kirkland, J. H. "The Obligation of the College to Society." The President's Address. AAC Bul., Vol. 11, April 1925. (XXIII)

Kotschnig, Walter M. and Elined Prys, eds. (See reference, Chaps. V-VIII) (XXIV)

Kunkel, B. W. and Donald B. Prentice. "The Colleges' Contribution to Intellectual Leadership." Sch. and Soc., Vol. 50, Nov. 4, 1939. (XXIII)

Lowell, A. Lawrence. *At War With Academic Traditions in America.* Cambridge: Harvard Univ. Press, 1933. 357 pp. (XXIV)

McBride, Katharine E. "A Community Service Performed by the College." Bryn Mawr Al. Bul., Vol. 18, April 1938. (XXIII)

Munro, Dana G. "School of Public Affairs." Princeton Al. Weekly, Vol. 39, May 19, 1939. (XXIII)

National Education Association. Educational Policies Commission. Syllabus on the School and American Democracy. Washington, D. C., 1937. (XXIII)

National Institute of Public Affairs. *Scholarships in Practical Government.* Washington, D. C., 1936. (XXIII)

National Research Council. *Directory of Industrial Research Laboratories.* 6th edition. Washington, D. C., 1938. (XXIII)

The Obligation of Universities to the Social Order. 2d edition. London: H. Milford, Oxford Univ. Press, 1933. New York: New York Univ. Press, 1933. 503 pp. (XXIII)

Osler, Sir William. *The Old Humanities and the New Science.* Boston: Houghton, 1920. 64 pp. (XXIII)

Poole, DeWitt. "Personnel for Public Service." Princeton Al. Weekly, Vol. 36, Mar. 27, 1936. (XXIII)

Prentice, Donald B. and B. W. Kunkel. "The Colleges' Contributions to Intellectual Leadership." Sch. and Soc., Vol. 32, Nov. 1, 1930. (XXIII)

"The Princeton Survey of the Government of New Jersey." Sch. and Soc., Vol. 36, Oct. 22, 1932. (XXIII)

"Research, A National Resource." *Relation of the Federal Government to Research,* Vol. 1. Washington: U. S. Govt. Printing Office, November 1938. (XXIII)

Richardson, Leon B. "Dartmouth College." AAC Bul., Vol. 21, May 1935. (XXIII)

Ridley, Clarence E. and Lyman S. Moore. "Training for the Public Service." Annals of the Am. Acad. of Pol. and Soc. Science, Vol. 189, January 1937. (XXIII)

Sanford, Vincent Steadman. "The University of Georgia." AAC Bul., Vol. 21, May 1935. (XXIII)

School of Government. Univ. of Southern California Bul. Los Angeles, June 1, 1938. (XXIII)

Shannon, John R. and Zola Moser. "Indiana University and Educational Leadership." Indiana Univ. Al. Quarterly, Vol. 23, Fall 1936. (XXIII)

Siegfried, André. *America Comes of Age.* New York: Harcourt, 1927. 348 pp. (XXIII)

Taylor, Graham. "The Social and Civic Responsibility and Opportunity of American Colleges and Their Graduates." AAC Bul., Vol. 11, April 1925. (XXIII)

Visher, Stephen S. "The Education of the Younger Starred Scientists." Jour. Higher Ed., Vol. 10, Mar. 1939. (XXIII)

INDEX